Pegasus Epitaph

The Story Of The Legendary Rock Group

Michael Stuart Ware

First published as *Love: Behind The Scenes* by Helter Skelter Publishing, 2003

This edition ©
Extradition Publishing / Cadiz Music & Digital Ltd 2020
13 Harmony Place, London SE8 3FE
and
This Day In Music Books 2020
Bishopswood Road, Prestatyn, LL 9 9PL

ISBN 978-1-9998627-1-8

Design by Ed Le Froy at Vive Le Rock! magazine
www.vivelerock.net

Cover design by Ed Le Froy

Computer files created by Brent Ware

The right of Michael Stuart Ware to be identified as the author of this work
has been asserted by him in accordance with the
Copyright, Designs and Patents Act, 1988

All rights reserved. No part of this publication may be transmitted in
any form, or by any means, electronic, photocopying, recording or
otherwise, without the prior permission of the publisher.

A CIP catalogue record for this book is available from the British Library

Printed in England

The publishers would like to express their gratitude to Jolene Firgens for permission
to use a photo from her collection for each edition of this book, a photo of LOVE
by her close friend, the legendary photographer, Earl Leaf.

The author and publisher gratefully acknowledge the permission granted to
reproduce the copyright material in this book. Every effort has been made to trace
the copyright holders of the photographs in this book but one or two were unreachable.
We would be grateful if the photographers concerned would contact us.

EXTRADITION PUBLISHING

Contents

Prologue   6

1.	The Palmer Springboard	10
2.	Only An Educated Guess	14
3.	The Invitation	20
4.	Fishing Trip	40
5.	Nighthawks at Canter's	44
6.	Transition	50
7.	The Flight of the Pigeon	56
8.	Da Capo	66
9.	The Bummer	72
10.	Hanging With Snoop	88
11.	On The Road	100
12.	Downtime	114
13.	The Trouble With Cars	124
14.	Forever Changes	128
15.	Kenny's Pad	138
16.	Daisy and The Bear	144
17.	Bristol, Wolfgang and The Hells Angels	150
18.	The East Coast Predicament	158
19.	LOVE (minus Arthur) Meets The Military	174
20.	"Arthur IS LOVE!"	182
21.	Endgames	194

Epilogue   206

This book is dedicated to Buddhist Zen Master, The Most Venerable Dr. Thich An Hue, who so eloquently and patiently taught his many students enlightenment and peace of mind through meditation, while leading the way along The Bodhi Path.

Prologue

ADORNED WITH paint the colour of ripe cantaloupe, my father's house stood serenely on a Los Angeles hillside, near the eastern end of Sunset Boulevard in Echo Park, on a street named Lucretia. At night, during his final years, we often sat on his couch and talked and watched through his living room window, as airplanes took off and landed at Los Angeles International and Burbank airports, regularly ascending from and descending into the twinkling lights of the Wilshire District. Funny, but they always looked like rising and falling stars, which is what you thought they were at first glance because from such a distance they moved so slowly that they appeared to not be moving at all. But then the realization… no, just another airplane.

The view being somewhat northwesterly, the early morning sky would begin to brighten only ever so gradually, and the porch lights from houses on adjoining hillsides would extinguish one by one, as residents awoke and prepared for the day. Most late-afternoon and evening sunsets bathed the sky, if only for an hour or so, in a soft and stunning explosion of crimson and orange and yellow cirrus that took your breath away.

In the daylight hours, the San Gabriel mountain range loomed magnificently on the northern horizon, and several miles straightaway, clearly visible even on a hazy day, the Hollywood sign and Griffith Park Observatory sat virtually side-by-side in peaceful coexistence. Only a few feet from the window, birds of prey routinely patrolled the skies, searching the terrain below for moles and gophers and lizards, glancing inside occasionally as they passed by, as if to ask, "What are you guys eating?"

Around ten o'clock, most weekend nights, from mid-spring through late-autumn, a massive fireworks display from nearby Dodger Stadium could be seen over the rooftops of the houses across the street; and every night, through the bedroom windows, the glimmering lights of the Los Angeles skyline dazzled brilliantly.

My dad had built a cactus garden greenhouse with a redwood chip floor, a green mesh ceiling for shade, and two chairs, down the back wooden steps leading to what would have been the backyard, if it had been a yard… which it wasn't. He had a lizard friend in the cactus greenhouse, and whenever he and I were down there watering or repotting or spreading new redwood chips, my dad would suddenly pause and say, "Hey, look," and there our lizard friend would be, perched on his rock, just watching. Curious creatures they are.

I was there when my father died, in March of 2009, and for months after, actually, doing routine maintenance, like painting and cleaning-up and pulling weeds and giving away to charity a few things, like empty file cabinets and the fold-up chairs my dad had stashed under the house, because you know… he kept them there for the birthday party he held for himself every year out on the patio, during the dog days of early September, when even the L.A. nights are really hot. He was big on birthdays, and you have to have a place for people to sit at a birthday party. Consequently the multitude of folding chairs. He had many friends.

When most of the maintenance was finished, I began thinking about heading home to Tahoe, but somehow I couldn't seem to actually schedule leaving. It was like when I would come to visit him when he was alive and we would find a project or two to work on… it was still that way after he died. My dad's physical being was gone, but his abiding presence held me there. He dwelled in all his remaining possessions... his books and his furniture, and in the house itself, and in the very atmosphere... therefore how could he not be there, as well? It seemed simply a matter of deductive reasoning. So we continued to hang out and do projects together, he and I, as we always had done.

It was during this time that my friend Dennis Kelley came for a brief stay. The first day he arrived, we just kicked back as usual and talked over old times, and then later we headed down the hill and grabbed a bite to eat at a nearby grilled chicken joint. He was still a little tired from his drive in from Las Vegas, so after we brought in all his stuff and watched an old movie on TCM, I got him set up in my Dad's old bedroom, and that was about it for the day. The next morning, as we sat drinking coffee and watching the hawks patrol the skies over Echo Park, Dennis asked me, "Hey, Michael, you want to drive out and visit Arthur today?," and I said, "Yeah, sure," because why not? It was a nice day and I knew Dennis hadn't been able to attend the memorial service back in August of '06. So, after a while, we jumped into my dad's Toyota Rav 4 and headed over to Forest Lawn. There was a guy at the front gate who gave us brief verbal directions and a map that showed Arthur's plot (complete with a helpful numerical designation) and off we drove again...up a windy little asphalt road, past a group of loved ones standing beside the grave of somebody newly-buried, then up further until we saw a marker like a street sign that approximated Arthur's location, so we pulled over and parked and began walking.

We started out walking together, but after two or three minutes of looking, we spread out, so as to cover more territory, because Forest Lawn is a big place and there are like a zillion graves, and a big part of the problem is that instead of standing upright, like the gravestones in film or on TV, the markers bearing the people's names lay flat, so that you have to walk right over and look down to read them. In other words, you can't read the markers from any distance at all, so we had to do a lot of walking and looking down, walking and looking down; and at first, as we walked, I tried to avoid stepping on the graves because it seemed disrespectful somehow, but it was kind of hard walking between the graves in such an exaggerated zigzag pattern, so after a while, I just walked.

Finally Dennis yelled out, "Michael, it's over here!," and he pointed down where he stood. I nodded gratefully and made my way over and looked down again for about the hundredth time, and there it was, at last... with the LOVE logo first and largest at the top, then directly below it, "Arthur Taylor Lee," the marker read. Then the dates he lived, and, "Son of Agnes and Chester," and, "Husband of Diane," and a few other things, and it concluded with a quote; "Love One Another Because Love On Earth Must Be. Signed A. Lee," and the grave was decorated with two flower pots near the foot... pots filled with flowers a few days past their prime.

I thought of Charles Laughton's wistful soliloquy to death in *The Canterville Ghost*: "To be buried in the soft brown earth, to have no today or tomorrow, to forget time, and to be at peace."

We sat next to Arthur for a while, one of us on each side of his grave, making small talk. I asked him how it was going and told him what a nice spot he had, because it actually was pretty nice... up on a little knoll overlooking a quiet valley; just the kind of place anybody would want to be buried. We asked him a few, "Hey Arthur, remember the time?"s and had some laughs, and then, after a brief lull in the conversation, Dennis abruptly and quite suddenly blurted out in a pseudo-confrontational tone, "Hey Arthur, where's my five hundred dollars?" Because, come to find out, Arthur had borrowed five bills from Dennis back in the early seventies and never paid him back; and Dennis, being an understanding friend, and the patient type, hadn't bugged him for it until this very moment. So now, he was finally mentioning it.

The funny thing is, Dennis always kept the cancelled check he wrote Arthur all those years ago, a check all properly endorsed with Arthur's childlike scrawl signature on the back. I mean, he didn't have it with him out at Forest Lawn or anything, but he showed it to me one time. Why did he keep it? He said it was because he figured Arthur might call him up after he cashed it and claim he never got the money and hit him up for it again... which is exactly what happened, of course. Why did he keep it after that? It's hard to say. I suppose because it was a visual reminder of a good story.

Anyway, Dennis was only asking for the five bills to hand Arthur a laugh, because he knew all along the truth of what his wife told him when news of Arthur's death broke. "Now you'll never get your five hundred dollars."

Chapter One

The Palmer Springboard

EAST TEXAS is the land of freeze-dried winter days and sweltering summer nights. June bugs congregate in vast numbers under porch lamp destinations, and fireflies help the stars light the evening sky, illuminating the backyard games children play. It's the part of Texas that features flat landscape, brick architecture and the best watermelon in the world. All in all, not a bad place to grow up.

My friends and I rode bikes and built model airplanes that flew. We fished a small stream and hunted giant grasshoppers with BB guns; played combat, and tied bath towels around our necks and became Superman and Batman. We played Cowboys and Indians.

The neighbourhood kids had been warned never to visit the local abandoned "haunted" house, because it was in constant danger of collapse, and because bums used it as a place to hang out and drink wine. But we went there anyway, every Saturday morning. My family was middle-class. My dad worked at an aircraft factory during the week and played piano with a jazz combo, "The Salty Dogs", on the weekend. Like a lot of children in our socioeconomic group, my sister, Gloria, and I were forced to take piano lessons, which she loved and I hated. Gloria has perfect pitch. She can listen to a doorbell go "ding, dong" and tell you what the notes are; when she was four she could play entire pieces and read music manuscript. Although Gloria went on to become an incredibly accomplished classical musician, I was never quite able to master even the most rudimentary principles of doing something so completely different with the fingers of both the right and left hands at the same time. I didn't have the concentration, or the digital dexterity or whatever, so after a few years of torture, I successfully begged my way out. My family listened to jazz artists like Ella Fitzgerald and Dave Brubeck, classical music, show tunes, almost everything. And my sister and I listened to rock'n'roll a lot. My dad laughed at rock. He called the Everly Brothers "the Everly Sisters" because they sang so high. Country music was the exception. We never listened to it at all, except for what they now call "cross-over", like the Everlys and Carl Perkins and Jerry Lee Lewis.

In fact, it's strange that country music is loosely associated with the South, because the whole time I lived there I never knew of anybody who listened to it, unless you count my great-grandmother, Grandma Ward. Grandma lived in a little house in the back of my grandmother's place in Texarkana, Ark. Her folks were settlers, the kind that travelled west in a wagon train. They stopped in Oklahoma and Arkansas and sprouted roots, setting up shop as ranchers and farmers. Grandma was their little girl.

Whenever my mom and sister and I visited Texarkana from the suburbs of Dallas, where we lived, my mom would send Gloria and me back to spend a little time with Grandma so that she wouldn't feel unloved or ignored. Because she never left her house. At all.

And the scene never changed. She always sat in her wooden rocker, wearing her settler's bonnet, as if posing for a painting by Norman Rockwell. Sometimes she churned butter as she talked, pausing occasionally to dip the end of a kitchen match into a jar of snuff and then quickly roll it into her mouth, between her cheek and gums, where it would do its work. Then, in a voice tired from age and from a lifetime of too many backbreaking chores, she told us stories of what it had been like, a long time ago. Tales of droughts and floods and gunfights, and feuds between our family and other families; feuds that spanned generations.

Occasionally, when the brown juice appeared at the corners of her mouth, she leaned over and spat into a jelly jar which rested on the floor, next to her rocker. Background music for these visits that Gloria and I paid to Grandma was provided by a small bedside radio that always played country and gospel music, songs recorded by The Stamps Quartet and The Sons of the Pioneers. Even her daughter, my grandmother, was too hip to listen to country music. She and her boyfriend liked the boogie-woogie.

So, people that associate country and western with the South, more than any other segment of the nation, are misinformed. Anyway, I have to rate the emergence of country music as "popular" as one of the most unlikely and downright shocking events of the Twentieth Century. And, apparently, the Twenty-first. Seriously. In its pure form, it has to rank right up there with professional wrestling in the How-in-the-world-could-this-have-happened? category. It's so danged corny.

When I was twelve, my best friend was Tony Holman. He was a couple of years older and good-looking and girls chased him, and he could dance cool. He also had a knack for turning the most mundane and unpleasant jobs into a once-removed kind of entertainment.

In most parts of Texas, the summertime air temperature reaches 90 degrees about an hour after sunrise, and on one such typical Saturday morning, I was sweating myself awake and rubbing the sleep from my eyes when the phone rang. A groggy voice asked, "Mike, you want to help me kill a chicken?"

The lady that lived next door to Tony had won a baby chick in a promotional giveaway at Safeway. She dug up a cardboard box and made the chick a little bed, which she kept next to her own bed, because the bird was supposed to be a pet. I think she was all alone. But when the lady woke up, the very first day after she brought it home, she discovered that somehow the chick had broken its neck during the night, and the head was hanging way over to one side at a very unnatural angle. So, she called Tony's dad and asked him if Tony would be willing to take the creature into the woods, somewhere, and put it out of it's misery.

Tony and I went to the lady's house, and she was visibly upset when she brought the chick to the front door. She was still in her pyjamas and she was crying, and the damaged chick was still in the box-home that she had made for it. She thrust the box into Tony's hands, "Take it, hurry!" she said. Then she turned away and closed the door. I looked down. Sure enough, it was a sad sight to behold. Head twisted grotesquely to the side, so that one eye looked downward and the other looked at the sky, the situation was clearly beyond hope. Unfixable, even by a chicken-surgeon's hand.

On the way to the wooded area, at the end of the street, we began to wonder, aloud, how the baby chick broke its neck. Maybe the lady got out of bed in the middle of the night to go to the bathroom and, forgetting the chick was there, stepped on it. It was, after all, the first night in its new home. But then, perhaps embarrassed and angry, the lady might have concluded, "Why cry over spilt milk? What's done is done. I don't know what happened. I woke up and it was like that, O.K.?" If she stepped on her new pet chick and broke its neck, the lady must have suffered, too. In the hours before daybreak. Tony and I took the baby chick into the woods and found a tree stump next to a large anthill.

"Michael, can you hold the chick over the stump?"

"Yeah, I guess," I answered. Pinning its tiny wings under my hand, I held the chick over the stump, as far away from my body as I could. Tony removed a switchblade from his jeans pocket and opened it. He took aim and, as he threw the knife, the chick seemed to look up at Tony with the one eye that could. He missed. He took aim and threw it again, this time severing the chick's head cleanly from its neck. The head rolled off the tree stump, and onto the anthill, where the ants, sensing an easy meal, began to immediately gravitate to it. After Tony sliced open the body to expose the organs, he cut off the chick's right foot and placed it in his shirt pocket. Then he threw what remained of the torso of the tiny beast onto the anthill.

"Ants gotta eat, too," he said.

Later, when he and I were back at Tony's house, watching TV and drinking Kool-Aid, I looked over and noticed Tony playing with the baby chick's foot.

"Hey, Mike." Tony held the foot up and pulled on one of the three small tendons dangling from the detached appendage. The claw curled and, as if from the grave, the chick extended its middle finger to me. The finger chickens use to dig in the dirt. After that, Tony carried the dead chick's zombied claw in his shirt pocket wherever he went, so he could use it to flip the bone to anybody that deserved it. "E-e-w-w-w! What is it?" the girls would ask.

Tony and I listened to a lot of rock'n'roll. Guys like Chuck Berry, Jerry Lee Lewis and Little Richard. Mainly Little Richard. I knew that his drummer's name was Earl Palmer, and that Earl Palmer had been a tap dancer before he became a session drummer. You could hear it, too, in his technique. I think that's what made him so special, that sound of Earl literally dancing those immaculate bass drum patterns. It was beautiful. To me, the drums provided the foundation, the heartbeat, the soul of every band on every record I listened to, and when I was alone, I began to visualize myself as the session drummer that recorded those hits with the rock legends I idolized. I started to want to be a musician. A drummer.

Chapter Two

Only An Educated Guess

NOT LONG before I turned thirteen, my dad accepted a job offer from another aircraft manufacturing company located in San Diego, California, and my family moved to the West Coast. This was a part of the world diametrically opposed to Texas in every way imaginable. To start with, there was no real summer and winter, as I had come to know it, except, I suppose, the San Diego fog burned off a little later in the day in the winter months. That's all. The streams with fish, giant grasshoppers, June bugs – all gone. In their place was the beach, and a beige-stucco junior high school environment that I was having a great deal of trouble adjusting to. Actually, the real problem had become my attitude, because suddenly, no matter how hard I tried, I could not make myself do my homework or study. As I entered my early teens, I found myself so obsessed with daydreaming while listening to music, that I really didn't do much of anything else. In fact, I quickly became one of those scholastic underachievers who comes to class every day unprepared, and, of course, suffers the consequences.

You know, the teacher says, "All right, everybody pass your homework forward," and I don't have mine, again. Then everything goes from bad to worse. Classroom humiliation delivered by somebody who's real good at it. It was very stressful. In fact, I still have the occasional nightmare where I suddenly find myself wandering through the halls of my junior high school, books in hand, in a daze. I'm late... I'm lost... I'm totally naked; and I don't need psychoanalysis to tell me it comes from that homework thing.

Eventually, I came to realize that, if I was ever going to turn my young life around and be happy in school, I had to become a better student. It was, in educational vernacular, a prerequisite. And as I embarked on this voyage of self-improvement, I decided this was a good time to channel my ever growing interest in music into something productive; something that would help me feel more at home in my new southern California, junior high school environment. I joined the band. The school band, that is. And I played the drums. It was fun, sure, and it was a way to meet girls and other people who loved music as I did. The school music organizations gave me focus and identity and a real good reason to be there.

More than that, it gave me my first opportunity to play music with other musicians... in concert. It harkened all the way back to the peaceful harmonies of the youth choir at the Episcopal church where I was a choirboy in Texas, the rehearsals of my dad's band, The Salty Dogs... wailing away in our living room, and the feeling I got when I heard the exciting sounds of early rock and roll on my little bedside radio... the sounds of Little Richard and Chuck Berry and the guys that backed them up on their records. It was the sound of musicians playing different things on different instruments all at the same time, and those individual sounds coming together and fitting so perfectly in a kind of magical auditory jigsaw puzzle, to form a musical creation as unique as a fingerprint. Music played and sung in concert was the ultimate and extreme example of the whole equaling more than merely the sum of the parts, and the prospect of being an integral component in something so special was nothing less than exhilarating.

The concept was simple. The program allowed each kid to select the instrument he liked and then, more or less, start from scratch and learn to play it by playing the songs the band played. This system of learning to play is the reason most junior high school band directors walk around with a slightly puzzled expression all the time. Like, "Why me, Lord?"

From the very beginning, I discovered I had what felt like a sort of spring-loaded elasticity built into the ligaments of my shoulders and wrists and elbows that allowed

me to generate a lot of energy and control. Like built-in electronic jackhammers, the sticks felt as if they belonged in my hands. Playing the drums seemed so natural, and, strangely enough, doing something so physical seemed to have almost no correlation at all to muscle strength or size. What I mean is, I was a real skinny kid with skinny arms. The kid who played the bass drum in the marching band was Kenny Larson, the push-up/pull-up champion of the school, and even though he was no more than fifteen, he was built solid, like an adult weightlifter. But, when he played the bass drum, no matter how hard he hit the thing, he sounded like a little girl. You know, "bong, bong, bong." No punch. He couldn't understand how to transfer all that muscle power into pounding the drum with the necessary enthusiasm to make it sound right. And, besides, he always hit it too near the rim, instead of closer to the centre, like he should have.

So, one day I took him aside, "Kenny, check this out. You see this place right here?" I pointed to a spot on the head of the bass drum near the centre. "This is the sweet spot, man. That's where you've got to hit it. And HARD, so everybody can hear it, all over the school. Every time you hit it, it's got to explode, man! It's got to start from the tips of your toes and travel up, and you have to put total concentration into every blow. Kill it, man! Whip it! I mean, you have to lay into it, really. Like this." I took the beater from Kenny and hit the bass drum four times, "FWOMP! FWOMP! FWOMP! FWOMP!" The air shook.

"Oh, I get it," he took the beater out of my hand, "like this?" He bit his lower lip and struck the bass drum with all his might, "bong, bong, bong."

"That's good, Kenny. Keep practicing," I said, walking away. No use. The instinct just wasn't there. He was muscle-bound.

My participation in these school bands and orchestras and choral groups continued into high school where it proved to be an effective way to accomplish my goals and have a good time. Along the way, my high school music buddies and I formed different kinds of bands to fit various occasions. We had a four-piece jazz ensemble that worked adult parties and local coffee houses, and a rock band that played the school dances. And subconsciously, even though we played for pleasure, I guess I was beginning to enjoy the financial rewards of getting paid pretty good money to do something I enjoyed. Something I would have done for free, anyway.

As I entered my senior year, I made arrangements to accept a scholarship offer to Pepperdine University, up the coast in L.A. One day, I got a note from my counsellor to come to his office to set up a preliminary first semester schedule for my college freshman year. I don't remember his name. He was, in every respect, the stereotypical high school administrator, locked into holding down what I perceived to be, at the time, a relatively boring and unimportant job at a place I was about to leave. But, I do remember he was a nice guy.

He welcomed me in and pumped my hand, as I sat down in the wooden chair near his desk. "Michael," he started, "first of all congratulations on having received the school's Outstanding Musician of the Year award, you've had a truly successful high school experience. I know you're headed to Pepperdine. You'll like Pepperdine a lot. It's a great school with a fine music program. By the way, I was a musician when I attended college, you know, like you. A professional musician. In fact, I was able to pay just about all my tuition with the money I made working nights and on weekends. I gave it up after a while, though. I wasn't lucky enough to qualify for a college scholarship. I hope you appreciate your good fortune. It's a wonderful opportunity."

I remember the feeling I experienced at that moment, sitting there in my high school counsellor's office. Pity, really. And alarm. You "gave it up?" You know, that's how careful you have to be. You can be cruising along, doing something cool, something you're proud and happy to do, something that gets girls; and before you know it, you're sitting behind a desk, wearing a wrinkled suit and working a dead-end job in a crummy high school. I remember thinking, as I walked out of his office at the conclusion of our meeting, "That's awful. I'll never let that happen to me." But perspective is a funny thing. It can change with the passage of time.

I would find out something really interesting about Pepperdine when I got there and it was too late. The catalogue described the school as a "liberal arts college with a small enrolment... partially funded by, and affiliated with, The Church of Christ." Small print, near the bottom of the last page.

George Pepperdine was the guy who founded the school back in the '30s with the money he made when he sold off his ownership in the Western Auto stores. He had a couple of little girls, and like all good fathers he began to worry about the time when they would go to college and he wouldn't be there to protect them, and I guess one day he thought, "Hey, wouldn't it be great if there was a college with a Christian influence and a wholesome environment? A place where parents wouldn't have to worry about their kids?" So he started Pepperdine. I wasn't concerned about the exaggerated moral philosophy. All I knew was, Pepperdine offered me the most lucrative scholarship so I took it.

Like I said, they didn't really play up the "wholesome Christian" concept in the literature. I think the school figured it might turn some potential students off, and they needed all the students they could get, so the administration, more or less, depended on the word-of-mouth church grapevine to get the message out. Because I know when I got there, I wasn't the only one surprised at the level of influence the church held over the school; and during the day-long "orientation" prior to the start of classes a lot of people were kind of looking at each other with expressions of amused disbelief and asking, "What's this...?" Because at Pepperdine there were three ironclad rules:

Rule number 1: "Each student must attend Chapel every Wednesday morning at ten o'clock. Chapel is mandatory. You miss three chapels in the same semester you lose your tuition, your scholarship (if you have one), and you get kicked out of school."

Rule number 2: "No booze-drinking. On or off campus. We find out you've been drinking booze, you lose your scholarship, your tuition and you get kicked out of school," and,

Rule number 3: "No dancing. We find out you've been dancing you lose everything and you get kicked out of school."

The chapel thing was no big deal. We went to the school auditorium and sat in our assigned seats for a half-hour and then we were free to go. We were even given two units toward graduation for showing up. Non-transferable units, of course. During chapel, the college big-wigs all sat on the stage in those enormous high-back chairs like you see on *The Hour Of Power* and, one at a time, each would get up and share a few words of wisdom and then it would be over. I mean, chapel was just like any other class, except it was shorter and there were no tests. I didn't mind it. The "no booze" thing? I wasn't really into booze. I didn't want any booze. "No dancing?" I was never much of a dancer.

The individual rules didn't bother me that much. It's just that the overall resulting atmosphere was so... repressive. You know, "If you don't be good, we'll throw you out of school and later you'll go to hell." Scare tactics never work. Everybody that wanted to drink, drank; and all the dancers danced. In fact, I began to wonder if the school meant business or if the rules were just for the benefit of the supporters. Then, on the very day I had planned to ask the really cute blonde who sat next to me in chapel for a date, I was greeted by an empty chair. So, I asked the girl on the other side, "Where's Cindy?"

She says, "Oh, didn't you hear? Charlie caught a boy in her room last night. They were having sex. Today, she's back home in Indiana."

Actually, I don't remember there being a "rule" prohibiting sex between students, so I guess it was just more or less understood, or maybe they were caught drinking and dancing, as well. Whatever, she was gone.

Charlie was our lone campus security guard. Had a lot in common with Barney Fife. All business, he made it his responsibility to protect all the girls from the evil intentions of the boys, even if they didn't want to be protected. Like, if he saw a couple sitting in a car, he would walk up and whack the rear bumper once or twice with his nightstick, just to let them know he was on duty and the guy better not try anything. Lew Grizzard once said, "Most security guards wake up every day wondering if they'll have the opportunity to shoot somebody." Because, you know, they're not really cops, so they have to be extra hard-ass to prove they're just as good. That was Charlie.

The Pepperdine campus was located in South Central L.A., close to Watts, and the local kids used to regularly play basketball in the school gym in the evenings. It was O.K. with school officials. They always left it unlocked and open to the public after classes were dismissed. The administration figured it was good for community relations. But one night, as a group of dudes was leaving the gym, Charlie figured he would "challenge" them and ask them to show some ID; for no reason, except he was bored, I guess, and it was within his authority to do it. So, while he was busy looking at somebody's ID, he absent-mindedly set the shotgun he always carried on the roof of his patrol car. What happened next is a matter of conjecture. Charlie claimed one of the basketball players made a grab for the gun, but what happened for sure was, Charlie shot to death an innocent thirteen-year-old kid whose only apparent plan when he left his home was to go to the Pepperdine gym, a few blocks away, and play basketball with some friends.

Like Charlie, the school big-wigs were well-intended. But several years after I had transferred to U.C.L.A., the president of the school was toodling along the Pacific Coast

Highway, drunk as a skunk, when he smashed into a car sitting at a stoplight and killed the other driver and a passenger. If he had been permitted to speak at chapel the next Wednesday morning, he probably would have said, "See? That's why we don't want you people to drink booze!"

U.C.L.A. was just the opposite of Pepperdine. They didn't care what you did there, at all. Knock yourself out.

Chapter Three

The Invitation

FOR A couple of years after moving to L.A., I followed the same pattern of participation in school production groups at Pepperdine and later, when I transferred in my junior year, at U.C.L.A. Fraternity parties were fertile ground during this period. I mean, these things could only be classified as "exclusive", I guess. You could definitely get hurt trying to get through the door unless you were a member of the fraternity or one of the girls they had invited or a member of the band scheduled to play that night, in which case, it was like, "Oh, the band? Yeah, sure, set up over there in the corner. Make yourselves at home. The booze is that way. The girls'll be here later." Almost every frat party I ever played was quite a bit like the one in the movie, *Animal House* – except I never saw a guy take a motorcycle up the stairs that I can remember. It was the kind of environment where, if you were on a break and looking for a place to kick back and relax, like a comfortable looking dark corner someplace... if you weren't careful, you could suddenly find yourself lying down in a pile of cold puke. Which I did, of course. All those frat dudes and chicks always drank too much, was the problem.

The fraternity parties paid fairly decent money, but almost without exception, they took place only on Friday and Saturday nights, and my band brothers and I started to feel like we should check out our options as far as playing during the week, as well. So, we decided to make the rounds of the little dives in Culver City and West Los Angeles and talk to club owners; and right away we ran into a difficulty we hadn't anticipated. The difficulty was that nobody in the band was 21.

Because the very first guy we talked to says... I mean the very first thing out of his mouth was, "I hope you guys are all 21. The state Alcoholic Beverage Control is in here almost every night checking I.D., and if I hire any underage help they'll jerk my licence to sell booze, and that will close me down and I wouldn't like that."

I think we all smiled and said something innocuous like, "Hey, we'll be right back," you know... so as not to raise any suspicion, like we were going out to the car to get our I.D.'s. Then we left and didn't go back to that joint at all. "The Party Doll," in Culver City it was. I made a mental note, so we wouldn't accidently go back. No party dolls there, however, just factory workers looking to bolt down a few quick beers after work, before heading home to the little woman.

But I mean, the whole thing really took us off guard, if you want to know the truth. Here we had been playing these fraternity gigs, where all they did was drink themselves into nauseous oblivion right out in the open for everybody to see, and the party goers weren't 21, the band wasn't 21... nobody was 21; and the cops didn't care, the state Alcoholic Beverage Control Board didn't care, the Dean of Students at the school didn't care... nobody cared; and now suddenly everybody in the place must be 21, including and especially us, or else bad things will happen, and someone definitely cares. The double standard was a bit confusing, to say the least.

So anyway, if we wanted to play clubs, our assignment was simple. Get some over-twenty-one identification somehow. The rhythm guitarist in the group said not to worry, he knew a girl who worked for the Department of Motor Vehicles and could get us actual drivers licences, so that's what we did. Problem was, because the licences were real, we had to get them in a name other than the one that appeared on our current I.D, or else somebody down at the DMV might notice. You know..., same face, same address, same hair colour, eye colour, height, weight, but a different birthdate? Red flag.

So that's how nineteen-year-old Michael Ware became twenty-one-year-old Michael Stuart.

The band? We called ourselves The Vectors, and after we got our new over-twenty-one driver's licences, it was a breeze. But finding the time to study and keep up with my classes at U.C.L.A. became a little more complex.

Eventually, I was offered an opportunity to tour, by a Hollywood production company, with a band comprised of members of various U.C.L.A. and U.S.C. rock groups. Unfortunately, the tour was smack in the middle of the spring quarter, and it soon became obvious that the only reasonable plan was to temporarily drop my classes at U.C.L.A., and re-enter school at a later date. Although I realized this was a dangerous thing to do, the temptation was too great to ignore. It was late 1964 and the influx of English power groups, like The Beatles, The Stones, Manfred Mann and The Kinks, was in full swing. The face of music history was about to change and I felt an overwhelming need to be a part of the new order. I knew this special time couldn't last forever and I didn't want to miss out. It had the feel of something that would never come along again.

It was the spring of '65. After I dropped out of school, I had lots of time on my hands to make the rounds of local clubs with some of my fellow musicians from the tour. Late one night, in January of 1965, we found ourselves sitting at a table in a beer bar in Santa Monica called The Mirage, watching far and away the best bar band I had ever heard: The Fender Four. But they weren't really a bar band, at all. In fact, the only similarity between The Fender Four and any other bar band I had seen, to that point, was that they happened to be working a bar. Their sound was tight-knit and powerful, and professional, and they had total command of their instruments.

The bass players in the rock bands I had been with to that point played real simple patterns. One-note sonatas. Change the note every couple of bars or so. The bass player in The Fender Four was banging out sophisticated runs that could only be described as "incredible". He was all over the fretboard, virtually defining the way an electric bass should be played. The group performed covers of some early Stones material and soul boogie, like James Brown's 'Night Train'. Their hair was really, really long and they had the stage mannerisms of a band that had been doing it long enough to be absolutely confident. And they had a following. The place was packed and the crowd was in the palms of their hands. At that moment I had to have been thinking, "Man, I would give anything to play drums with The Fender Four." I mean, they were dynamite.

During a break, the group members sat at a table with their girlfriends and talked to the patrons who came over to buy them drinks, and they looked all sweaty and happy and satisfied. Pretty soon, it was time for the next set to begin and they got back on stage and, after somebody killed the jukebox, The Fender Four commenced to knocking 'em dead again.

After a couple of songs, I felt somebody slide into the chair next to me and a female voice asked, "Are you guys in a band?" I looked over and was surprised to see the girl who had been sitting with the bass player. Smiling, stunningly beautiful. "I'm Donna." She held out her hand and we shook. Then, without me even asking, she began to tell me about The Fender Four. Because she was real outgoing.

Suddenly, the next song began, "All the guys are from Baltimore!" she shouted over the din. "Except the drummer. They found him here in L.A. They call themselves 'The Fender Four' because the lead guitar player, Randy, hustled a deal with Fender to get free equipment in exchange for free publicity."

I thought, "Jeez, free equipment? This dude Randy must be a damned fine hustler."

Donna looked up at the group and leaned over close to me. "Quite honestly, I don't think they're completely happy with the drummer. They're sort of looking to replace him, eventually. You don't happen to play the drums, do you?"

I wanted to grab her and kiss her and hug her but what I did was admit, matter-of-factly, "Yeah, I play drums." So, she took me over to where Randy's wife was sitting and she introduced me and told her I played the drums and they both acted real happy to have found me. But, as we sat at the table and talked, I began to get the impression that there might have been a little more to the story. Like, maybe a little personality clash or something, because the dude playing drums with The Fender Four was a good drummer. I didn't really care. For whatever reason, it looked as if I was maybe about to get a shot to play with the best rock group I had ever seen. After the set ended, Donna introduced me to Mike and Randy and told them I was a drummer, and they said something like, "Well, hey, maybe we can get together and jam, sometime," and they took my number. But it was understood they were talking about an audition.

So, I thanked Donna, and on the way out of The Mirage, my buddies from the U.C.L.A. frat band I had come in with, were asking me, "Hey, what were they talking to you about, Michael? Did they offer you a gig? Are you gonna be in The Fender Four?"

I said, "I don't know." But I was hoping and praying.

The next day, Randy and Mike called and asked if I wanted to jam, and I said, "Sure, come on over, we can jam here at my house, no problem," which was crazy. I still lived at home, and things were already a little on the shaky side, what with me having dropped out of school; the "tour" having long since concluded, I had no regular means of support. But what I did have was this hair that was getting longer by the minute. More and more, my folks were beginning to give me this look that said, "What's the matter with you?"

We lived in Ladera Heights, a very quiet, upscale suburban neighbourhood. No loud traffic or stereos or barking dogs or anything. In fact, on any given day the only noise of any kind would be, maybe the chirping of the birdies, that's all. Seriously.

So, around noon, Mike and Randy pulled up to the curb in front of my house and unloaded their equipment and brought it in and set up, and in a little while we started to play. And, whoa, it was amazing! And ear-splitting. I guess my dad was at work, but I think my mom and sister jumped in the car and left, because they were probably afraid or embarrassed of what they figured was about to happen. You know, police intervention, or whatever. I only know after the first tune they weren't around any more.

I mean, when Mike and Randy played onstage at The Mirage in front of a crowd, they cranked the volume on their amps up all the way, to pump everybody up and achieve maximum excitement – and when they played in neighbourhoods on nice, quiet suburban streets, they cranked it up all the way then, too. They always cranked it up all the way. The walls of my folks' house literally shook. Hey, truth be told, I was only slightly self-conscious about the noise. I just wanted the gig, that's all. I figured, one way or the other, I had to move out pretty soon anyway, and we sounded good and got along well. Nothing else was important, especially the tranquillity of what would soon be my ex-neighbourhood.

After running through a few tunes, Randy and Mike set guitar and bass down, lit a couple of Viceroys, and we sat around and talked for a while. Then, in a minute, Randy looked up and told me, "Michael, this group's going to the top, and we want you as our drummer. How about it?"

Oh, yeah.

As soon as I joined up with Randy and Mike and Jac, we moved into a house together in Pacific Palisades and began to play the beer bar circuit. We played Cisco's, in Manhattan

Beach, and The Mirage in Santa Monica, and the Warehouse IX in West L.A., and a few others; and we continued to build a following.

One night, when the group was playing the Beaver Inn in Westwood, we got word that a Hollywood entrepreneur named Kim Fowley was coming down to check us out, and he would be bringing some friends with him. They didn't call them "hippies" back then, but that's what they were. We said, "Who's Kim Fowley?"

The club manager laughed, "Remember The Hollywood Argyles? 'Alley Oop, Oop?' Well, that's him."

"You mean, 'There's a mayun in the funny papers, we all know/Alley Oop, Oop. Oop. Oop-poop/He don't eat nuthin' butta bearcat stew'?"

"That's it. That's the guy."

"O.K.," we said. "We'll be looking for him." Kind of an odd song, though, 'Alley Oop'. Not exactly rock'n'roll.

The Beaver Inn was a real popular bar, close to U.C.L.A., and we packed the people in every night. Line around the block and a long wait. So we left Kim's name at the door. The clientele of this club was a straight, tough crowd. No long hair or drugs. Just beefy, beer-guzzling frat football players and their gorgeous, beer-guzzling sorority girlfriends.

About eleven o'clock the next night, there was a small commotion at the door and in walked a dude that we all knew right away had to be Kim Fowley. He stood about 6'6", and weighed maybe 145 pounds; he wore a gothic robe and a faraway expression, and was accompanied by nine or ten beautiful young girls wearing leather sandals and love beads. When they walked through the door, we had just finished a song, and it was kind of quiet momentarily, except for the normal room noise of people milling about. When they spotted Kim, conversation stopped and all eyes turned to the newcomers. Suddenly, you could hear a pin drop. You could feel the beer drinkers thinking, "What in the hell is that?" But as we launched into our next tune, the party atmosphere resumed, attention reverted back to the beer and everybody started dancing. You could tell, though, the regulars were still keeping an eye on Kim.

And, I guess, so as not to disappoint the crowd, Kim and his girlfriends began to perform. They moved slowly to the music, out to the centre of the floor, past the football players doing the Frug and the Boogaloo and the Watusi and, when they reached a place where they could be seen by everyone in the room, they began a strange dance. First, the girls circled around Kim, and he started to writhe and squirm; and then he took an imaginary arrow from an imaginary quiver and loaded it into an imaginary bow. He leaned back and, eyes closed, shot the arrow into the ceiling of the Beaver Inn. It was all performed in slow motion to the music of some Stones song we were playing. When Kim opened his eyes, he discovered what the rest of us already knew. The football players and their girlfriends had all stopped dancing and had moved back to form a giant circle around the group of hippies. You know, like a spotlight dance, but mean-spirited. No happy faces. In fact, they were all glaring at him. Now, his friends joined the rest of the crowd and backed off the dance floor, leaving Kim out there alone. So, I guess he thought, "Well, hey, I'll give them a little show."

Like a huge praying mantis, he glided, gracefully and slowly, in patterns only he understood, sliding and weaving, arms akimbo, implementing his theatre of the absurd for this unappreciative roomful of drunks. Forcing it down their throats. Hate permeated the atmosphere. People don't like what they don't understand, and they most definitely did not understand Kim. He looked so strange and out of place in The Beaver Inn. Alien, really.

Suddenly, Kim spun around and, facing us, slowly and deliberately drew his right forefinger across his throat, the universal signal musicians use to bring a song to its conclusion. His eyes were wide. "Cut it short," his expression read, "I can tell they don't like me. Time to leave."

I don't remember what happened right after the song was over, I mean, they didn't jump on Kim and beat him up or anything, although they probably wanted to. It was just kind of quiet. I do remember that at the break, he met us over by the edge of the stage and introduced himself and told us he liked the group and he thought he could get us some work in Hollywood. Then he said, "Hey, 'The Fender Four' is a dog shit name, man. You guys should call yourselves 'The Sons of Adam.'" He said it with a flair. And then, Kim Fowley and his girls left. We had the club bouncer follow them out to make certain they got to their cars all right. I don't think Kim realized how far south of Hollywood The Beaver Inn was.

Pretty soon we began to attract more of the hip crowd into the beer bars we were playing and, before long, we got an offer to play a club that was actually located in Hollywood: Gazzarri's on La Cienega. Later, Bill Gazzarri asked us to open his new club, on Sunset. And we did.

Mike and Randy and Jac, the group's rhythm guitarist, were characters. In Baltimore, they had all dropped out of high school and worked as cab drivers and shoe salesmen. When they decided to come to California and become rock stars, they didn't have any money saved. So, to finance the trip, they told me, they got hold of a pink slip to a car that didn't run at all, didn't even have a battery; and they pushed the car to the top of a hill. Then, they all jumped in and rolled it down the street into this used car dealership that had advertised it would pay two hundred bucks for any car, as long as it ran. It was a noisy corner downtown, with tremendous traffic, so the salesman-buyer probably couldn't hear much, but it certainly looked like it was running, because they pulled into the lot and got out of the car and all walked over to the office together, easy and natural, like a bunch of friends out for a drive, who just happened to stop in on the spur of the moment. To sell their car.

The dealership manager strolled out of the office and approached Randy, "Help you guys?"

Randy smiled, "Yeah, we want to sell our car for two hundred bucks, like you said in the ad."

He gave the car the once over. "It sure looks like a piece of shit, but it runs O.K., huh?"

And Randy said, "Well, of course it runs. You saw us drive it in, didn't you? Sure it runs. How do you think we got it here?" So the guy bought the car and gave them the two bills and that's how they got the money to get to California. That's what they told me, anyway. Yeah, I know.

Like I said, they didn't do well in school but they had "street smarts".

Randy Holden was the leader of the Sons of Adam, tall and thin, with angular features and long, jet-black hair, grown down past his shoulders. He brushed his hair back, off his forehead, not down to his eyebrows, like everybody else. Sometimes, club owners would take me or Mike or Jac aside during a break. "Hey man," they would implore, "can't you get Randy to wash his hair and turn the volume on his amp down?"

We always said, "He washes it every day, that's just the way it looks and, no, we can't get him to turn down. He's the leader of the group. He can play as loud as he wants." In fact, he sounded good playing loud. It just meant the rest of us had to play loud, too, to try to keep things even. Besides, the music brought customers in from several blocks away, so I still don't know what they were snivelling about.

We had a gig at The Cinnamon Cinder in the valley for a couple of months, back in early 1966, when it was owned by Bob Eubanks, the game show host. He came in the club one night and the place was jammed-packed with paying customers, and we were playing loud, as usual. As soon as he walked through the front door, Bob went over and grabbed the bartender by the arm and he was all red in the face and yelling at him and jerking his thumb in our direction, and in a minute he left, holding his hands over his ears and shaking his head.

When the song was over, the bartender hurried over to the edge of the stage and said, "Hey, guys, Bob said to tell you to tone it down some. You're way too loud." So Randy nodded and told him, "no problem", but about halfway through the next tune he turned it right back up again to about one decibel shy of blowing the speakers. I mean, Bob was gone.

We were the Cinnamon Cinder house band. Every Wednesday night was "guest star" night and we would serve as the back-up band for whatever star showed up on Wednesdays. The really astounding part of the plan was the lack of preparation involved. The star would just show up about twenty minutes before the set and we would meet in the dressing room during the break and run over a few songs, and then we would go out and introduce the star and the star would emerge and take the stage with us. Then we would back them up on their hits and a few other songs and that would be it. It was an O.K. system, I guess, I mean we never had any major foul-ups that I can remember, other than an occasional wrong note. No big deal. The Sons of Adam were pretty good at picking things up the first time.

Glen Campbell was the guest star one night, after he had had a hit or two, but before he had his TV show, *The Glen Campbell Goodtime Hour*, or whatever. He was a pretty nice guy... that is, he didn't seem to have an overinflated ego or anything. We met in the back room before his set, like we always did, and he showed us some of his tunes and we went out and did the guest set, just like we were supposed to. Everybody knew, before he became a successful single act, Glen had been a real busy session guitarist, playing on a lot of Beach Boys stuff, and for Phil Spector and even Frank Sinatra. He could read music. So, when we were in the back room working on the material, we were more than a little surprised to discover that Glen hadn't even bothered to bring his guitar with him. He just planned on borrowing Randy's guitar for one of the tunes when he needed to play the intro. But when we got onstage and Glen put Randy's guitar on, it hung down real low and cool, arms extended, like rock guitarists wear their guitars now, instead of chest-high hootenanny-style, like guitar players in most of the groups wore their guitars at that time. So Glen turned away from the microphone and looked down at the guitar, and then looked over at Randy and laughed, "What are you trying to cover up here, buddy?" The audience laughed, then Glen laughed some more. It was a pretty good ad lib, I guess.

Earlier in 1965, The Sons of Adam had played a gig at the Long Beach Auditorium with The Stones, during their first American tour. Dick and Dee Dee were on the bill as well. You know, 'The Mountain's High'? (Dee Dee sang the regular woman's voice part and Dick sang the higher falsetto part.) The Dick half, Dick St. John, had been impressed as hell with the group and thought we had enormous potential so, ever since the Long Beach gig, he had been in on-and-off negotiations with Randy to manage and produce the group. His partner was Mike Post, the dude who would go on to hit it big writing countless theme songs for TV shows like *The Rockford Files*. Mike had just been released from the United States Air Force and he still had the buzz haircut and the girl-starved serviceman attitude. If we were sitting in his car, waiting for a red light to change, and a really cute black chick was walking across the street, Mike would kind of lean out his window and say, "Whoa, I feel like changing my luck" loud enough for her to hear. Dick and Mike had been doing some preliminary recordings of The Sons of Adam over in the garage studio Dick and Dee Dee used to record their stuff, and the group had been doing some hanging out over at Dick's house in Santa Monica, the one he shared with his mother.

During the first visit, Dick had just returned from a European tour he and Dee Dee had done with The Stones and we were in his bedroom listening to some demo cuts from an unfinished Stones album, when we suddenly heard a lot of explosive yelling coming from the other room, "Look out, damn it! Tear his head off! Break his legs! Kill him!" Dick waved it off. "Ignore that. It's just my mom. She's a big wrestling fan. She's watching TV." We never met her because she always stayed in her room when we were there. Dick had a real nice boot collection. About fifty pairs of hand-made Italian and English boots he bought when he and Dee Dee were European-touring. Always nice to bring something home with you.

Problem was, like a lot of the people who had designs on the future of The Sons of Adam, Dick St. John and Mike Post kept trying to turn the group into something we weren't, something we knew we could never be. Dick even overdubbed his voice onto one of the demo cuts the group did over at Dick's garage studio in Santa Monica. The group was hard-rocking and cooking and then, right in the middle of it all, Dick laid a real gutsy, high-pitched "Ooh, hoo!" in there, right where it didn't belong. Sounded really out of place. Dick and Mike Post thought it sounded great. When we were listening to the playback, Dick and Mike were saying stuff like "All right! That really makes it!" and they were grinning and shaking hands with the engineer and slapping each other on the back, but I could see the look on Randy's face that said, "We're heading into uncharted waters, here. Where's the nearest exit?"

Not sure what Dick's real agenda was. I once read that The Rolling Stones had backed Dick and Dee Dee on two songs they recorded in England, 'Blue Turns to Grey' and 'Some Things Stick in Your Mind', so maybe Dick St. John saw The Sons of Adam as a way to shoehorn himself into the new rock scene that was taking over popular music. Whatever the case, it finally got to the point where Dick and Mike Post didn't want to invest any more time or money into The Sons of Adam without us signing a contract. Dick had mentioned a few times that he expected us to sign one pretty soon; so one night Randy called Dick up on the phone and gave him the bad news that we weren't interested. The next day Randy told us the phone call hadn't gone well: "Yeah, he was real upset about it. He was yelling and screaming that we had wasted his time and then he hung up on me. So, to hell with him, he's a jerk." And that was that, sort of.

Because on the final week of the Cinnamon Cinder gig, we were on break between sets on a Tuesday before our normal guest celebrity Wednesday night, when the club manager walked up to Randy and handed him three 45s. "You guys might want to run over these tunes before tomorrow night. Dick and Dee Dee are the guest celebrities. You remember them: 'The Mountain's High'?" It got real quiet.

"Yeah, O.K." Randy took the 45s from the club manager and set them on the top of his amp.

Next night, Wednesday Guest Celebrity night, Dick and Dee Dee arrived at the Cinnamon Cinder about twenty minutes before their set was to begin and we all got together in the back room to do a quick run-through of the songs they planned to do. The atmosphere was business-like and professional. Not friendly.

When the guest set started, we took our places on stage and began the intro to 'The Mountain's High'. Then the club manager introduced Dick and Dee Dee, and they climbed the stage steps and took their places behind the two microphones, finger-popping and moving their bodies to the beat, nodding their heads and smiling to acknowledge the applause of the crowd. But as soon as they started to sing, it became obvious what Dick had in mind. No way was he going to forgive and forget, as we so naively assumed he might. Dick immediately turned and waved his arms at us and frowned, like, "No, no, that's not right!" Then, he looked out at the audience and shrugged and shook his head and laughed. His body language said, "Jeez, this band is crappy, isn't it? What can you do? When you're a big star, this is the kind of thing you have to put up with all the time." Kept it up throughout the set.

Finally, mercifully, we played the last note of the last Dick and Dee Dee song, and then they exited the stage and were gone. He "got even" with us, I guess – in his own mind, at least. Except that several regulars came up to us after the set and said stuff like, "What the fuck was wrong with that asshole? You guys were playing it right."

I mean, it was our audience. The Sons of Adam were the mainstream entertainment at The Cinnamon Cinder. Dick and Dee Dee were an "oldies" group, visitors from the past.

Randy not only looked unique, but his playing style was unique as well. He taught himself to play the guitar, note by note, from records, and then he taught Jac and Mike their rhythm guitar and bass parts for each song. Extremely focused, Randy was a dynamic and powerfully talented guitarist. Blessed with blazing speed, his hands always shook just a little when he wasn't playing, as if they couldn't wait, such was the level of his intensity; and he hit the right note every time. He was a consummate perfectionist who hated leaving anything to chance. A groundbreaker of heavy metal, his product was fire and the guitar his incendiary device. He was awesome every night.

Jac Ttanna was our rhythm guitarist. The showman of the group. Great stage presence and personality. Conjure up a mental image of Frank Sinatra, with long hair and glasses, and you'll have a rough visual concept of Jac. In fact, he even had a framed picture of himself in a Frank Sinatra pose on his bureau. Head tilted casually to one side, sports jacket draped over his shoulder, looking back at the camera. Walking out the door, smiling nonchalantly. Like the publicity shot used for *Come Blow Your Horn*.

Jac talked to himself in the mirror a lot, if he thought nobody was around. Like, if he was in the bathroom combing his hair, working real hard, trying to get it to look good.

"Now, if I can get this to stay over here, on the right... yeah, that's it. Who do those people think they are anyway? I'll show 'em they can't mess with me!" But, you know, non-stop, jumping from one subject to another in a running monologue. I think it was an emotional release of some kind, self-administered psychotherapy. If he heard footsteps, of course, then he would put it in pause, get real quiet, wait until the coast was clear and, when he thought he was alone, he would start rapping again.

He wore those flip-up/flip-down shades over his glasses. The rest of us soon began teasing him by flipping them down whenever we could get close enough to sneak a hand in. Very disrespectful. One day he discovered the flip-ups were cracked and made us all chip in to buy him a new pair. Total cost was, like, three bucks, but you could tell he got a charge out of us having to cough up the money to pay for our sins. He probably broke the shades himself – on purpose, to teach us a lesson. I guess his strategy worked, though, because we all stopped messing with his glasses after that. Jac was a hell of a good singer. Carried a tune, right on.

Somehow, Jac fell into the habit of constantly being late for rehearsals. After a while, it got to be so bad that it led to a new rule: whoever was late for rehearsal had to pay fifty bucks to the other guys. Of course, Jac was the only guy who came to rehearsals late, so the rule was for him. The very next day after the rule was implemented, Jac came running through the door at Gazzarri's, breathless. Fifteen minutes late.

"All right, man..." Randy started.

"Wait, wait, wait, you don't know what happened!" Then, Jac began a long and convoluted story of having been run off the road by a couple of big guys in a big car, and they ended up on somebody's front yard, where they all jumped out of their cars, and the big guys started to beat on Jac, but he, knowing a little karate, was able to kick their asses and drive away, unscathed. He won the fight. I guess we were supposed to be proud of him for scoring a knockout victory for long hairs and not fine him the fifty bucks, like we normally would have, if he hadn't just performed such a heroic act.

Then, as he neared the conclusion of the tale, his brow furrowed. "And the first thing I thought about after the fight was over, and I was driving down Sunset, was the fifty-dollar fine I was gonna have to pay. I realized, for Christ's sake, now I'll be late for rehearsal and it's not even my fault," Jac concluded, looking at the floor, then pausing silently for effect. He was trying really hard to avoid paying the fifty-dollar fine and that was a pretty good story he made up, so Randy let him off the hook. Besides, Jac was never late again, so... I think it just took him one more time to get into the new, "don't be late" groove.

In spite of what I said about him resembling Frank Sinatra, Jac was not, by traditional standards, a "pretty boy." I mean, he was good-looking but his rugged features gave him the look of a man slightly older than his years, and girls were fond of telling him to his face how much he reminded them of the character of Paul's grandfather in *A Hard Day's Night*, like it was a compliment. One night when we were on a break at Gazzarri's, Jac was working a really beautiful girl for her phone number; after the break was over, he came back up on the stage with a big smile and a piece of paper. "Hey, check it out, I got her phone number," and he showed it to me: "Mary... Beechwood 4-5789." That's what she wrote.

But, like I said, Jac was a good-looking dude and, even though he didn't get Mary, he had a whole lot of beautiful women chasing him – and he was talented.

Mike Port was our bass player. Thin, soft features, baby face, gentle expression, but the other guys had filled me in. As a kid, Mike was forced to fight his way through one of the toughest neighbourhoods in Baltimore every day, to get to the store and buy his mom a pack of Camels, so he got tough.

One week, on a break from our steady gig at Gazzarri's we were offered a five-day booking in Hayward, California, back when it was a ranching community and thronging with drunken cowboys any night after ten o'clock. On one such night, about three in the morning, we had gotten off work and were trying to grab something to eat in a nearby coffee shop when a size extra-large wrangler walked over to our booth and threw a couple of pink women's styling combs down on our table. Then he leaned over in Mike's face and said, with a smile, "I'll be waitin' for you outside when you're done, honey."

Maybe I can help you fix your hair." Then he laughed and walked out through the front door and disappeared. Mike didn't look over at the cowboy or acknowledge him at all. He just took another bite of his cheeseburger and stared straight ahead. I mean, the sudden threat of an after-dinner fistfight didn't seem to ruin his appetite, or anything.

Sure enough, after we paid the tab and went out to the parking lot, there he was, waiting by our car with a bunch of his friends. Laughing and joking.

"You can't leave yet, little girl," he said to Mike. Without a word, Mike took off his coat and handed it to me. Randy nudged me with his elbow, "Don't worry, Mike can take care of himself." I couldn't help but worry a little. Mike was soft and kind of fragile-looking and the cowboy was big and tough.

The cowboy's friends stood in a large group, maybe ten or fifteen strong, shouting stuff like "Kick his ass, Jim. Kill the little fruitcake." Followed by much laughter. But when they came together, Mike immediately began peppering the cowboy with short, lightening-quick jabs. And, as each jab connected, the cowboy's head lurched back. It was visually misleading. The jabs looked so harmless at first, but they were keeping Mike's opponent off balance and, being drunk, the guy couldn't seem to get off a shot. Finally, the cowboy threw a wild right hand that sailed about six inches over Mike's head. The crowd cheered. But then Mike resumed the jabbing, and before long the cowboy's nose started to bleed from both nostrils. He began to kind of walk backwards on unsteady feet, all the while smiling and shaking his head, as if to say, "This doesn't hurt." But you could tell it did.

"C'mon, Jim," a solitary voice in the crowd tried to cheer him on but, only forty-five seconds or so into the ass-kickin', the cowboy seemed to be in big trouble. Cut over both eyes, he was disoriented, becoming blinded by his own blood. His face was a crimson mess and he was staggering around like a bull with a sword through his heart.

Mike refused to let him get his bearings. His hands, like pistons, never hesitated. He was relentless. It was a professional fighter against a drunken, uncoordinated, over-confident amateur. Jack Dempsey versus Andre the Giant. It was target practice and the cowboy had put himself smack dab in the middle of the target. He was being cut to ribbons.

I caught a glimpse of Mike's face. Unmarked, it was expressionless. He was on autopilot. Emotionally detached. Not even breaking a sweat. Soon, Mike began to lean into it, hitting the cowboy, already weakened by the jab attack, slower, and harder, and more deliberately, with crushing blows you could hear land; and with each one, he asked, "Give up? Give up?"

Jim was nodding, and gurgling a response in the affirmative, but Mike continued to lay in a few more shots, as if to say, "I can't HEAR you," like Gomer Pyle's drill sergeant. I think Mike wanted to make certain the cowboy was totally and permanently comfortable with his decision. He wanted to punish him, and make him quit in front of his friends. The crowd, which had long since lost its enthusiasm, was beginning to yell things like, "Somebody stop it. He's had enough." And, finally, "Jim, you all right?" No, he was not all right. His face, and the reputation he had enjoyed as a local tough guy, were being systematically and methodically taken apart by a soft-looking musician about half his size. The girls calling for somebody to stop it were only fooling themselves. The other Sons of Adam band members didn't want to stop it. We liked it. And the cowboy's buddies appeared to be reluctant to get too close to Mike. So, for the moment, at least, it continued.

But, then, without warning, Mike paused, put his hands down and stepped back. The cowboy dropped to his knees and began blowing blood bubbles out of his nose which, by now, was all swollen and crooked. The fight was over. Elapsed time: about a minute and a half. The cowboy's friends rushed in, lifted him by his arms and led him back into the restaurant.

"Let's go," Mike said quietly, as I handed him his coat. What remained of the crowd, parted to let us pass, and their body language seemed to say, "I guess we better give these guys a wide berth. There might still be some unburned plutonium lurking somewhere near the surface."

On the way out of the parking lot Randy said, "See? I told you not to worry. Mike was one of the best fighters in Baltimore." But this was just one time. He seemed to attract trouble. Mike was in a bunch of fights, when I knew him, all under similar circumstances, and he won them all. I don't remember him ever getting hit. Not once. It was always more or less total annihilation of the opponent by what was, essentially, a fighting machine. He couldn't be beat. It wasn't only that he had been one of the best fighters in Baltimore; he was one of the best fighters in whatever town he happened to be in. He had to be. It was a dangerous time, and his soft, delicate looks gave him the appearance of a pretty girl, from a distance, in the dark; which is the way most drunk dudes saw him for the first time. But looks can be deceiving.

After the Hayward gig, we returned to L.A., where we resumed our running schedule as the house band at Gazzarri's on the Strip. It was a cool environment for us because, among other things, of the variation in our fan base. A lot of people who came to see us were professionals in the movie and television industries, while others were simply art students and hippies. One night while I was standing outside the entrance on a break, the veteran character actor, Arthur O'Connell, approached me and struck up a conversation.

"You know," he said, "I'm a pretty old guy, so I've had the chance to see some of the really great big band jazz drummers, over the years, and I want to tell you something. You're the best I ever saw." So, we talked for a while, and I told him I was from Texas and he told me his favourite effort, *Bus Stop*, was shot in Texas and he looked forward to going there again someday, then we shook hands and he turned and went back inside to his table. Of course, Arthur was drunk when he paid me that compliment, but so what? He was probably drunk when he saw the other guys, too.

David and Rick Nelson came in several nights a week with a few of the actors that played their frat brothers in the TV show, *The Adventures of Ozzie and Harriet*. They said they were forming a production company and wanted us to be their first act. Never happened, though. David came in with the other guys, one night, and told us Rick decided he wanted to resume his recording career, so the production company was being put on the back burner.

The director, Sydney Pollack, saw the group one night and decided to cast us as the club band that would appear in a film he was about to begin, featuring Anne Bancroft and Sidney Poitier, *The Slender Thread*. We shot our part on an enormous sound stage at Paramount Studios, in Hollywood. On the first day, as we approached the main gate, the guard in the security booth challenged us with a hard look. "Can I help you guys?" he asked us.

"Sons of Adam. Sydney Pollack is expecting us," we told him.

He looked down at his clipboard, then he waved us in. As he slid the gate open, I noticed a dude sitting on the steps next to the main entrance. He had several weeks' growth and wore the expression of a man who needed a drink and a shower. But as I stole a second and third glance, I realized there was something very familiar about this down-and-outer. He was a guy I had grown up watching on TV, one of my favourite actors, in fact: Billy Gray, "Bud Anderson" on *Father Knows Best*.

So, I was curious. "What's the matter?" I asked the guard, nodding toward Billy.

"Aw, a couple of months ago, they caught him on the set, smoking a marijuana cigarette," the guard obliged. "They fired him, and now he can't get a job; nobody wants to take the chance. The bosses told us not to let him on the premises under any circumstances, so now he just hangs around, hoping for some kind of break."

I thought, "How odd." I mean, where was the justice in that? "He smoked a joint, so now let's end his career? Let the punishment fit the crime!" Was that their reasoning? If that's the case, why stop there? Why didn't the studio heads just burn him at the stake?

Billy Gray was a hell of an outstanding actor. A few years before he did the *Father Knows Best* TV series, he played the part of the kid in the sci-fi classic, *The Day The Earth Stood Still* – and he nailed it. If actors today were a fraction as good as Billy Gray had been, the entertainment world would be a much better place. But he smoked a joint, so now it's all over. Is that what they decided? That's stupid. Talk about cutting off your nose... What I mean is, actors that can act are hard to come by.

"You guys are over on soundstage C," the guard pointed to a large white airplane hanger down the asphalt path. Randy, Mike and Jac and I started off in the direction he had indicated, and the gate clanged shut behind us.

Sidney Poitier wasn't scheduled to appear in our scene, therefore we didn't see him at all during the two or three days we were on the set, but Anne Bancroft was there the whole time. She was so beautiful and polite and personable; she didn't hide in the dressing room between takes. She sat right in her movie-star chair, with her name on the back, chain-smoking and chitchatting with the little people. She was real human.

We didn't actually play when they were filming. The group had gone into the studio and recorded the soundtrack a few days before our scene was shot, so all the extras were dancing and gettin' down to a record, while we pretended to be playing. Because it was a nightclub, it was supposed to be real smoky, and to simulate the effect of being in a smoky nightclub, a little man with a "smudgepot" kept running around just before the camera began to roll, pumping the hell out of the smudgepot and fanning the smoke into everybody's eyes. He ran real low, all hunched over, because smoke rises and Sidney didn't want it to rise above the camera angle before the scene was finished. Each "take" only lasted about fifteen seconds.

"Cue the smudgepot! Cue the music!" Sydney yelled before each take. "Roll 'em!" Every time the moment for on-camera conversation arrived, the sound engineer would de-cue the music and Anne Bancroft and Steven Hill would talk to each other and say their lines and smile and nod in unison, and pretend they were digging the music. But there wasn't any. Just the sound of shuffling feet and the dude occasionally pumping the smudgepot to keep it smoky in the "nightclub".

Several months later, when the film was released, The Sons of Adam were invited to the premiere. It was the first thing Sidney Poitier had done since taking home the Academy Award for Best Actor in *Lilies Of The Field*, so it was a big deal. The story of a woman on the brink of suicide and the rookie suicide-prevention counsellor who is trying desperately to bring her back. If you're wondering how the writers could shoehorn a rock'n'roll band into a movie like this, we were in a flashback-to-happier-times scene, when Anne Bancroft and her husband go to a disco together to try and have a good time and work out their problems.

I didn't think the film was that great, really, but at least Sydney Pollack had the artistic insight to shoot it in black-and-white, so there was a visual dark mood and depth of character that gave the story a lift. If they ever do a remake, it'll probably star Winona Ryder and Leo DiCaprio and they'll shoot it in Technicolour, naturally. Anyway, the black-and-white version, featuring The Sons of Adam, is on Turner Classic Movies once in a while. We even got billing in the closing credits. Check it out.

We were getting other kinds of gigs, as well. We landed a clothes-modelling assignment for *G.Q.*, which we shot at the Whisky, and we shot an advertising poster for Leslie Speakers and another for Fender Guitars. Also, our manager moved us up the street to the Whisky a Go-Go, because Gazzarri's and the Whisky were both the same kind of mainstream Hollywood nightclub that would help us make contacts in the industry, and get us other work.

But for months, many of our art student-type fans had been bouncing back and forth between the Whisky and Gazzarri's and a small club on the eastern end of Hollywood called Bido Lito's.

Hollywood embodies the same contradictions that all cities experience, only to a greater extreme. The neon and glamour is so exaggerated that, at first, that's all you notice. And in 1965, Hollywood and Sunset Boulevards were still everything a tourist could hope to see on a first visit: clean, well-maintained shops and restaurants, no prostitutes or panhandlers or grime to speak of. Only nice stuff.

The Ivar Theater, and some great jazz clubs, did business on Ivar St. and Cahuenga, where they run parallel, just south of Hollywood Boulevard. So, a long time ago, city planners made an alley between the two streets to accommodate supply deliveries. They named this alley "Cosmo Street". Eventually, the owners of the bar located at the rear of the Ivar, concluded that an entrance from Cosmo might be convenient for their patrons, so they knocked out a door in the rear wall of the theater and thus was born the club that would eventually become Bido Lito's. Or something like that. It was really just a separate entrance for the customers of the bar that was affiliated with the Ivar Theater. And, to this day, it's the only business that I know of ever to have existed on Cosmo Street, in the heart of Hollywood. Because, only a block long, Cosmo is an alley, not a street, and you don't usually put the front door to a business on an alley.

But the club was there long before it became a hippie joint, because I've been told Lenny Bruce cracked jokes on the stage and shot heroin in the restroom there, in the late fifties or early sixties.

One day in late '65, an elderly gentleman and his wife (Bill and Dorothy) and their two grown kids (Linda and Tommy) pooled their resources and bought the lease on

this small piece of real estate to try and make some money off the hippie movement. So, they took the first two letters from each of their first names and called their new enterprise "Bido Lito's". Except, this was a family of otherwise normal people who lived in the San Fernando Valley and who had never owned this type of business before, so they ran it kind of funny. There seemed to be no plan or anything. They, more or less, made up policy as they went along. For instance, when it was time for the band to start, around 9 o'clock, tickets would be five bucks. Then later, when the place started to fill up, tickets would go up to ten or fifteen. By midnight, if the place was packed and there was still a line of freaks waiting to get in, Bill and Dorothy might raise the price of admission to twenty or twenty-five bucks a pop, whatever they felt they could get. But Bido Lito's was, if nothing else, an afterthought, so regimentation was not the order of the day or the night here. From the beginning, the level of appeal of Bido Lito's to the members of the artistic underground that comprised its clientele was remarkable and unpredictable, and the lure of the club and the action inside was absolutely magnetic.

The contrast between Bido Lito's and the more successful straight clubs in Hollywood was more than remarkable. It was incredible. The Whisky and Gazzarri's had chandeliers and red carpeted staircases, valet parking and neon marquees – and business addresses on one of the most famous streets in the world. They were nightclubs whose patrons were doctors and lawyers and actors and entertainment industry executives and other people, who somehow had made a lot of money.

Bido Lito's was something out of a Nelson Algren novel. It was a dimly lit, dirty and chipped red brick building with a big wrought-iron gate. The entrance was marked with a flimsy sign overhead in the shape of an arrow, illuminated by sequentially firing light bulbs that directed the customers to the front door. It looked more like an adult bookstore than a nightclub. A hand-printed piece of cardboard resting on the lid of a garbage can near the gate announced, "Bido Lito's Presents" and the name of the group appearing. Tickets were sold by an old man in a trench coat who occasionally accepted whispered advice from his wife on how much to charge and who to let in for free. Parking for Bido Lito's was in a small, unattended lot, down at the end of Cosmo on Selma. When you got back to your car, after the club closed, you always felt relieved if it hadn't been burgled. Narcotics officers in unmarked police cruisers circled the block every ten minutes. Sometimes they simply parked across the street from the front door and waited.

Some of the fans who came to see us at Gazzarri's and The Whisky also went to Bido Lito's: the things they told us tweaked our interest. They told us rock groups playing other clubs in Hollywood often went to Bido Lito's on their nights off, to sit in and do guests sets for free; and the house band, LOVE, played a unique style of hard-rockin' folk, and they said the group had an album coming out soon. The Sons of Adam knew something else about LOVE, too. Their drug use was already legendary. Occasionally, around midnight or one o'clock, people would show up at Gazzarri's with stories of what was happening at Bido Lito's. They would tell us that they had to abandon the line because ticket prices were raised to thirty bucks. Or five minutes after finally getting in, LOVE's singer, Arthur Lee, was dragged off stage and taken away by the police. Nobody had gotten a refund. Or that LOVE's drummer, Don Conka, didn't show up for the gig again, so now they had a new drummer named Snoopy, a guy they pulled out of the audience one night.

The Sons of Adam weren't into drugs. Some of our fans had offered us pot and hash and speed, but we had always very diplomatically declined. "I mean, if you want to, that's cool, but no thanks," we always said. We had always thought of drugs as something for the people to use who came to listen to the music, but as far as trying to do something intricate and creative and physically challenging, like play an instrument, wouldn't being high interfere with your ability to do it well? And we understood drugs had the ability to make you feel better. Well, we already felt great. The Sons of Adam were professional musicians in Hollywood, and we were having just about as good a time as any four guys should ever have in this life. We didn't need drugs to feel good. We would end up doing them anyway – but not for a while.

Mike and Jac and Randy and I decided to go ahead and arrange a guest set at Bido Lito's on our next night off at Gazzarri's. LOVE was playing, so Bill and Dorothy had to get an O.K. from Arthur. Soon we got word that Arthur knew of The Sons of Adam and liked the group and we were welcome to play the guest set anytime. Later, Bryan would tell me that some of the fans we shared with LOVE used to recount some of the stuff that was happening at Gazzarri's and the Whisky when they went over to Bido Lito's. I mean, we weren't getting jerked off the stage and arrested, but we usually had a pretty good time, and members of LOVE respected our musicianship, and like I said, we shared fans.

When we arrived on the night of our guest set, we could hear LOVE playing all the way to the parking lot on Selma. As we approached the big wrought-iron gate, Bill and

Me on my Ludwigs at Gazzarri's on the Strip

Sons of Adam outside The Whisky for a GQ modeling assignment

Dorothy introduced themselves and told us they had heard of us, and if the set went well, they would be getting in touch with the group about a booking for pay. LOVE was doing 'You, I'll Be Following'.

At a time when using drugs was something that was played close to the vest, it was a song about Arthur trying to find some dope, at Johnny's and Conka's and Cisco's, in Frisco. Two narcs sat in their car only a few feet from the club entrance. They were diggin' it.

When we went inside, Bido Lito's was bedlam, wall-to-wall hippies, a whole club of unique individualists, all in a desperate struggle to achieve the time of their lives at any cost.

Onstage, Arthur was decked out in his signature multi-coloured sunglasses, combat boot (one only) and scowl, and he was banging the hell out of his tambourine. Kenny Forssi, the bassist, was a technically accomplished musician, kind of normal-looking compared to the other guys. Standard long straight hair, like The Sons of Adam wore. Johnny Echols was the lead guitarist. He resembled Johnny Mathis a little, I guess. Johnny had a guitar style like no other. Loud and frantic, soft and melodic. Jazz, rock, classic, flamenco... He could do it all. Played a double-neck Gibson, 12-string and 6-string: he was equally accomplished on either neck. Skin-tight pants and Indian moccasins, you got the feeling he was in total control of his instrument and his destiny.

Bryan Maclean, adorned with boyish freckles and curly reddish-blond hair, sat in a chair on stage. Eyes closed, his head tilted down almost to his chest, he appeared to be fighting to keep from falling off while he played, or as if he was about to let go with a drool.

"Whoa, Bryan's got a good buzz goin' tonight," somebody said. When they finished 'You, I'll be Following', Arthur said, "We wanna dedicate this next song to The Sons of Adam. They'll be doin' a set up here later." Then, Arthur started the tambourine intro that led into the hit single off their first album, 'My Little Red Book'. The crowd went crazy. No doubt about it, LOVE had Bido Lito's in the palms of their hands. This was LOVE's place.

But then it was time for our set. There's something about only having to play six or seven songs in a strange club that gives a group a tremendous advantage, because you don't have to hold back. You're not a little tired from the three sets you've already played, and you feel inspiration from playing to a packed room full of people, some of whom have never seen or heard you before. And that night, we were on fire. The audience responded and we took it away from LOVE. We could see it in their eyes. We played some hard-driving, heavy metal rock'n'roll and it was beyond perfect. Midway through our set, I looked over to my side of the stage and Arthur and Bryan were standing together, arms outstretched to me, grinning fiendishly and wiggling their fingers and grabbing the air, like when you knead bread dough with your hands.

After the group had finished its set, I made my way to the bar to get a cold drink. Arthur was sitting on a stool, waiting. He shook my hand. "Hey, man, you guys were out of sight. But can I tell you something? The Sons of Adam are never gonna go anywhere. They're just another band. My group LOVE is about to record some shit that's bound to blow everybody's mind and I want you to be the drummer on those records. We want you to be our new drummer." I wasn't shocked, or surprised, or anything. It was no secret that the group considered Snoopy an interim member and that, collectively, they hated his drumming and were looking for a replacement, but Arthur had picked the worst possible time to ask me. I had never been happier in my life, and my brothers in The Sons of Adam were a part of that. Besides, we had just got through kicking their brains in. Really. The Sons of Adam were the better band that night. Bill and Dorothy were over pumping Randy's hand and offering us a contract at that very moment. So, I turned Arthur down flat. Thanks but no thanks. And then I forgot about it. Sort of.

Over the course of the next few months, Arthur began to regularly drop by The Sons of Adams' house in Laurel Canyon, to hang out and exchange ideas.

Sons of Adam playing at Gazzarri's on the Strip

Sometimes he brought Johnny or Bryan with him, sometimes he came alone. One day he said, "I have a song I want to give you guys. It's perfect for The Sons of Adam," and then he picked up his black Gibson acoustic and played us '7 and 7 Is'.

"Naw," Randy said, "It's a little far out for us. We don't want it." A few months later LOVE recorded it with Snoopy on drums and it became a big hit. Needless to say, I was somewhat miffed.

Chapter Four

Fishing Trip

THE FIRST time I heard '7 and 7 Is' on the radio, I began to fully understand the magnitude of Arthur's imagination. Absolutely without limit. When Arthur tried to give The Sons of Adam '7 and 7 Is', we didn't understand it because it's not a song: it's a production number. Arthur was banging his acoustic Gibson and yelling the words and we all thought, "What the hell is this crap? Certainly not rock'n'roll." It just didn't make sense to us. That he seriously thought The Sons of Adam could do justice to it was a tribute to Arthur's high opinion of our musicianship. This was a creation that resulted from the same kind of explosive energy that fuelled the minds of Stravinsky and Sibelius. It was a modern-day concerto of incredible power, and Arthur and LOVE were the only people who could have recorded and performed it adequately. No record like this had ever graced the Top 40 and none ever would again. The vocal work on 'My Flash On You' and '7 and 7 Is' laid the foundation, but the relatively tame work of today's artists never lived up to the potential of what Arthur set in motion. It defies category. He called this vocal style, "preaching". It was more than that. Like film clips you've seen of Adolf Hitler pumping-up the massive throngs of The Third Reich to a fever pitch, it was threateningly ferocious. More like "inciting to riot" than "preaching".

But things other than his compositions and vocal style set Arthur apart. Take a look at pictures of groups that were successful during this period: small, white dudes, maybe from tough neighbourhoods, but not physically threatening by any stretch of the imagination. Arthur was a riveting, scowling, menacing presence. An anomaly in the music scene of the sixties. Kind of a big dude, he never seemed to be onstage to have a good time but to do business, to fulfil his destiny. Visually fearsome: Sonny Liston, not Sugar Ray Leonard. Combat boots, not Beatle boots.

'7 and 7 Is' could have been Arthur's theme song. When he was on stage, he always looked like he wanted to hurt somebody.

The Sons of Adam liked to enjoy life, not hurt people. We were still regular dudes with standard interests. No drugs, yet. We liked to have normal fun.

One night before we left for our Gazzarri's gig, Randy said, "Hey, let's go fishing in the morning. We'll have to be down at the dock at 4:30 a.m., so that's good. We don't have to wake up early, or anything. We'll just come home from Gazzarri's and eat breakfast and change clothes and go. What do you say?"

We said, "Yeah, well..."

The next morning it was as cold as it gets in southern California – and foggy, as you might expect down by the ocean. The fishing boat was a commercial half-day charter out of Santa Monica that was scheduled to leave the pier at 5 a.m. and head back around noon. When we boarded, Mike and Jac and Randy and I found ourselves on the boat with about thirty other dudes, all retirees in their sixties and seventies. They were cool though, they didn't stare at our long hair and make snide comments, or anything, they were just there to fish. At five sharp, the deck hand slipped the rope holding the boat to the pier off its mooring, and we headed out to sea; and about fifteen minutes after leaving the dock, the captain stopped the boat and dropped anchor. It was barely dawn.

"Okay, we're right in the middle of a school of bonita," he told us, "Go ahead and bait your hooks and drop your lines." So, with the help of some of the old guys who knew what they were doing, Jac and Mike and Randy and I baited the hooks on our rented gear with the wiggly little minnows we had bought back on shore and dropped our lines. And hey, we were fishing! Right away, everybody started catching bonita. The ocean appeared to be full of them. But they're pretty strong fish. After each guy hooked one, he would get dragged around the perimeter of the boat as he reeled it in. So there was a lot of walking around sideways with the poles, bumping into each other, and shouts of "Look out! Coming through." A little bit of confusion and all, but we were catching 'em and, before long, we each had four or five fish. Big ones.

After a while, we hit a lull. Suddenly, nobody was catching anything. The Sons of Adam glanced at the old guys for a lead on what to do and most of them had attached their poles to clamps, and were perched up on the boat railing to wait it out, so we did the same.

By now, it was only about 6 a.m., still real cold and foggy, and everybody's butts were hanging over the railing, freezing. Suddenly I heard somebody yell, "Hey, is that a wallet?" We all twisted around and gazed out through the fog, to where the deck hand was pointing. Sure enough, about ten feet from the boat, a brown wallet bobbed, floating, temporarily at least, as if trying to gather the courage to sink. Adrenaline surged. Thirty-four hands slapped for their wallets, and thirty-three fishermen breathed a huge sigh of relief. One hand came up empty.

"That's my wallet!" Randy hopped off the railing and stood staring, wide-eyed, out to sea. Only ten feet, but it may as well have been a hundred. His hand still clutched the hip pocket where the wallet had lived for so many years. "Everything I own is in that wallet!" he declared. His face was ashen. The deck hand raced over and reached out a pole with a net on the end, but when he extended it as far as he could to try and grab the wallet, it was still a good two feet away. "Here, let me," Randy said. Snatching the pole from the deckhand, he climbed over the railing and extended the net pole as far as he could, grasping onto the rail with one hand, and holding the pole with the other. The rest of us felt helpless. I mean, barring forming a human chain across the surface of the ocean out to where the wallet bobbed, what could we do? And, to make matters worse, every time Randy slapped the water with the pole, the ripples pushed the wallet a few inches further away.

Randy stretched and strained and reached, his expression contorted with desperation. I thought, "You know, if he leans out much more..." Just then, Randy did a perfect 360 into the ocean, conked his head on the bottom of the boat, and came up bleeding. Then, he swam out and grabbed his damned wallet. Which was a pretty good trick because he was wearing a heavy overcoat and, soaking wet, it probably added around a hundred pounds to his body weight. So, the rest of us fishermen threw him a line and pulled him back into the boat. Then, we wrapped him in wool blankets and stuck him over in a corner, on a little stool, where he sat clutching his wallet... for the next five hours. Randy looked real pitiful, all wet and bleeding, and naturally, he couldn't fish anymore. But the boat captain didn't feel sorry enough for him to take him back to shore. Besides, he was a little upset. During the rescue operation, he started yelling that half of us had to get back over to the other side of the boat because it was listing badly to the right and we were about to capsize. Then, we would have all gotten dumped out into the ocean. That would have been a pretty picture. And, of course, the captain would have lost his boat. So he didn't have any mercy on Randy at all. Like the sign said, this was a "half-day charter," so we were going to stay out a half-day, no matter what.

After we got back to shore, I asked Randy, "What's in the wallet?" I mean, I couldn't help but wonder what was so important about its contents.

"Huh?" He was still soaked to the skin and shivering.

"You said everything you owned was in that wallet."

"Oh, you know, driver's licence, phone numbers, stuff like that."

We never even ate the bonita we caught. We left them on the boat, actually. Everybody but Randy. He remembered his because he had them sitting in a bucket at his feet the whole time. But as we walked across the parking lot on the way back to the car, a game warden stopped Randy and confiscated his fish and wrote him a ticket for fishing without a permit.

Sons of Adam publicity shot for Decca Records

Chapter Five

Nighthawks at Canter's

AFTER THE clubs closed in Hollywood, usually around 2 a.m., everybody, musicians and patrons alike, met at an all-night restaurant. At first, Ben Franks on Sunset was the place to be. By 2:15, you could head west on Sunset, round the slow curve to the right and, as Ben Franks appeared, get the impression you had stumbled onto a "Love-In". Parking lot packed, a hundred hippies standing around, shooting the breeze, because of the half-hour wait for a table inside. But, it wasn't long before Ben Franks became like what Yogi Berra said about a New York restaurant once. "Nobody goes there anymore. It's too crowded." Besides, there was another, even bigger, problem with Ben Franks: the police discovered it almost as soon as the hip crowd did. That parking lot situation made the cops' job incredibly easy. The Sunset Boulevard location made going there so convenient for them too because, at 2 a.m., they simply moved all their stakeout operations from where ever they had been, right down the street to Ben Franks. We had to find a new place.

Canter's Delicatessen and Restaurant, on Fairfax Boulevard in south Hollywood, is the home of the best Kosher cuisine anywhere in the country. In fact, whoever said "There is very little perfection in life" never ate at Canter's. It ranks right up there with the world famous Jewish deli restaurants in New York.

The menu is all the standard fare. Lox and bagels, Matzo ball soup, corned beef sandwiches and a lot of other stuff. My own personal favourite after-the-gig meal was Lox and Eggs and Onions, chased down with a banana split. It was so good, I was never tempted to try anything else. Anyway, Canters became the crowd's new choice for the after hours joint.

Sons of Adam publicity shot for Decca Records

As much as the cops loved to roam Sunset Boulevard, they didn't seem drawn to south Fairfax whatsoever, and in all the time I went there, I never once saw a cop car, black and white or narc, anywhere near Canter's. Which was strange, because Canter's was open all night, just like Ben Franks, there were about three hundred drug-carrying hippies loaded out of their minds on any given morning after 2 a.m., just like Ben Franks, and, like Ben Franks, the atmosphere was one of unbridled enthusiasm. It was loud. So why no cops? I don't know, I guess they just liked to be up on Sunset, where it was glamorous, and where they thought the action was.

In fact, if anything, Canter's was the home to less restricted and more outrageous activity than Ben Franks, where the waitresses were known to call the police in to clear out a table of customers, even if they were only suspected of something as innocuous as being the kind of people who might not leave a proper tip. I know, because The Sons of Adam were once escorted out of Ben Franks by the L.A.P.D. under that exact set of circumstances. On the way to the parking lot, when Jac Ttanna had the nerve to try to interject some kind of polite question, preceded by an "Excuse me, officer", one of the cops wound up and swatted him real hard on the butt with his clipboard. "POP!" Then he said, "Keep walking, hippie, they don't want you here." It was almost as if the management at Ben Franks figured if they were real rude to the hippies, the regular crowd might return. What they didn't realize was that the hippies WERE the regular crowd. The new one. They just didn't recognize them yet.

At Canter's, if something disruptive happened, everyone was cool enough to pretend not to notice. One night, a dude fresh from one of the clubs, tripped on the very top step of a long staircase, leading down from the restrooms. "Clumpity, clumpity, clumpity, clumpity, clump." Head over heels, all the way down to the main floor, so loud it could be heard well above the din of the unruly eaters. After he hit bottom, he lifted his head and looked around, then he picked himself up and walked over to his table and sat back down with his friends. For the few seconds he lay there, nobody ran over to ask him if he was all right, or expressed any concern at all. Everybody figured that kind of attention would have just further embarrassed him, so we all looked the other way and kept eating. The dishes and silverware never stopped rattling and clanking, and the conversation never ebbed.

On another night, as The Sons of Adam stood in the foyer waiting for our table, the wife of a local art guru, Vito, "Vito's Sue", wife of local art guru, Vito Paulekas, got up from her table, where she sat with her husband and friends, and, out of the blue, hopped on Mike Port's back, and started bobbing up and down and yelling, "Giddyup!" Nobody knew what to do, especially

Mike. He just stood there in shock, with a girl on his back. I mean, how do you plan for something like that? Mike's wife, Donna, although beautiful, was the violent, jealous type. She could only stand there with her mouth open, a volcano poised to erupt. Vito, like almost everybody else in the room, never even looked over. He just ignored it and continued eating; and finally, after what seemed like a very long time, Vito's Sue got bored of the ride, dismounted and went back to her table without a word. No big deal. Mike was wearing his favourite maroon velour outfit that night. It was the last time I saw him in it.

A guy named Johnny who suffered from Tourette's Syndrome was at Canter's almost every night, shouting what sounded exactly like "fuck!" repeatedly at the top of his lungs; there was so much other noise, you didn't really notice, unless you were sitting at the next table. He had a lot of friends but was nonetheless referred to as "Johnny Fuck-Fuck" by patrons and staff alike.

Phil Spector was there all the time with his bodyguards sitting on either side of him in his private booth, so that no one could try to engage him in idle chit-chat or try to be his buddy.

But mostly what was at Canter's was really good food.

While LOVE and The Sons of Adam were working the Los Angeles club scene (sometimes on the same bill), there was activity up the coast in San Francisco as well, with bands like Jefferson Airplane, Big Brother, The Grateful Dead and other Bay Area groups, doing a lot of work for a production company headed up by Chet Helms. Chet was a laid back, friendly sort of guy, tall and with long, long hair. He once told us that he and Janis Joplin had hitchhiked out from Port Arthur, Texas together.

The Sons had recorded a single and B-side at RCA on Sunset, using the Stones' engineer, Dave Hassinger, and their studio. Our manager, having great hopes for the success of this single, had booked us with LOVE to work a weekend for Chet's Family Dog Productions in the old Fillmore Auditorium. An "All L.A. Show" they called it. Chet arranged for the two groups to stay in different homes as a courtesy. So, as soon as we hit town, on Friday afternoon, we decided to hang out at the guest pad for a little while and relax before heading over to the Fillmore. But, right in the middle of our relaxation time, the hunger bug bit, and after talking it over, we decided to grab dinner. The Sons of Adam were used to before-the-gig meals consisting of the average quality stuff they served at places like Denny's, so we felt pretty confident of our chances of finding a restaurant in the same general category, someplace close by, this being a large city and all, like L.A. Only San Francisco is a large city not like L.A. It's way different.

As Chet was about to leave for the Fillmore to help coordinate the setup for the light show, that night, Randy said, "Hey, Chet, where can we get something to eat?"

He smiled, "Oh, that's easy. There's a great little cafe, right down the street at the end of the next block," he jerked his thumb in the general direction.

After Chet left for the Fillmore, we struck out to find what we hoped would become our new favourite, conveniently located place to eat. Just like Chet said, at the end of the next block, we spotted a hand-painted wooden sign hanging over the front door to what looked to be nothing more than a converted ground-floor apartment. "Frank's Cafe", the sign read. When we walked in, we were stunned. Eight, straight-back wooden chairs lined up in front of a make-shift counter, marked the customer seating area. Cans of individual sized Campbell's soup lined a crooked shelf over a hot plate. That was the menu. That was the total set-up.

"Have a seat, fellas, I'll be right with you" a voice from a back room directed. Through the half-open door we saw the owner-cook putting on his pants.

Cursing the small bell attached to the door that had signalled our arrival and departure, we quickly made our way out to the sidewalk to continue our hunt for a Denny's. There wasn't one, at least not within walking distance. When we got back to the guest pad, Randy asked Chet's buddy, our host, if he knew of any other restaurants in the area.

"Oh, no!" He seemed embarrassed. "Did Chet send you down to that greasy spoon on the corner? You guys have to forgive Chet. He's a functional eater, and to tell you the truth, he's just about the only one who eats at that dump, that I know of." Then he directed us to a more conventional coffee shop-type place a little further away, a place like good old Denny's.

I appreciated that concept, though – because we're all functional eaters to some degree. Like when you grab a burger from McDonald's, your third one that week, instead of holding out for something better. Same thing. You have to eat or die. And if your philosophy of functional eating is liberal enough, you might even find yourself sitting in a straight-back, wooden chair and staring down into a single serving of Campbell's soup. Because, I know, that's where Chet found himself every day. That's what the guy said.

That night, April 8, 1966, The Sons of Adam were scheduled to go on first, LOVE naturally having top spot on the bill. When we arrived and walked into the main ballroom, I was blown away by the spectacle. The group wasn't supposed to begin playing for over an hour, yet the cavernous Fillmore was already jammed to capacity. Freaks and hippies jumped and writhed and squirmed to the recorded music from Jefferson Airplane's first album, being powered through the gigantic "Voice of the Theaters" that lined the stage – and to the pulsating light show. Droplets of coloured oil in dishes of water, magnified and projected onto giant screens, resembled amoebae, spasmodically lurching to the rhythm of the music. The massive strobe lights, which alternately over-illuminated the hall, then plunged it into near-total darkness, made it difficult as hell to walk a straight line, but eventually we found the staircase that led up to the dressing room.

We climbed the stairs. Inside, we were greeted by a young girl who warned us, "No smoking, guys. Fire department rules. Bill Graham is the building manager, here, and he's a real hard-ass about the 'no smoking' thing. He'll probably come up and check on you later." She lit some incense and placed the sticks in a holder located in a corner of the room. Then she left. We all found seats on the over-stuffed sofa and kicked back to relax a while before our set. Randy and Jac were busy tuning their guitars through a small amp, when we heard heavy footsteps coming up the stairs. The dressing room door burst open abruptly, and there stood the only normal looking person in all of Haight-Ashbury: in pin-striped shirt, button-down collar, neatly pressed khakis and hair barely long enough to comb, the dude exhibited the body language of a pissed-off banty rooster, patrolling the perimeter of the henhouse. Then, he lifted his nose and began suspiciously sniffing the air. "You!" he suddenly pointed to me. "What's that smell?"

I was taken aback. "I don't know. Incense?"

"No." he shot back. "Not incense." His voice dripped with sarcasm. "Marijuana!" he snarled. "You guys have been smoking marijuana, right?"

Without waiting for a reply, he launched into a tirade, waving his arms and yelling at the top of his lungs. "You know, I've told Chet again and again, that he can only use my building for his hippie dances if nobody smokes in the dressing rooms. Doesn't he realize I could lose my lease if the Fire Department catches you guys smoking grass or anything else up here? Tell him if this happens one more time, no more dances!" And he walked out, slammed the door behind him, and pounded back down the stairs.

We just looked at each other.

There was no grass. Just incense. Incense smells like burning perfume, and marijuana smells like burning horse manure. That's why they call it "shit". How could Bill Graham have confused the two? I'll tell you how. It was what you might call an "uneducated guess". Deductive reasoning gone awry. At that time, he just didn't know what weed smelled like, that's all. But he figured somebody in the building, somewhere must be getting high, and we were all alone in the little room, upstairs, with all that funny smoke, so, therefore, we must be smoking pot and that odd smell must be marijuana. Simple as that.

After a while, it was time for The Sons of Adam to go on, and we were dynamite. We blew the crowd away. We had it working just like the night we did the guest shot at Bido Lito's. An ovation after every song. That old thing about playing a brand new room where nobody has ever seen you before was working full bore. You always get up for it. By the time we had finished our set, LOVE had arrived. We were on our way back up the stairs to the dressing room when we bumped into Johnny and Arthur coming down. We nodded and said "Howdy," and Arthur nodded back and said, "Great set, man." Then LOVE went on stage and they blew the audience away, just as we had done. Like the old time Battle of the Bands. It was a hell of an "all L.A." show.

Around a year later, when I was playing drums with LOVE, Bryan would tell me, "Man, when we walked into the Fillmore to do our set and saw you guys on stage, we knew we had our work cut out for us. It was like you belonged up there and we didn't. It was your place. We had to try and take it back."

For the next several months, The Sons of Adam bounced back and forth between L.A. and San Francisco, promoting the single we had recorded, 'Mister, You're A Better Man Than I'. Our legion of fans continued to grow. Nevertheless, Arthur's prophecy for the future of the group was about to manifest itself in the present. The Sons of Adam's time together was about to come to an end.

Chapter Six

Transition

RONNIE HARAN booked the talent for the Whisky. Beautiful and articulate, she was a native of New York and, soon after moving to the West Coast, developed the business acumen necessary to go head-to-head with the toughest agents in the business. She had, over the course of time, become a kind of unofficial group manager for LOVE. "Unofficial" only because, although she was doing a great deal of work for the group, it was all being done "piecemeal", one booking at a time, with no firm business arrangement or contract that I knew of, and for very little appreciation. Over the course of our association, she even had the strength and diplomacy to guide LOVE into decisions that were based on intelligent planning, some of the few decisions that would actually prove beneficial. Of course, as the booking agent for the Whisky, she had formed a close working relationship with members of The Sons of Adam, as well, so I wasn't really surprised when I got a call from her, one night, asking me to meet her in her upstairs office at the Whisky. "Michael, I have to take a run up to Terry Melcher's house to talk over some business," she said. "My car's in the shop, feel like giving me a lift?"

Terry lived in Benedict Canyon, one of the mountain districts that separate Hollywood and Beverly Hills from the Valley, a labyrinth of winding streets, lined with architecturally unique houses and inhabited by deer, raccoons, owls and celebrities. I had never met Terry Melcher but I knew of him. He was Doris Day's son and he had produced The Byrds' first album. That's all I knew, actually.

It was almost midnight when we left the Whisky. As we wound our way up Benedict Canyon, Ronnie reached over to turn my car stereo down. "You know, Michael, Arthur really wants you to join LOVE."

I nodded, "Yeah, I know, Ronnie, but what about Snoopy? He did a great job on '7 and 7 Is'. He sounded fine to me. Are you sure they want to get rid of him?"

"Does a bear shit in the woods?" Which is what Ronnie always said when the answer to a question was "Yes, absolutely!"

"The session was a nightmare," Ronnie explained. "They had a hell of a time getting it right. Arthur hates Snoopy's drumming and they're totally committed to making a change as soon as possible. LOVE is about to break new ground on their next album and they want you in the group really bad, before they go into the studio. You're the only drummer they're looking at. Every time you guys play on the same bill, all Arthur can talk about for days is your drumming. He even told me he had a vision, a dream that you were going to be LOVE's new drummer. You should consider it, very seriously, Michael. It's a tremendous opportunity to take a step up."

Frankly, I had already been thinking about it. For the last few months, The Sons of Adam had been in a kind of holding pattern. No movies, no modelling assignments, our record deal had gone flat, and lately we had found ourselves playing the same old clubs over and over. But more importantly, our lack of a really outstanding lead singer was becoming more of a noticeable detriment than ever before. It seemed to be something we simply couldn't get past. Our manager had even mentioned it. Not that a rock group couldn't achieve success without one.

The times were changing, competition was getting tougher and fuses began to grow short at The Sons of Adam's rehearsals. In this, the summer of 1966, an offer from Arthur to join LOVE was beginning to look tempting.

But LOVE had problems, too. For one thing, they sometimes played a little out of tune. When the group was playing live in concert or at a club, it wasn't quite as noticeable to the average listener but, nevertheless, on the first album, it was pretty obvious – to other musicians anyway.

The thing is, getting used to playing in tune is fundamental. It's a rudimentary facet of musicianship that becomes, after a while, practically automatic. For most people who play an instrument it starts early, like in school. If the band director hears somebody off key, he may shut everything down and listen to the offending section one person at a time until he isolates the responsible criminal. Because once he finds you that's how you're treated. If you're the guy, look out. You just wasted everyone else's time and you're fair game for an ass-chewing. So, learning how to tune up quickly and accurately is something you learn to do early on, in self defence, if you have a proper musical background.

You know that flair for sarcasm that is such an integral part of being a high school teacher? Well, with band directors, it's a part of the job description. Handed down and refined from one generation to the next, until it becomes razor sharp. Then again, The Sons of Adam were always right in tune and they didn't play in any school bands at all. So I don't know. With some people it's more of a priority than with others, I suppose. Or more natural.

But, as Ronnie and I continued up Benedict Canyon, I mentioned this tuning problem to her. "You mean they play out of tune?" she asked, incredulously.

"Sometimes, yeah."

"Well, Michael, look at it this way. The important part is what the fans see and hear. They buy the records. That tuning problem is a musician thing, not a fan thing."

Her reasoning was unbelievably simplistic but, in a way, she was right, I guess.

O.K., she had convinced me. The bottom line was, I trusted her judgment. The tuning thing was probably not a real big deal in the grand scheme. They could always learn to tune up; but there were several other matters I had to come to grips with before I could jump into this commitment, without so much as a backward glance.

LOVE's drug reputation was ominous. They were the Pied Pipers of self-destruction by any means available. To them, no drug was unsafe. Everybody knew about Conka: the widely held opinion in Hollywood was that he was merely the first to go where the others in the group would soon follow. My own drug philosophy was at the opposite end of the spectrum. I was, by this time, content to smoke a joint or two with friends during an evening of screwing around and listening to music. That was about as close to the edge as I cared to be. Did the group think my own drug views were closer to their own? Maybe so. The friend-fans who came to see me play had often told me that my appearance on stage was misleading... that my eyes were glazed, that my expression was one of an individual high on a chemical much stronger than any of the smoking dopes. I've seen pictures of myself taken while I was in a musical groove and they were absolutely right. But I wasn't loaded. The feeling I had when I was playing live, in front of people who were in that groove with me, was indescribable – or describable only to the extent that it was the best feeling imaginable. It's why you become a musician. Drugs make you feel different so, if you feel bad, then the drugs make you feel good, but only because good is different than bad. Music makes you feel good. If you start out feeling good, then music makes you feel great.

No chemical can approach the power of music when the goal is mind and mood elevation. That's the only reason I looked the way I did on stage. Music, not drugs. But, the misconception had been irrevocably formed. Members of LOVE probably already felt I was one of them, in spirit and in drug philosophy.

As Ronnie and I neared the top of Benedict Canyon she began squinting at the street signs. "Slow down, Michael. Terry's street is right around this next curve." This section of the canyon had no streetlights. In fact, except for the headlights of my car, there were no lights to be seen at all, anywhere. We were in the forest, really. What moonlight there might have been was obscured by the trees clustered overhead like umbrellas.

"It's the next street," Ronnie said, suddenly. "Turn right. That's Terry's security gate. He lives up that private driveway."

When I stopped at the gate, a voice cracked over a small speaker affixed to the top of a post, "That you, Ronnie?"

She leaned over and yelled through my window, "Yeah, Terry. It's me and Michael." A small electric motor began to hum, the gate slid open, and we started up the final fifty yards of our journey.

As we pulled into the driveway and I brought my car to a stop, I saw Terry walk out onto the porch. He stepped down and approached my car.

"Hi Ronnie." He smiled and gave her a hug. Then, turning to me, "Michael, I'm Terry." We shook hands. "You guys, come on in, I just got some high quality weed. Let's try it." He opened the door and we went inside, where he gestured to a large sofa in front of a riverstone fireplace. Canyon rustic, the interior of his living room rested under a large beam ceiling. Terry reached for a metal box sitting on the coffee table, opened it and removed a baggy of weed and wheatstraw papers and rolled a joint. Then, he took a long hit and passed it to Ronnie.

"Hey, Michael," he said finally, "I understand you're considering an offer to become LOVE's new drummer. You should grab it, man. They're great, a very unique group."

For the next twenty minutes or so, Terry filled us in on an upcoming project, and, then he glanced at his watch. "I have to meet some people at a private screening room down on Sunset. Why don't you two come with me?" He gathered up the baggy of weed and the wheatstraws and we left.

The next time I saw Terry's house was several years later, on the evening news, only he didn't own it anymore. Roman Polanski did. I couldn't help but think how the peaceful and tranquil atmosphere we had enjoyed in Terry's living room that night was only a temporary mask, in sharp contrast to the unspeakable hell that would eventually take place there when Charlie's girls came to call on the new residents.

The day after we met with Terry, Ronnie called, "Michael, the group has a weekend gig in Fresno and they want you to fly up with us. You know, just come hang out. It'll be fun. Shall I make the arrangements?"

So I agreed to take that little plane ride to Fresno with LOVE and Ronnie. My buddies in The Sons of Adam knew what was happening but they understood. Arthur had made no secret of the fact that he wanted me to join the group, and I had been spending a lot of time with Ronnie. More importantly, Randy, Jack and Mike were as aware as I of the insurmountable difficulties facing our group. Each of us was looking for a "Plan B" and, as far as I was concerned, LOVE was quickly becoming mine. That weekend in Fresno would prove to be the catalyst for the decision I had to make regarding my future because, during the next few days, I would come to know Arthur and Bryan and Kenny and Johnny well enough to realize, for the first time, that I might one day feel as close to them as I had with the members of any group I had played with professionally... in spite of the drug fables that were such a big part of LOVE's reputation. "Besides, everybody knows rumours have a way of growing beyond the truth," I thought.

The day of the Fresno flight, we all met in one of the lounges near the airline boarding area at LAX. In a preview of things to come, I discovered we were running a little late. We had all just ordered something to eat when I saw Ronnie trotting up to our table.

"What are you guys doing? Are you crazy? Don't you know they're holding the plane for us? You don't have time to eat! Let's go, c'mon!"

Without a word of protest, we all jumped up and broke into a dead run, following Ronnie through the maze of corridors that led to our plane. Occasionally, Ronnie would half turn and yell over her shoulder, "Hurry!" The funny thing is, as many times as we were destined to repeat this scenario, there was, to my recollection, never a good reason for us not being someplace on time. It just seemed to usually work out that way. Like, when I was in the bad groove of not doing my homework in school, I never actually decided not to do it. I just kept putting it off until it was too late.

After we made our way to the plane and climbed the rollaway staircase that led into the cabin, we all entered and walked down the aisle to the only remaining seats located near the back. The plane was packed with our fellow passengers who had arrived on time and were already seated, and who seemed to regard us, not with anger for holding up the show, but with curiosity. Their expressions were more like "Who are they? They must be important for them to have held the plane" than "Who the hell do they think they are?" But, actually, the airline held the plane because Ronnie convinced them it was the right thing to do. She would have made a real good lawyer or politician.

We settled into our seats, Arthur and I directly across the aisle from each other, the cabin door was secured, and the plane taxied into position for take-off. Several minutes into the flight, the "No Smoking, Fasten Seat Belts" sign was turned off and, as if on cue, all the smokers began to fumble through their pockets and purses for a cigarette. Out of the corner of my eye, I noticed Arthur reaching for a cigarette, as well. At least, I thought it was a cigarette. Instead, he removed a hash pipe from his coat pocket, packed it, lit it, and took a hit. Then he reached up to the small overhead fan located above each seat and turned it on. Now, I was beginning to see where the outrageous stories of LOVE's drug use came from. They flaunted it. I mean, hash has a very distinct odour, not as powerful as weed perhaps, but it's nothing like cigarette smoke. It smells dank and musty and unique. And that tiny little fan didn't do much except disperse the hash smoke all around the cabin. A closed cabin, packed with about 150 normal travellers who probably felt this nation's drug laws served a noble purpose and should be upheld. This was practically begging to get busted.

"Here you go, Michael," Arthur exhaled, extending the pipe to me across the aisle. A small wisp of smoke rose from the almost closed fist he held around the pipe. I looked around briefly. None of our fellow passengers or flight crew seemed to be looking our way, so I took the pipe from Arthur and, after first reaching up to turn on my own little fan, of course, I took a hit. Then, I passed the pipe to Bryan, who was sitting next to me, eyes closed, listening to the earphones, apparently unconcerned. He took a hit and passed the hash pipe forward to Kenny. We smoked hash all the way to Fresno. Nobody noticed.

At the first gig on Friday night, the atmosphere was filled with the kind of magic you expect when a great rock group comes to perform in a town like Fresno. As soon as we walked in, we knew the audience was pumped. LOVE indeed had that something special which almost always captured the imagination of any audience: a unique style and power that foretold a level of future success with virtually no limit. I told Ronnie later that night that I would give my notice to The Sons of Adam when we got back home.

However, during the Fresno trip, I began to see that certain aspects of membership in LOVE would take a little getting used to. For one thing, Arthur and the other guys had something of an "arm's length" relationship. There seemed to be a cutting sarcasm to the sense of humour they shared, and you could tell none of them ever really let his guard down. Like, each guy thought it was real funny to work out some kind of plan to somehow shaft the others. When we arrived at the Fresno airport, for instance, and got into the limo for the ride to the hotel, Johnny tried to ride shotgun, but Arthur managed to ace him out of it by pretending to have trouble putting his guitar in the trunk. He called Johnny, "Hey, man, come back here and give me a hand with this axe, will you? The case is too big to fit in here." Then, when Johnny got out of the limo, Arthur ran around the front, jumped in the passenger seat, slammed the door and locked it. Everybody laughed long and loud – except Johnny, of course.

Then, after the group got to the hotel, we all went to the coffee shop to grab dinner. When we were almost finished, Bryan pushed his chair back from the table and said, "I gotta go to the bathroom," but he never came back. He split. So we all had to chip in to pay his part of the bill. Like, he shafted us. Pretty funny. They didn't really have that "brotherhood" type friendship that I shared with my partners in The Sons of Adam. In fact, it seemed to be more of a "don't-let-your-guard-down-or-you'll-be-sorry" kind of a relationship than anything else.

The first night back in L.A., I had to take a run down to the Sunfax Market to buy groceries. It was pretty late so I was able to find a spot right out front. I parked my car and went inside. As I pushed my cart down the frozen food aisle, I heard an unfamiliar voice call my name. "Hey, Michael, what's happening?" I stopped pushing and turned around to find myself face-to-face with LOVE's very first drummer, Don Conka. He was approaching with his hand extended, "I'm Conka, man. How's it going?" I recognized him, so even though I had never seen him play, I guess I must have seen him before someplace, or at least seen his picture.

I smiled and said, "Hi, Don." As we shook hands, the irony was palpable. Conka was reputed to have been one of the great rock drummers in town. Mutual fans told me his solos were unparalleled. That he was one of the truly great solo artists.

"You should have seen it, man," they would say. "He started out over here on the floor tom and then, fast as lightening, worked his way to the snare and the cymbals. Powerful, man! Explosive! You couldn't even see his hands. It was awesome!" They would dissect it, sometimes bar-by-bar. And I was always a little bit jealous, of course, because these were knowledgeable fans. Conka must have been really good.

Yet, with LOVE perched on the verge of success, ready to record their first album and being touted as the next big L.A. rock group, Conka had simply stopped showing up for performances. He had, without a second thought, chosen drugs over music. If not for his addiction he would doubtless still have been LOVE's drummer. No Snoopy, no me.

He grasped my hand and looked me squarely in the eye, "Michael, when Arthur told me you were going to take over, I couldn't have been happier, man, because I know you're the only drummer in Hollywood who can handle it. I saw you with The Sons of Adam a couple of times, at Gazzarri's. You got great chops." He didn't seem jealous or resentful, at all. We talked for a little while longer, then he wished me luck and turned and walked away. It wasn't that Conka didn't love music and playing the drums, but that he simply loved the high more than anything else in the world. More than music, more than freedom.

Bryan once told me Conka's favourite song was 'Double Shot of My Baby's Love'. So, in his own mind, at least, he wasn't a tragic figure playing a pitiful role in life's one-act play, or anything melodramatic like that. Conka didn't care. He laughed about it. He liked being who he was. He, more or less, had a philosophy of humour and destiny about his predicament. But, whether or not he realized it, he was the original "Man With The Golden Arm".

Chapter Seven

The Flight Of The Pigeon

THE PLAN, I soon learned from Ronnie, was not to kick Snoopy out of the group after all, but to move him from drums over to keyboards instead and add a woodwind guy, Tjay Cantrelli. Seven guys total, not five. This instrumentation would suit the new direction LOVE was taking on its second album, *Da Capo*. The first order of business for the reinvented LOVE was to get the new material ready to record as soon as possible, therefore rehearsals were to begin immediately. After all, we only had a couple of weeks.

Most of the rock musicians in Hollywood lived in Laurel Canyon, and the members of LOVE were no exception. Like Benedict Canyon, it was located in a small mountain range that helped to separate West Hollywood from the Valley – the main difference being, the houses in Laurel Canyon were somewhat more plentiful and less expensive than those in Benedict. More importantly, however, to the folks who lived there, Laurel Canyon was directly above the centre of Sunset Boulevard, close to the clubs and recording studios, and Harry's Open Pit Barbecue. They delivered. About halfway up Laurel Canyon Boulevard, there was a small mom-and-pop market called The Canyon Country Store. Not the sort of place to do major shopping, but a good spot to grab a gallon of milk or a loaf of bread if you wanted to avoid driving all the way down the hill to the Sunfax.

I had already struck up a friendship with the group's bassist, Kenny Forssi, at a few of the gigs LOVE and The Sons of Adam had played together so, on the first day of rehearsal, I picked up my new bandmate, Kenny, and we started off in the general direction of Arthur's pad, up near the top of Kirkwood. As we approached the Country Store, Kenny said, "Michael, stop for a minute. I told Arthur I'd bring him some orange juice."

So I pulled into the lot and Kenny went in and bought the O.J. When he came back out to the car and crawled back into the passenger seat, holding the paper bag with the O.J., I thought I'd give him the business a little bit.

"Hey, uh, Kenny. This isn't part of the gig, is it? I mean we're not expected to bring Arthur his food and drink on any kind of regular basis, are we?"

Kenny glanced over as we pulled out of the lot, "Sorry, Michael. I thought you knew about Arthur's problem he had here, a while back. That thing with Barry."

"Huh, uh. What do you mean, 'problem'?" I asked. "Who's Barry?" So, Kenny proceeded to fill me in.

He told me Arthur had negotiated a price of a few hundred bucks (back when weed was cheap) for delivery of a pound with a local supplier-buddy named Barry, a guy that often scored drugs for the musicians in the Canyon. It had been arranged for Barry to bring the dope up to Arthur's house in the afternoon. "But listen, man," Arthur told him, "I might

Me and Tjay Cantrelli in Johnny's garden in Laurel Canyon. Shot taken by a reporter for *The KRLA Beat* magazine, Fall of '66

The Flight Of The Pigeon 57

have to run a couple of errands. So, if I'm not here when you come by, just look in the mailbox. The money'll be in an envelope with your name on it. Take the money and leave the pound in the box, O.K?" But, predictably, when Arthur got back from his errands and opened the mailbox door and looked inside, no envelope... and no pound. Naturally, Arthur picked up the phone right away to give Barry a jingle to find out what happened.

"I don't know what you're talking about, Arthur," Barry said. "I took the envelope and I left the pound, just like we agreed. If somebody swiped the pound from the mailbox, that's your problem. What do you expect me to do, just lose the pound and give you your money back? Sorry, that's not how I do business. It was your plan, remember? I can't help you."

So, they ended their phone conversation with Arthur really steamed and feeling ripped off. About a week later, Arthur was toodling up the hill in his black Porsche, past the Canyon Country Store, when he saw Barry, sitting on the wooden railing out front, where the hippies often congregated, laughing and talking to a couple of girls. It was too much. He immediately turned into the lot, parked his car, got out and walked over to where Barry was sitting. Without a word, Arthur jerked him down off the railing, threw him to the asphalt and began giving him a decisive beating. He had Barry on his back, punching him over and over. The girls were screaming, traffic on Laurel Canyon Boulevard was slowing down to watch the action and Barry was bleeding profusely. All in all, I guess it was a pretty violent and disturbing scene.

Bill, the elderly gentleman who owned the store, saw what was happening through the front window and, abandoning the cash register, ran outside and began trying to pull Arthur off the nearly unconscious Barry. "Stop it! Stop it!" he yelled, holding onto Arthur's arms.

"All right, I'll stop, motherfucker – for now," Arthur huffed and puffed. But then, turning back to Barry, "Better stay out of my way, man. I'll kill you, next time."

The owner, Bill, was a tough old bird, though, and he swung Arthur around with authority. "I'm gonna tell you once." He was red in the face and all out of breath, from the struggle, "Get off this property and don't ever come around here again! Because if you do, I'll call the police and have you arrested! Understand?"

Arthur nodded, and then he turned and walked back to his car and drove home. He had been 86-ed from The Canyon Country Store. That's why Kenny and I had to stop and buy him his orange juice.

When Arthur wasn't wearing his signature one combat boot and one bare foot, he wore a pair of black Gestapo boots that buckled up the side, skin-tight black Levi's, short silk scarf around his neck and black leather jacket, an outfit that helped convey the attitude that was such an important part of his on-stage persona. It worked, too. The fans loved it. Especially the boots. He always left them unbuckled because he was a free spirit and nobody could make him buckle them up if he didn't want to. But, as Kenny and I pulled up and stopped in front of Arthur's house on that first day of rehearsal, I noticed the Gestapo boots sitting in the carport next to the garbage cans, neglected and already beginning to collect dust. We got out of the car and, Arthur's front door having been left wide open, walked inside. "Hey, Arthur, you here, man?" Kenny yelled.

Arthur emerged from a back bedroom wearing a pair of Hush Puppy-style, suede loafers and neatly pressed slacks. "Hey, Kenny, did you remember the orange juice?" he asked.

"Yeah, Arthur. Here you go." He held the bag up. Arthur took it, opened it, and drank from the carton. In a few minutes, Snoopy came in from his place downstairs, then, before long, Bryan, from a separate unit he rented, also downstairs. About ten minutes later, Johnny and Tjay arrived in the same car.

For an hour or so, we sat around and smoked hash and listened to the first Cream album and some other stuff, and talked music. Then, Arthur picked up his black Gibson. "Well, I may as well show you guys some of the tunes I've written for the new album. 'Da Capo' is a sheet music direction to return to the beginning of the passage. That's what this album is all about... returning to the beginning. I call this first one, 'Stephanie Knows Who'. It's in threequarter time, about a girl Bryan and I both had a little experience with. Right, Bryan?" he laughed, but Bryan ignored him, removing his own guitar from its case and beginning to pick absent-mindedly. As Arthur played "Stephanie" all the way through, I began to plan the drum part.

While the guitar strings still rang with the final chord from 'Stephanie', Arthur immediately pressed on. "I call the next tune, 'Que Vida'." He started it with a finger-picking configuration, followed by a strumming kind of syncopated "bossa nova" rhythm. He sang the lyrics in a pure, clean style, in a voice again one-step evolved from the vocal style he used on the first album. Then, he played 'She Comes In Colours'. Then, 'The Castle': an elegant, orchestral-renaissance number. And, again, the high, sweet, beautiful vocal style. I wondered if the disappointment was showing on my face. It was all so sophisticated. What the hell was this? I had already played symphonic, orchestral music, and jazz and show tunes in high school and college. They were all great and worthwhile experiences and I wouldn't have traded my background for anything. But I had already done those things. That was then, this was now. I was ready to move on to something a little more mainstream-contemporary. I was ready to keep rockin' for a little while longer, too.

And, as Arthur played each song that was to appear on *Da Capo* I began to realize just how thoroughly LOVE was about to abandon the raw, hard-rocking folk style that established the huge underground fan base that had bought the first album. I suppose I had simply assumed that the stuff that would comprise *Da Capo* would bear some similarity to the previous material that had met with such universal acceptance. If this was the new direction the group was taking, I, for one, was going to miss the old style. I really loved the violent and powerfully unique product LOVE had embraced in the past and had become known for. I kept waiting for something off the new album to kindle a spark of recognition but, so far, nothing.

"Wait a minute," I told myself, "Ronnie said Arthur was breaking new ground on this album, so he could have some more stuff up his sleeve. Something he hasn't shown us yet. Something a little more exciting, like 'My Flash On You' or 'You, I'll Be Followin'." Maybe, maybe not. It didn't really matter, because, in fact, Arthur WAS breaking new ground. Just because I wanted to keep rockin', that didn't mean that's the way it was supposed to be. Arthur was the songwriter. He knew what all great artists know. Imagination and change has to be the guiding force. Creative lethargy is the kiss of death. If you write music, you have to explore new worlds on a regular basis. I just played the drums. Besides, in the context of what was going on in popular music at that time, this material was unique; it was new and different and exotic. It was something the music critics and the more sophisticated fans could appreciate. Our regular old rock fans? Not so sure.

A few years down the road, of course, I would develop an appreciation for the songs that Arthur had written for *Da Capo* but at the time, quite candidly, the material seemed a little too different. It was anti-mainstream. Aggressive and inventive, the album was a landmark in sonic and lyrical experimentation. Frankly, it was a lot of things. Definitely not rock'n'roll. Truth be told, it totally defied every category except "futuristic". So, I guess you could only be safe in saying that Arthur, true to his position as the leader of an underground group with a cult following, wrote music for future generations. That was our audience.

He set his guitar down, "We'll go over 'Orange Skies' tomorrow. I want to give Tjay a chance to practice the flute part first. That's it for side one. Side two is gonna be something the fans have never heard before. It's gonna be different, man. The whole side will be one long John Lee Hooker jam. Nobody's ever done anything like it. We'll each take a long solo. It'll cook, man. It'll blow their minds."

"Woops," I thought. "Did he say, 'each take a long solo'?" Because, personally, I was never crazy about drum solos in rock. Especially the ones that go on and on. Never liked listening to them, even as a kid, when I thought I was supposed to enjoy all that whacking, banging, crashing and booming. Most of the time, they just didn't sound good to me, so I never learned to do it. Sorry. The American Heritage Dictionary defines "percussion" as "The striking together of two bodies, especially when noise is produced."

"Noise." They said it. In the first place, a long solo by any instrument only sounds good if it's successfully woven into the fabric of the total composition, and then performed with systematic accompaniment. That especially applies to drums. The thing that bands do, where everybody else abruptly stops playing and, sometimes even, walks off the stage, leaving the drummer to play all alone, is amateurish and stupid, like a high school rock group performing at an assembly.

Sure, there's room for drum solos in certain situations. Short drum breaks used to tie stanzas together? That works. The sensitive, heartfelt solos, born of genius, like the ones Elvin Jones takes on 'A Love Supreme'? Nothing finer. I'm not talking about that. But the John Lee Hooker jam was a rockin' boogie, not jazz, by any stretch of the imagination.

The Bible says, "It's harder for a rich man to get into heaven than it is for a camel to pass through the eye of a needle," or something like that. Same analogy could be drawn with drum solos. The ones worth listening to are really rare. I honestly don't think God planned for drums to be a solo instrument.

However, I could tell that Arthur had planned *Da Capo* to include a drum solo and I didn't have quite the seniority to argue the point, this being my first day and all. So, a drum solo it would be.

But, the more we explored the material, the more I formed the impression that this album was being used as an interlude, a breather. These songs, although intricate and, for

Individual KRLA Beat shoot

the most part, melodically cosmic, had the feel of music that was being recorded as a part of an agenda, a master plan to perhaps fulfil an obligation, something to take up time and space while Arthur worked out the nuts and bolts formula for a future, more important effort. Whatever, I had to keep pluggin'.

During a break, Arthur began to pack the pipe, "Tell you guys a little secret. I plan to retire before I reach twenty-five." He fired it up and passed it to me. Then he stood up, hunched over and began coughing his lungs to ribbons. Walking to the sliding glass door that led to his rear deck, he opened it, cleared his throat and hung one over the railing.

"Really?" I wondered. "Retire from what? Rockin' and rollin' and getting high?" And what would he do in retirement? Go out and get a real job? Watch TV? It's my understanding, you have to work a little before you retire. I mean, when musicians play, they call it "work"; when actors act in a movie, they call it "work". But it's not work, really. It's playing and acting. It's not work, in the conventional sense, like digging trenches in 110 degree heat, or pulling telephone cable fifty feet up a pole in a driving rain, or teaching school. In fact, it's just the opposite. It's getting paid big money to have fun, is what it is. And, besides, even the people who do real work don't start looking forward to retirement when they're only 22 years old. It's not natural.

But as this first day of rehearsal drew to a close, Tjay and Johnny said their good-byes and left. Bryan went back to his downstairs unit to listen to his own music on his own stereo. Kenny and Snoopy and I stayed around a little while longer to go over a few more tunes and smoke some more hash. Before long, Arthur rose from the couch and re-opened the door leading out to his rear deck. Turning toward me, he asked, "Michael, are you into pigeons? Check these dudes out." He signalled me to come to the door, then he walked to a large screened enclosure at the far end of the deck, opened the door to the coop, and removed a white bird with a lot of feathers on his feet. "I've kept pigeons since I was a kid, man. Watch what this one can do."

Suddenly, he threw it over the railing, into the air, over the portion of the canyon that stretched out below his house. At first, the pigeon flew magnificently, soaring and rising up through the thermals. Then, without warning, it stopped flying and went into what looked like an out of control death spiral, twisting, and fluttering toward the canyon floor. Only a few feet from certain disaster, the bird pulled up, regained control and resumed flying again. He soared back up to Arthur's deck and landed on the railing, next to the coop. Arthur picked it off the railing, placed it back inside the coop and closed the door.

"Pretty impressive, man," I said. "Did you train it?"

"Naw, nobody trained it. It's a Tumbling Pigeon. They do that automatically. They're born knowing how to do it. It's a defence mechanism they use to draw predators away from the nest in the wild." He walked back to the coffee table, picked up the pipe and lit it.

But Kenny was still staring through the sliding glass door in the direction of the pigeon coop. "Is that part of the defence mechanism?" Arthur and Snoopy and I went to the sliding door and looked out. The bird was lying on the bottom of the cage, under his perch, feet up, his little eyes closed. Arthur stepped quickly out onto the deck, reached in and lifted the body of the pigeon. The head hung limp.

"He's dead, man," Kenny announced. "Maybe he hurt himself when he did that trick."

Arthur squeezed the pigeon to see if there was any sign of life. When he did, the bird let out a little squawk.

"Involuntary reflex," I thought. Then, he squeezed him again. The pigeon squawked again, but this time his eyes fluttered, then opened briefly and he seemed to be struggling to bring his head erect. But a moment later, the head began to droop and the eyes closed.

Arthur squeezed him. Eyes opened. He squawked. Arthur had stumbled onto a early form of avian cardiopulmonary-resuscitation, the "squeezebox technique," I guess. As long as Arthur held the pigeon in his hand and squeezed, the bird lived. And squawked. Occasionally, he placed it back on its perch to see if it could stand on its own, but each time, as soon as he let go, the bird would keel over, close its eyes and fall to the floor of the cage.

Arthur soon became resigned to the task of squeezing the pigeon, nonstop, and the squawking sound eventually became an integral and unnoticed part of the background. For the next hour, or so, Kenny and Snoopy and Arthur and I, went over the *Da Capo* tunes with Arthur working more or less one-handed, occasionally pausing to pass the bird to one of us, while he packed the pipe or demonstrated a passage on the guitar. But, for the most part, it was Arthur squeezing, his left hand having been transformed into a miniature iron lung, and gesturing with his right, when necessary, to make a point. Otherwise, it was business as usual.

After a while, Snoopy left and Kenny and I prepared to do the same.

Arthur rose from the couch, still caressing the pigeon. "Michael, tomorrow before practice we have to meet at Schlessinger and Tabor's office so you can sign a contract, and then I want you to go with Johnny and me over to the Elektra offices for a short meeting with a company rep. Give me a call around ten, O.K.?" As Kenny and I left and walked out to my car, we both took one last look back. Arthur stood in the doorway, squeezing the pigeon with his left hand and waving bye-bye with his right.

We climbed into my Porsche and Kenny immediately picked up a shoebox full of weed from the passenger side floorboard. "Where's your papers, man?" I pointed to the glove compartment. He retrieved the papers, then rolling a joint on the lid of the shoebox, he shook his head and smiled, "Tell me, Michael, do you give that pigeon much of a chance?"

As we pulled away from the curb, I laughed. "Not unless he has it surgically attached to the palm of his hand."

The next morning at ten o'clock sharp, I called Arthur. He told me that the offices of the group's attorneys, Schlessinger and Tabor, were located in The Crossroads of the World business complex on Sunset. You couldn't miss Crossroads of the World. Shaped like a tugboat, Crossroads was a group of professional bungalows that was built in the Old Hollywood architectural tradition of round-corner stucco, accented with the translucent crystal blocks, so popular during the 1940s and '50s, in a style now called "art deco". But you couldn't miss it because of the rotating world globe, which had been erected near the centre and high above the development, clearly visible from several blocks away, proclaiming the spot "The Crossroads of the World". Crossroads was as much a landmark as it was a location. The name? I don't know, I guess it might have been because that part of Hollywood is usually cursed with a lot of gridlock.

We met around eleven, and Arthur introduced me to Tabor. Portly dude with a moustache, dressed in a dark suit. Schlessinger wasn't there that day, or any other, throughout our association, so he could have been made up, for all I know, just to make the name of the law firm sound better. I mean, just, "Tabor?" No, that doesn't make it, but "Schlessinger and Tabor?" Sounds cool. Very impressive.

While Arthur and Tabor talked, Tabor's secretary sat me down at a table near the window, and had me fill out some forms that would enable them to send a weekly salary check to me, and pay all my utilities out of a central fund. I suppose it was an effort to narrow my frame of responsibility and make sure nothing would be turned off when the group was out of town. Of course, I had learned to handle that sort of thing myself when I entered my adult years and moved out of my parents' house but, "O.K.," I thought, "you guys can pay my bills from now on, if you want to."

When I was finished, she handed me another multi-page document. "This is the contract to record for Elektra. It entitles you to one percent of the earnings on everything you record with the group, LOVE. Standard 'Equal Member's Share' contract." I signed. Then, she laid what appeared to be a duplicate contract on the table in front of Arthur and tapped it once or twice with her finger. "Don't forget to take this to Tjay. We need to get both contracts back to Elektra's New York office before the end of the week."

Arthur picked Tjay's contract up off the table, folded it, and put it in his inside coat pocket. "Yeah, I'll get it to him today." Then we said our goodbyes and walked out to the parking lot, where Johnny had been patiently waiting in the passenger seat of Arthur's Porsche. A copy of the band's first album rested on his lap. "Come on, Michael. Let's take my short," Arthur suggested. "Johnny and I can bring you back here after we get through at Elektra." He pulled the driver's backrest forward, so I could crawl into the back seat. Then, Arthur fired up his Porsche and the hash pipe and pulled out of the parking lot. Turning right, we headed west on Sunset. On the way over to Elektra's West Coast offices, he and Johnny explained the purpose of the meeting.

"Here's what's happening, man," Arthur began. "Elektra Records is brand new to the popular music industry. A year ago, they were just a novelty label. They had, like, fifteen volumes of sound effects and a couple of folk groups, that's all. In fact, that's where we got the explosion at the end of '7 and 7 Is'. It's a gunshot, recorded and then slowed down a hundred times, or something. They have some other bullshit I want to use on 'Que Vida', by the way, a jingle bells and a cork popping. But anyhow, we're their very first rock band and they've been sort of learning on us, using us as their guinea pig."

"They don't know what the fuck they're doing yet," Johnny interjected. "Their promotion and distribution is too weak to handle a major group, like us." He reached for Arthur's pipe and put a new match to it.

Arthur continued, "But Jac Holzman just signed these new guys, The Doors. So, now that we're not their only rock band anymore, I'm hoping they'll listen to reason and be grateful for what LOVE has done for the label, and that they'll let us out of our contract. That's why we're going over there now, to talk about it."

"Let's see..." I thought, "I definitely heard him say we were going from gunshots and explosions, to jingle bells and popping corks."

"Do they know what the meeting's about?" I asked, taking a hit off the hash pipe.

"Nope."

"This ought to be fun," I thought.

Before Elektra built their new West Coast corporate offices on La Cienega in the late sixties, the company did business out of a place that looked a little like a small re-vamped two-storey apartment complex, just down the street from Crossroads of the World on Sunset. In fact, it was so close, we were there already. Arthur pulled into the lot and we got out of the car. "Don't forget the album, man," Arthur instructed.

"Got it right here," Johnny held it up. The three of us took the elevator to the second floor. When the doors opened, we were greeted immediately by the company rep with whom Arthur had scheduled the meeting. He introduced me to the rep, who shook my hand and welcomed me to the label.

"Glad to have you with us, Michael. Come on, guys. Let's go out on the terrace. Hell, it's a nice day, no reason at all to sit inside." He gestured through the sliding doors, to some chairs scattered around a glass-topped metal table on a patio overlooking Sunset. Arthur joked around with the rep a little, to throw him off his guard, and then he got right to it.

"Listen, man," Arthur said, leaning forward and suddenly turning serious. "There's something we have to discuss with you. It's about our future."

A look of concern swept across the Elektra rep's face. "What do you mean, Arthur? What's wrong?"

"Well," Arthur continued, "we're really disappointed in the lack of promotion and distribution the company gave our first album. I mean, I have friends in Tennessee that have never even heard of us, much less heard any of our songs on the radio, because I don't think the disc jockeys have heard of us either. We've lost confidence in you guys. We just don't think Elektra will ever have the size or the resources to do for this group what needs to be done to put us on top. The company is too small, man. We've decided we want to do what ever we have to do to get out of the remainder of our contract with Elektra. Tell us what needs to be done, man. We want out." Then Arthur leaned back in his patio chair and lit the cigarette he had been fishing out of his pocket during the last few words of the speech. The company rep appeared stunned.

Johnny seized the opportunity. He removed the group's first album from its cardboard cover, held it up and, using both hands, snapped it in half. "Look, man, you can't do that with albums manufactured by other companies." He tossed the two halves on the table in front of the rep. "Elektra uses cheap materials."

If Arthur's speech and Johnny's demonstration were designed to shame the Elektra guy into agreeing to set us free, the plan proved woefully inadequate, because by now, having regained his composure, he smiled a fatherly smile and said, "Guys, there's no way the company can erase the contract. You've known from the beginning that we're not big, like a Columbia or a Capitol or an RCA. Granted, our distribution isn't what it will be someday. But we always have, and always will, put your welfare and success above all else, and the company will do everything in its power to promote the group and get it the international attention it deserves. No matter how many rock bands we manage to sign, Elektra will always have the highest regard for LOVE. You guys are very important to us, and I'm sure I speak for Jac when I say, we will not let you out of your contract prematurely, under any circumstances. You have to record the remaining three albums you owe the company, and that's final." But he smiled diplomatically one more time to show there was no hard feelings. That's just the way it was. Actually, his tone of voice and his demeanour was so calm and quiet, and his response was so measured, that the traffic noise from the street below drowned out an occasional word, here and there. But we got the message, loud and clear.

Arthur fixed him with a glare for about ten seconds, and then he got up from his patio chair, shook the rep's hand with a half-hearted hand shake and, turning to Johnny and me, grumbled, "Come on, we'll be late for rehearsal."

Then we all stood up and the rep shook Johnny's hand, "It was nice seeing you again, Johnny," he said. He meant it, too; you could tell. And as we walked back toward the elevator, he shook my hand again, and again told me how glad they were to have me with the label. Then we left.

It was a nice try, I guess.

Chapter Eight

Da Capo

CONSIDERING THE INTENSITY of the effort put into this ill-fated escape attempt, I thought the mood might be slightly on the dark side, during the ride back to the Crossroads parking lot. But it wasn't. More philosophical. Like: "Oh, well, nothing ventured, nothing gained. At least we gave it a shot."

When Johnny and Arthur and I arrived at Arthur's house, Kenny and Bryan and Snoopy and Tjay were all waiting out front, standing around and talking and smoking a joint. "We have an album to do," Arthur said, motioning us inside. "Let's go to work."

As we set up for rehearsal, Arthur opened the sliding glass door to his deck. "Check out the patient." He gestured to the pigeon coop. "There he is. The white one, remember?" Sure enough, the bird that appeared to be a certain goner, only the day before, was back up on his perch, side-stepping, like they do, bumping into the pigeon next to him on purpose; you know, giving him a hard time. Fit as a fiddle. At least, Arthur said it was the same bird. Pigeons all look pretty much alike to the untrained eye.

Over the next few weeks, rehearsals for *Da Capo* intensified, and I began to learn more of the musical character of my new bandmates. My fellow inductee, Tjay, was a jazz musician, pure and simple. He had probably never played a rock'n'roll song in his life. LOVE had decided that the new direction the group was taking needed additional instrumentation to carry it where it had to go. The creative woodwind fills that Tjay had written for the breaks in the songs on Side One, were the perfect solution to the problem of what relatively inexperienced rock and folk musicians could do to make this thing sound right. Tjay's parts were downright soft and imaginative and beautiful. In contrast, his solo on Side Two, 'Revelation', could only have been classified as "intense and powerful." Free-form jazz. Groundbreaking stuff for that time period, for music that was marketed as "pop" or "rock." He wanted to be the "new John Coltrane" of popular music. He idolized Coltrane. So much so that he patterned his life style, as well as his playing style, after him. And, like John Coltrane, Tjay had battled the drug devils.

The group's bassist, Kenny Forssi, was the founding father of the driving folk-rock bass he pioneered on the first album. But he was so technically flexible and deliberate, he would have no trouble adjusting to the new material, whatsoever. At every practice, he showed up with his part memorized; after every practice, he went home and rehearsed the bass parts he would need to know the next day. His approach was to be thoroughly prepared, leave nothing to chance and thereby avoid any unpleasant surprises. When you listened to him play what he had composed, you were left with the impression it was written down, because the progressions were so well thought out and consistent. But, to my knowledge, anyway, the bass parts were only written in his head. I don't think Kenny could read or write a note.

Moving Snoopy from drums over to keyboards was a masterful stroke of convenience. He was already in the group, and his training in classical piano gave him all the expertise he would need to handle the tunes on *Da Capo*. I had wondered from the beginning if there was any resentment on his part because I had been brought in to take over the drumming; but the conversations I had with Snoop during breaks at the early rehearsals made me realize that he was relieved to be out from under the gun. He was content with the new set-up that put him back into the keyboard environment, where he felt more comfortable. The year of being dogged by everybody in the group about his lack of experience and power behind the drums had taken a severe toll on his confidence, and he was more or less glad it was over. As much as anyone in the group, Snoop welcomed my arrival, and we soon became best friends.

Bryan had come from the world of folk music, and his finger picking background had been greatly responsible for the strong folk influence on the first album. The technique that defined his musical identity transferred well to the sound Arthur had chosen for the group's new direction, and his voice and compositions were a vital component to the total package. Remove Bryan from the mix and it wouldn't be LOVE anymore. It would just be the individuals that remained.

Johnny was a guitar master. He was comfortable with almost any guitar format, and was recognized as one of the top musicians in Hollywood. Instrumentally, he was a legitimate free spirit, and he almost never played any song the same way twice. The new stuff was very structured and required each guy to play his part exactly as he had played it the time before, but Johnny had no trouble meeting the challenge and making the adjustment to the regimentation demanded on the material Arthur and Bryan had written for *Da Capo*.

From raw and emotional to clean and sophisticated is a big leap but most of the fans would make the transition to the new sound with no trouble at all. Others would have difficulty embracing, or even becoming remotely interested in, the "new direction" and would never be able to understand why LOVE had abandoned the style that had brought it so much success in the past. To a certain extent, that was a problem.

The first album had dealt with subject matter that was easy to comprehend and, for the young record buying public, natural to identify with: worry over the fear of nuclear war ('Mushroom Clouds'), the frustration of trying to find drugs ('You, I'll Be Following'), a lament for a friend hopelessly hooked on smack ('Signed D.C.'), and love songs like 'Message To Pretty' or 'No Matter What in the World You Do' were all common-bond concepts that linked people together during that time period. The first album was one you could sing along with.

Da Capo? Poetically beautiful, innovative and different? Of course. A new direction, after all.

Although LOVE and The Doors were the only two rock groups signed to Elektra, there was never much interaction between the two. I mean, we didn't hang out with each other. There was, however, a brief period when Jim Morrison and Bryan had started to cultivate a friendship. Jim would come over to Bryan's little pad downstairs from Arthur's to listen to music: they would talk and smoke dope. I think Bryan's unit just had a hotplate and a mini-fridge. No real kitchen. Separate entrances and bathrooms. That meant all Bryan's friends could come and go without having to say "howdy" to Arthur. There was a swimming pool located about a hundred feet down the hill from the house, at the bottom of a long wooden staircase, and in plain view of maybe ten or fifteen other houses in the neighbourhood. One day, we were at Arthur's, running over 'Stephanie Knows Who', but softly, with acoustic guitars, when Arthur frowned and kind of cocked his head to one side, as if to listen better, and then waved at us to stop playing and be quiet.

He looked at Bryan, "Hey, man, I think I hear somebody down in your pad."

Bryan looked unconcerned. "Oh yeah, that's Jim. I told him he could stick around 'til we were finished with practice, then we're gonna hang out for a while. He's trippin' on acid."

So we went back to 'Stephanie'. None of us thought any more of it until about twenty minutes later, when Arthur happened to walk past the window which overlooked the pool. He stopped and did a serious double take. "Uh, Bryan, your buddy, Jim is down at the pool."

Bryan kept picking at his guitar. "So what? I told him he could go down there. Is that all right with you?" he asked sarcastically, not looking up.

Arthur continued to stare out the window. "Yeah, well, he doesn't have any clothes on. You know, no bathing suit or anything. He's naked."

Bryan looked up. "Oh?"

Arthur started to pace back and forth, working himself up into a lather. "The nerve of that asshole! He comes over here, he uses our pool, and then he parades around naked in front of all the neighbours and grosses everybody out." Reaching the boiling point, he shook his head. "I don't care. Acid or no acid, I'm going down there and give that motherfucker a piece of my mind." He whipped open the sliding glass door leading to the rear deck and started jogging down the stairs.

"No, man, don't," Bryan pleaded, but it was too late. We couldn't hear everything that was being said, but only halfway down and Arthur was already yelling and waving his arms. I picked up a few words here and there, like "Get your god-dammed clothes on! How could you be so fuckin' stupid, man?" Diplomatic stuff like that.

So, Jim quickly scrambled out of the pool, grabbed his clothes and trotted up the wooden stairway. As he passed the window, I caught a glimpse of his face. He was wide-eyed, terrified. After that, I don't think there was even a superficially polite, moderately diplomatic, nodding acquaintanceship between the two groups. All the times we bumped into each other while playing on the same bill or using the same recording studio, working with the same engineers, producers... nothing. Maybe we nodded at each other occasionally, but that's about it.

Any other two groups signed to the same label might have sat in on the other dude's sessions or contributed in some other way to the success of the other group's album. But the swimming pool incident squelched that. In future years, Bryan would occasionally mention to Arthur how he had screwed up the budding friendship he had with Jim Morrison – you know, kind of kidding and kind of serious at the same time. But Arthur never appeared to feel guilty, or anything like that. In fact, every time Bryan brought it up, Arthur would always just shrug his shoulders, as if to say, "I don't care. Too bad. He shouldn't have been in my pool naked."

Another *Da Capo* rehearsal had concluded and I was sitting in my car, giving it the necessary warm-up. "Hey, Michael, can you give me a ride home? My car won't start." Johnny stood at my window, jerking his thumb, with disgust, in the direction of his vintage black Jaguar sedan. It was in pretty good shape – visually – but, like a lot of older things, it wasn't quite as dependable as it was when it was young. The group was nearing the end of the few weeks we had been given to work on *Da Capo* before heading into the studio, and it occurred to me I had never had a normal conversation with Johnny. One not associated with the arrangements, I mean. We had never really hung out.

"Yeah, sure, man. I'll give you a ride home. Hop in." I leaned over and unlocked the passenger-side door and Johnny put his guitar in the back seat. After he got in and closed the door, he reached in his shirt pocket, pulled out a fat joint, fired it up and passed it to me.

On the way home, Johnny asked me, "Michael, you like jazz, right? You want to take a run down to Shelly's Mannehole later tonight?"

I don't remember who he said was on the bill, but it didn't matter. Only the top names in jazz played there. Shelly Manne himself was a tremendous talent, having done, among other things, the drumming on the greatest movie soundtrack album of all time, Elmer Bernstein's *The Man With The Golden Arm*. The club was a Hollywood meeting place for the rank and file, as well as the stars of the jazz world.

We pulled up to Johnny's house and he reached into the back seat and grabbed his guitar. As he climbed out, I told him, "Hey, I'll pick you up at ten, but what about your car? You want me to call the Auto Club?"

"Naw," he shook his head, "It'll be all right. Anyway, the piece of shit'll start tomorrow. Thanks for the ride, man. See you at ten." He waved and walked up the driveway to his front door, and I left.

But, actually, his car wouldn't start the next day or any other day, for that matter. In fact, it would sit in that very spot against the curb, in front of Arthur's house where Johnny had parked it, until one day after rehearsal, we walked out to get in my car so I could give Johnny a ride home as usual, and discovered it had been towed away. Funny thing is, Johnny didn't seem to mind. In fact, he appeared almost relieved. Like, whew, now he didn't have to deal with it. Of course, he wasn't dealing with it anyway, but now he didn't have to feel guilty about not dealing with it anymore.

What you have to realize is, all the precautions and celebration that most people heap on a car – like waxing the finish regularly to protect the paint job, using exactly the right oil in the engine, stuff like that – just didn't make any sense to Johnny. He thought of a car as a convenient way to get from point A to point B, that's all. The "upkeep" crap was a burden.

When I got back to Johnny's house that night around ten, I pulled into his driveway and flashed my headlights at his living room window a couple of times to let him know I was there. A minute later, he opened the door and stepped out on the front porch, paused, and lit a joint. Then, he walked over to my car, crawled into the passenger seat, took a hit and passed it over to me. He flashed the happy-go-lucky grin he almost always wore. "You ready to go listen to some good music, Michael?" he asked in that funny voice you have to use when you're holding a hit.

"Oh, yeah," I nodded, then I backed out of his driveway and we headed off down the hill into Hollywood.

Johnny dressed in buckskin and velvet and sometimes a bowler hat, and smoked weed in public all the time, because he knew he'd never get caught. He had a carefree outlook on life and never worried about a thing. Always ready to have a good time. Always ready for something different.

Even before Johnny's car got towed away, his girlfriend used to drop him off at practice, sometimes. She was strikingly beautiful, and every time I saw them together, it was obvious he was her world. She watched him constantly with adoring eyes.

Winding our way down Laurel Canyon, I reached over and turned down the car stereo. "Hey, Johnny, who's your girlfriend, man? She looks familiar. Does she come to the gigs?"

"Oh, that's Nancy Harwood, Michael. I've been going out with her for a while. She's a *Playboy*'s Playmate of the Month. Last July, I think. Lotta fun, real nice, but she hangs around a little too much. She's been smothering me, man. Seriously. Lately, when she calls, I've been telling her I'm busy with rehearsals but she doesn't take a hint too well and, like, she comes over anyway. I don't know, I don't want to be mean to her or anything, but I'm starting to feel like I need a little space. I guess I'll have to say something to her pretty soon in language she'll understand."

I thought, "Yeah, you're right, man. You got to set the ground rules early on." Those *Playboy* Playmates can be a pain in the butt sometimes.

A few minutes later we got to Shelly's, located only a few blocks from Bido Lito's. After the valet took my Porsche to its temporary home in the lot, Johnny and I paid admission, then the guy working the door seated us at a table near the stage. Before long, a waitress took our drink order. The house group was on a break and recorded jazz was being piped in softly over the P.A. All the regulars were sort of milling around and hobnobbing and buying each other drinks and yucking it up. So, after our drinks came (two drink minimum), we sat there, just checking out the goings-on, with a good buzz working from the weed, adding to it with the booze and waiting for the live music to restart.

Suddenly, Johnny punched me in the arm. "Hey, Michael, look, man!" He gestured to a group of people being seated at a table, maybe ten feet away. The conversational volume in the room began to rise. The people at the other tables were all focusing their attention on the new arrivals, too. "It's Miles Davis and Tony Williams, man! Can you believe it?" They were with two or three other dudes in suits and, even before they sat down, the waitress was right there to take their order. Just about the time the girl got back to their table with the drinks, the house band took the stage, and hurriedly stormed into their eleven o'clock set, fuelled by what must have been an awesome level of inspiration and enthusiasm. I mean, you're a jazz musician and Miles Davis is in the audience, for God's sake!

So, the house band started playing some great stuff and they were, of course, cranking it up and sounding good. Miles wasn't listening though. From the moment he and Tony sat down, Miles was deeply involved in some kind of informal, impromptu business meeting. Something that probably started out as "Let's go have a couple of drinks at Shelly's and talk it over" but quickly was escalating into another thing altogether. Several members of his party, the guys in suits, were trying to reason with Miles about something, but he didn't want any part of it. He occasionally jabbed his index finger in the direction of the faces of his associates to make a point, as he tried to yell over the din of the music. Watching him, I thought back to the hours my bandmates and I, in high school and college, had spent listening to the Miles Davis classic albums, *Sketches of Spain* and *Kind of Blue*. They were magical works of art. And Miles, physically diminutive, was the biggest man in the world of jazz. Larger than life. His playing style was so cool and calm. Notes long enough to span the universe. He was superhuman.

Eventually, the heated discussion between Miles and the dudes (who appeared to be label execs) cooled, everybody relaxed and the suits went off in different directions to socialize with the folks at other tables. While Miles and Tony talked, some of the other patrons got up from their tables and stopped by Miles' table and were trying to buy them drinks, or something, but Miles and Tony looked, each time, as if they were politely declining the offers. Then the people would nod and go back to their tables, where they belonged, and Miles and Tony would continue talking to each other. It wasn't too long before Miles started looking real bored. Staring off in the distance, occasionally stifling a yawn and looking more and more aggravated every time a stranger tried to talk to him or buy him a drink. One by one, the suits stopped by his table and said their good-byes and drifted out the door. The meeting was over.

For the next hour, Johnny and I sat there and shot the shit and listened to the house jazz group and watched the people try to hobnob with Miles. And I began to notice two things. Miles didn't want to be there, and Miles never smiled. Not once. In fact, he looked miserable, as if he wanted to be anywhere else than in Shelly's Mannehole at that moment. "Why," I found myself wondering, "is he here?" It didn't make any sense. He never once looked at the stage to give even the slightest encouragement to the group playing its heart out for him: so, he wasn't there to listen to the music. He wasn't hobnobbing. Why didn't he just meet with the label execs, say what he had to say, and then take off?

"Go on home, man." I wanted to tell him. "Go home where you can be happy. This isn't the place for you." Did he crave the attention? Is that why he was hanging around?

After a while, Johnny and I left the Mannehole, and as we drove back in the direction of Laurel Canyon, he leaned forward and picked a roach out of the ashtray, and, holding it carefully between the tips of his thumb and forefinger, he lit it. "Michael, you want to go up to Arthur's house for a while? Conka's gonna be there. He got out of Corona last week, and he's got some dynamite smack. I told him we might come by for a taste and he said there would be enough for you, if you want some."

"Sure, man, let's swing by."

Chapter Nine

The Bummer

AS SEPTEMBER of 1966 approached, preparations for *Da Capo* drew to a close and time was booked at RCA studios on Sunset Boulevard. Like The Rolling Stones – and The Sons of Adam – we were to use Studio B, with Dave Hassinger, considered the best in the business at that time, engineering the session.

On the final day before the group was to begin laying down the instrumental tracks, we were all at Arthur's house for one last run-through on a couple of the tunes. After rehearsal, when everybody was leaving, Snoopy approached me.

"Hey, Michael, I gotta move out of the house I'm staying in, and I know you're still living with The Sons of Adam. You want to get a place together?"

Sounded like a good idea to me. Even though Randy and Mike and Jac and I were all still friends, I knew in my heart it would be better and more natural if I roomed with one of my new bandmates in LOVE. So I followed Snoop over to the Beechwood area of the Hollywood Hills to check out a pad he already had picked out. It was way at the top, close to the Hollywood sign, on a little street so remote and difficult to navigate that nobody in his right mind would be on it unless he was lost or lived there.

He led me up Durand, a winding series of twists and turns so harsh that some of them might have had to be taken in two swipes, if the driver was unfamiliar with the area or was driving a car with a limited steering radius. Essentially a single-lane road, it was most safely travelled at night, when headlights warned of oncoming traffic. In the daytime it was a head-on collision waiting to happen. The only way two cars could pass each other, going in opposite directions, was for one car to pull over and stop. In fact, Durand was such a bad road, it was almost surprising it was even paved, or on a street map. Which it was. But the accompanying isolation and the view were exquisite, and at night the silence and the twinkling lights from the city below, gave the atmosphere a dream-like quality impossible to describe.

The architectural style of the house itself was kind of Spanish-modern white stucco with a typical southern California red tile roof. Immediately inside the oversized double front doors, a foyer led into the upstairs living room, with an adjacent kitchen, dining room and guest bath located on the same floor. A sliding glass door provided an exit out onto the veranda and upper-level deck.

Over the foyer entrance, a large crystal chandelier illuminated a red-carpeted staircase leading down to two adjoining bedrooms, each with its own bath and terrace, and separated by a laundry room. The living room and bedroom terraces overlooked a canyon dissected by a small stream, a stream I never saw, only heard. All in all, a very opulent and serene environment. The house came totally furnished, so Snoopy and I were able to move in the very night of the afternoon I first saw it. And that's exactly what we did.

The next day, September 27, 1966, we met at RCA to start *Da Capo*. When we walked in, the engineering and production guys were already spacing the mic stands and talking over the preliminary settings they would use to record the instrumental tracks.

Dave Hassinger looked up and gave us a wave. "Go ahead and start setting up, fellas. We'll be ready in a few minutes."

We all brought our instruments in and began to set up behind the large baffles that kept the sound from one instrument from leaking over into the microphones meant to pick up only the others. Kenny rolled his amp into one of the baffle cubbies, removed his bass from its case and started tuning up, as did Johnny and Bryan. Snoopy sat down at the electric harpsichord they had brought in for him and began running through his solo on 'The Castle' while Tjay doodled never-ending arpeggios on his soprano sax. We were all gettin' ready for this thing. Serious business. Except, the hash pipe was being passed around the whole time, of course.

As I unpacked my drums, Arthur leaned his black Gibson acoustic and his solid body electric side-by-side against the wall, and sat down on a stool directly in back of me, by the vocal booth. From time to time, during the long process of assembling my equipment, I could see him, out of the corner of my eye, furiously scribbling notes on a sheet of paper. His guitars were within reach of us both but closer to me than him.

Then, without looking up, "Michael, hand me my guitar, will you? I want to show you something I added to 'The Castle'." He reached out.

"Here we go," I thought. "Now, I'm supposed to stop what I'm doing so I can hand him his guitar. And he's just taking it for granted I'll do it. Is he testing me, or what? Is he seeing if I'll fall in line with the rest of the guys?" I put the cymbal stand I was holding down on the floor and grabbed the neck of the acoustic I knew he wanted. "You mean this one?" Then, just as he started to nod, I let go of the acoustic and grabbed the neck of the electric. "Or this one." Then, when he started to shake his head, "No," I re-grabbed the acoustic. "This one? Or this one? Which one, man?" Finally, after five or six times, I handed him the black acoustic, "Here you go," and went back to setting up my cymbal stand.

He started to absent-mindedly strum a few preliminary chords, "Michael, you know how to put a motherfucker on."

Actually, I didn't really want to hand him the guitar at all, so I kind of turned it into a little joke. But what I was saying was, "Man, from now on if you're in a hurry for your guitar, maybe you better get up and get it yourself, O.K.? I mean, what's next? Maybe you'd like me to stop and buy you some orange juice at the Canyon Country Store."

Kenny and Bryan were huddled together, going over some last-minute stuff and, in a minute, Kenny put his bass down in the stand by his amp and lit a cigarette, but not before sticking it in one of those plastic, disposable aquafilters that he always used. The ones that cool and saturate the smoke with water, so you don't get lung cancer. "I'm gonna go get a Coke," he said, and went out into the hall.

Bryan unplugged his guitar and carried it over to where Arthur and I sat. He stood in front of Arthur and began to pick on the big strings. "Hey, Arthur, check out this new part Kenny wrote for 'Que Vida'. It's pretty good."

Arthur turned away. "I don't care what Kenny wrote," he sniffed. "Kenny doesn't know if he wants to take a shit or eat a peanut butter-and -jelly sandwich." He laughed long and hard, then went back to scribbling. Bryan gave Arthur a look that said, "What's wrong with you, man?" then he shrugged and walked back to his baffle cubbie.

After a while, we started laying down the tracks. The first day, we did Bryan's composition, 'Orange Skies'. We put 'Que Vida' off until the next day, September twenty-eighth, then, on the twenty-ninth, 'She Comes In Colours'. September thirtieth: 'The Castle'. Then, on October first and second: 'Stephanie Knows Who' and 'Revelation', the John Lee Hooker jam. Five days, all done. It was all pretty well thought out and structured, except for 'John Lee Hooker'. That one was just the opposite.

It was like, Arthur said, "O.K., first I'll start out on guitar, 'ga danga chink, ga danga chink...' and then all you guys'll kick in, and Johnny'll be over in the vocal booth, and he'll do his vocal, and I'll play his guitar for a while, then Johnny and I'll trade places, and I'll go in the booth and he'll come out here and play the guitar. Then I'll take my harp solo, see? Then, I'll come out and Tjay'll go in the booth and take his solo, then when he's done, Kenny'll take his bass solo, then Michael'll take his drum solo, and then, Snoopy'll take his harpsichord solo, and we'll be finished."

I mean, to be honest, I don't remember if that was the exact sequence or not – and I'm not going to listen to it again to find out, either. That day in the studio was the first time we had ever played it together. It was a jam, orchestrated on the spur of the moment. Certainly not the kind of material to take up the whole side of an LP. I felt like I had just joined the group, and we were already starting to cut our own throats. Arthur and Bryan had a bunch of great songs written and all ready to record, but it was as if Arthur wanted to prove something to Elektra. Who was boss. "All right," he was saying. "The company won't let us out of our contract, huh? Well, O.K., here you go. Check out Side 2. It's special. Just for you guys." But, in the long run, I believe that little plan of retribution (if that's what it was) may have hurt us more than it did them. The last I heard, Elektra seems to have survived.

Or: 'Revelation' was a powerful force, a painting on a jazz-rock canvas, accomplishing something that no one had ever even attempted before, a driving force, bringing the two worlds together on an explosively unique and innovative platform inspired by the works of the all time blues great granddaddy, John Lee Hooker. A rare opportunity for our fans who were limited to listening to us on record, to experience what it must have been like to hear us play live in a club like Bito Lido's. It cooked!

Take your pick. I thought it was a mistake to use a whole side of an album for it, myself. So, I don't know. Whatever the motivation, the way it was used on the record has its merits, I guess.

When the *Da Capo* sessions were finished, the company and our management group immediately arranged a series of local gigs in the Hollywood area, and short tours around the western United States, to promote the new album. But all the gigs were on the weekends. For instance, right after the album was released, we debuted it at the Whisky, on a Friday, Saturday and Sunday. Then, for a week or so, nothing. Then, we did a weekend at The Hullabaloo, and the next Friday and Saturday we flew up to do a weekend at The Fillmore. But Mondays through Thursdays, we were usually free. The group was finished rehearsing, for a while, so it gave Snoopy and me a lot of free time to hang out and have fun. He had this red Corvette that he loved to drive, so we went out clubbing and driving just about every night.

In 1965, there was a real popular L.A. disc-jockey named Dave Hull, the Hullabalooer. I mean, his mom and dad called him Dave Hull and then, later on, he made up "The Hullabalooer" part. Every time he came on the air to do his show, a pre-pubescent-sounding chick group sang his theme song, "Dave Hull, Dave Hull, The Hullabalooer, Dave Hull, Dave Hull, The Hullabalooer, He's a wild and crazy guy..." or something like that. One day, as a financial experiment, he bought the lease on the old Hollywood Moulin Rouge building, near the corner of Sunset and Vine. Back in the '50s, the old *Queen For A Day* TV show was taped there; in the '70s, it became The Aquarius Theater; in the mid-to-late-sixties, it was The Hullabaloo Club. It was cavernous, for being a "club". In fact, it held so many people that Dave Hull figured that, in order to exploit its potential to the fullest, he should book only top groups. So, right from the beginning, you could go to The Hullabaloo Club and see bands like The Yardbirds, featuring Jeff Beck on guitar, The Animals with Eric Burdon, Van Morrison and Them and, of course, LOVE. All the big groups of that period played there. Like I said, it was one of the places we introduced *Da Capo* to the public. But the funny thing was, incredible as it may seem (Dave Hull being a D.J. and all), the publicity for these concerts was apparently lacking, because the place was rarely more than about two-thirds full. And these performances were monumental. The members of these groups were at the top of their game, just hitting full stride, musically. Not strung out, or past their prime, tired of the grind and just hanging in there for the duration of their popularity. In fact, at the time they were booked into The Hullabaloo, most of these bands were as good as they would ever be. It was so powerful, but it was slipping past everybody.

Our concerts there were packed, as far as I could tell, but I think that was only because our management group was in town to see to it that the debut process for *Da Capo* went smoothly and, trusting nothing to chance, had not left all the advance publicity responsibilities up to

Dave Hull. But you could almost read it on the faces of these giants from England when they were on stage looking out into the darkness. "Where are the people?" they seemed to ask. It wasn't merely a visual letdown. After they would finish the last note of one of their mega-hits, no thunderous, rousing ovation from an appreciative throng. Scattered applause by distracted fans, that's all.

Several factors contributed to this unlikely scenario. Aside from Dave Hull's apparently limited publicity budget, he had decided to access his AM radio airwave pipeline to the teenagers of Los Angeles, and make The Hullabaloo Club alcohol free. The "no booze" policy equated to a huge savings in overhead and a customer base of a lot of underage girls. And young girls don't go to a nightclub to see great groups. They go to a club like The Hullabaloo to be seen, and to meet boys. And Snoopy and I started going there on, more or less, a regular basis to... well, sure, it was to see The Yardbirds, too.

Dave Hull was too busy to actually come down and run the club himself, so he hired a young upcoming local promoter named Brent Dizak to manage the place for him. Brent, in turn, hired a couple of dudes, Skip and Paul, to help him actually do it. Skip and Paul had participated in the building of Gazzarri's on Sunset, where The Sons of Adam had played. That's where I met them. And they had been friends with Arthur, and the other guys in the first LOVE group for a long time, as well. They had been in Hollywood since high school and so they knew where to get the hard drugs. In fact, I think Arthur had directed the words to 'My Flash On You' at Skip and Paul, among others. That's what Bryan told me. They worked the door at The Hullabaloo a lot, so when Snoopy and I would show up, we were always greeted warmly and ushered in like the big shots we thought we were. That's another reason we went there. It was a good ego trip. I mean, if we had gone over to Shelly's Mannehole we would have had to pay admission and nobody would have recognized us and there wouldn't have been any underage chicks inside. So, we didn't like to go to Shelly's Mannehole on any kind of regular basis. We liked to go to The Hullabaloo.

Skip and Paul would do just about anything for a laugh. During the week, bands that nobody ever heard of played The Hullabaloo. The Palace Guard was the house band. They wore uniforms like the ones worn by the palace guard at Buckingham Palace in England and played all the hits made famous by groups of that era, like the Stones and the Beatles and all those guys. Actually, most weeknights were amateur night, because there would always be a quick succession of bands like the Palace Guard, but without the uniforms, playing hits by the hitmakers, you know, clones of groups.

The Hullabaloo had an enormous revolving stage, maybe a hundred feet in diameter. As the curtain rose, whatever group was playing would launch into its first song of only a five-song set at the rear of the stage, facing away from the audience; and then, as the group rotated to a position near the front of the stage, the revolving part would grind to a halt. And there they would be. Very dramatic. All the garage bands played there for free just to take a ride on that revolving stage in front of an audience. I mean, Dave Hull didn't make it a "Battle of the Bands" type thing and give away a prize to the winner, or anything. He just let anybody who wanted to do it, come to his joint and provide free entertainment while he made money.

On any given night during the week, you could walk in and see a Jim Morrison lookalike in front of a bunch of "Doors", dressed in black leather, doing his own special rendition of 'Light My Fire' or watch a "Mick Jagger" doing the "Jagger walk" across the stage while belting out, "I cain't git no, satisfaction, no, no, no!" It was funny as hell, really. Much more entertaining than seeing the real guys, live. Which I did, a couple of times.

One night Snoopy and I even caught the act of a garage band LOVE clone, doing our songs off the *Da Capo* album. Their drummer even had my stage mannerisms down pat, which was a little disconcerting,

Love backstage at the Hullabaloo

and he took a drum solo that was pretty close to the one I had played. So, it was always fun to go there. You never knew what you were about to see.

But, Skip and Paul hated the garage band amateur night concept because, I think, it made them a little embarrassed to work there. One night Skip met me at the top of the steps, near the front door entrance. "Michael, can you give me a ride over to Hollywood Ranch Market? There's a band coming up in this next set I gotta anoint with a tomato."

I thought, "Oh, right. You're about to throw a tomato at a guy standing on stage, like in the movies?" But, even though I didn't really think he would do it, I figured I would call his bluff and gave him a lift to the Ranch Market. When we got there, Skip bought five or six great big fat juicy ones and then we headed right back over to The Hullabaloo, where, once inside, we went our separate ways. I found Snoopy over by the snack bar sipping a Coke. There was no noise coming from inside, so I realized we had gotten back while the bands were changing. I signalled him to follow me to where we could see the stage.

"What's happening, Michael? Where did you and Skip go?" He took another sip of his Coke.

I gestured toward the stage. "You'll see, maybe." Because, by this time, I was starting to think Skip might actually do it. When I last saw him walking away with the bag of tomatoes, he had a look of determination on his face. Like he had a job to do. An assignment.

The next group started to play and the curtain began to rise, the stage revolved into position and stopped. It was another Rolling Stones look and sound alike, which was always a lot of fun. Mick Jagger was so easy to ruin. The singer was even able to somehow puff his lips up, real big, like Mick's – maybe he was born that way, I don't know. They did a couple of the Stones' hits, and then, the lights were turned down low, to set the mood. Then, with only the spotlight on the Mick Jagger clone lighting the stage, they began to ease their way into 'Lady Jane'.

The Bummer 77

The singer grasped the microphone, closed his eyes and tilted his head back. You could hear a pin drop. It was a very dramatic moment. He began to sing the quietly emotional words, accompanied only by a single acoustic guitar and a tambourine.

Suddenly, just as he finished the phrase that ended 'Lady Jane', the first tomato came sailing down through the spotlight and landed with a resounding thud at his feet. It was real loud, too. More like a boom, than a thud. Everybody stopped what they were doing and looked up at the stage to see what had happened. And then, another tomato came down, and another, until they were all gone. You've seen old newsreel footage of night time Allied bombing raids on Germany during World War Two, the bombs descending, one after another, through the spotlights on their way to their targets. It was like that. Skip's accuracy was incredible, I guess because, as I later found out, he was behind the Hullabaloo's spotlight, using it as a kind of laser sight. But the singer never stopped singing, dodging from side to side to avoid getting hit, he simply leaned the mic stand where it had to go to stay next to his mouth. And, except for squinting up into the glare, trying in vain for a glimpse of the next projectile, he never outwardly acknowledged the tomatoes at all. I mean, he didn't complain or anything.

It's almost as if this tomato business had happened to him before. Like he was saying, "Hey, I worked long and hard to get centre stage at The Hullabaloo and this is a big moment for me. I'm sure as hell not going to let a few tomatoes spoil it." But I think Skip connected at least a couple of times, because I seem to remember during the last song, the kid had a big red stain on his pants.

Snoopy didn't really like Skip and Paul. He had once bought a lid of weed from Paul and it was short. That's what he claimed, anyhow. So, Snoopy never had much to say to either of them. He usually, just smiled and said, "What's happenin'?" when they met up. Never made conversation beyond what was necessary.

When the commotion died down and the members of the Stones clone were revolved to safety, Snoopy nudged me and, opening his extended hand, showed me two sugar cubes. "Look what a couple of girls gave me. Acid. You want to take one with me?"

I had taken acid only a couple of times before, when I was in The Sons of Adam. When you take LSD, you see a lot of unusual visual images, your level of emotional sensitivity increases dramatically, and listening to music becomes a powerful and exciting physical experience. And other stuff. Then, around 5 a.m. you find yourself laying in bed, feeling really drained, trying desperately to fall asleep, and watching the acoustic cottage cheese on your ceiling become alphabet soup. At least, that's the way it was for me. Maybe everybody's different.

When you're on it, even though you may be having a good time, you have to be careful. There's this feeling of vulnerability and isolation. Like, you're trying to hide it from the normal world. You, and the people you're high with, are strangers in a strange land. Aliens amongst the regulars. And the whole time, you have to hold your mug, no matter what happens, because remember, whatever it is that's blowing your mind probably isn't even really happening at all. So don't make yourself look like a fool. Don't over-react to outside stimuli. Like, if you're kicking back, listening to music, and everything's real peaceful, and suddenly you feel something, and you open your eyes and there's a cockroach on your leg, don't reach down and brush it off or yell or anything. You have to wait until somebody looks over and says, "Hey, there's a cockroach on your leg." Then you can brush it off. But cool.

My first time, I took it with Jac, The Sons of Adam's rhythm guitarist, and a few other dudes at the house we shared. There were four or five of us in the group, and we decided right away to just stay right there at the house and be safe and enjoy the high. Listen to music, or whatever. But, no matter what, we wouldn't go out and drive around, especially if it got late, because that's how you can get busted, a bunch of long hairs all piled into one car, driving along Sunset

Boulevard in the wee hours of the morning, is begging for it. The man is on the alert for that sort of thing. That's how they train those folks over at the police academy. So, we wouldn't do that. Definitely.

But as time passed, during this first acid experience with The Sons of Adam, I was beginning to wonder what all the hubbub was about. I mean, it had been about forty-five minutes since Jac and I had eaten our cubes and, nothing. The topic of conversation had begun to revolve around the subject of us perhaps having been ripped off, when I started to notice a tightening in my jaw. Jac had already said, "I think I feel something." But we had all shrugged it off.

"You don't feel anything but the weed, man," we told him. "This stuff is nothing but sugar." But then, the tightening – and the wavy lines and the music. Them's 'Mystic Eyes' started to pulsate right through my body and suddenly I had that feeling you get when you're perched right at the top of that first big drop on a roller coaster. Then the descent. Everybody started saying "Wow!" at about the same time. A few minutes later, we were all into it and having a lot of fun.

The thing is, an acid trip can be like a deep, dark scuba dive in the ocean…exhilarating and beautiful, but at the same time a little scary; and it seems like every time I took LSD, somebody with me decided it was a little too scary, and he didn't want to be there. But, unlike a dive in the ocean, there's no pulling your way back up the anchor line to safety. You're there for the duration, man, unless you want to go to the hospital.

So, a couple of hours into this first trip with The Sons of Adam, we were all having a pretty good time, when Jac reached over and, turning down the stereo, nodded over to one of the guys, standing in the corner, with his head down, like he was being punished. Then we heard him quietly sobbing, and all of us, realizing things weren't going well for him, went over to check it out and see what could be done.

"I want a glass of milk!" he finally cried out loud, and he started blubbering and shaking, and a few of the guys put their arms around him and tried to settle him down a little, but it didn't work. He still wanted a glass of milk, bad. We didn't have any milk. All we had was Pepsi. So, we all had to go get some milk, because an acid trip is like a journey. If you take acid with four other guys, then you all have to stay together. One guy's problem is everybody's problem. One person couldn't go get the milk. We all had to go get the milk. If only one of us went, some unspecified, indefinable bad thing would happen to us, each and every one.

And on this night, in the wee, small hours of the morning, we did exactly what we swore we wouldn't. The group piled into a beat-up Volkswagen Beetle bustmobile and headed off in the direction of The Sunfax Market, where the milk was. And toodling down Sunset, the only car on the road, we were most predictably, and almost immediately, spotted by the man and pulled over. I mean, it was like waving a red flag. He hauled us out of the car and checked our identification and shined his flashlight in

The Bummer 79

our eyes, and I figured, "Well, we're all going to jail on acid," because we looked real messed up... high on drugs, no doubt about it. But after a while, for some inexplicable reason, he handed us all back our I.D.'s and paused and looked at us real hard, like he was thinking it over, and then he finally said, "All right, get out of here." So, we got back in the car and drove on down to The Sunfax and got the baby his milk, and when we got back to the house we poured him a big glass and he drank it right down. Didn't help at all.

The rest of the trip turned into a baby-sitting adventure, with each of us taking turns trying to calm down the dude that was freaking out. Because every time we started to groove to some music or be happy for any reason, he would start up with the crying real loud, like, "I want us all to be on the same trip. I want all you guys to be on my bummer with me." Going to get him the milk had been a complete waste of time. I felt like dumping the rest of it over his head. The fun part was the first couple of hours, I guess.

The second trip was a lot like the first, only the dude we had to worry about that time kind of froze, leaning against the kitchen counter in a position reminiscent of Rodin's The Thinker but standing up, instead of sitting on a rock. We didn't know anything was wrong at first, until somebody noticed he hadn't moved for a long time and was standing in a puddle of pee. So, the rest of that trip, we had to look after him and be concerned because we were afraid he might fall over and damage himself. He was sort of in a coma. All night long.

But that was then and this was now. Standing there in the middle of the Hullabaloo Club, I figured Snoopy was my new best buddy. If he wanted me to take the acid with him, I would. "Hey, maybe this time will be different," I told myself. There were only two of us, after all. That simplified things quite a bit. I popped one of the cubes in my mouth and Snoopy did the same.

"Michael, what did you think of my aim, pretty good, huh?" Skip was at my elbow, wearing a big grin. "I hate that little twerp. Some of the little girls that come in here think he's as good as Mick Jagger. Can you believe it?" I detected a hint of jealousy in his voice. "I nailed him a couple of times, at least. Did you see it?"

"Yeah, you had him dancing, all right, but who's gonna clean up all that tomato puree?"

I noticed Snoopy had moved off and was talking to some people in another group, so I hung out with Skip and Paul for a while and forgot about the acid. Everybody knew half of it you got on the street was no good anyway. A few more bands were revolved on and off the stage and then, in the middle of a Kinks clone set, I started to feel the familiar tightening in my jaw, and I remembered. I walked back to the front door where Skip and Paul were taking tickets. "Seen Snoopy?" I asked.

Paul looked up and nodded out to the parking lot, where quite a few hippies were standing around, generally shootin' the shit and making drug deals. "I think I saw him out there someplace, a minute ago," he said.

Suddenly, I caught a glimpse of the yellow shirt I remembered Snoopy had worn that night. He was smack in the middle of the lot, standing in a small oasis of date palms, his back to most of the crowd, head slumped to his chest, shoulders rounded, and with his hands clasped low in front of his body like a man in prayer. Which is exactly what I thought he was doing. I got over to him as quickly as I could. "Snoop, what's up, man? Are you O.K.?"

"Michael, they're going to kill me." Without turning around, he jerked his head in the general direction of a place somewhere over his shoulder. He was obviously scared to death. No wonder. A large group of tough-looking dudes on motorcycles seemed to be staring at Snoopy, giving him the bad eye.

"Oh, yeah, Snoop, I see 'em. Don't worry, we'll be O.K." But I wasn't a hundred percent certain.

Snoopy looked up at me, and then, impatiently, "No, man, not them. Them!" He nodded

Love onstage at the Hullabaloo

furtively over to where Skip and Paul stood at the front door of the club, innocently taking tickets.

"Skip and Paul? They're not gonna hurt you, Snoop. They're our friends." He shook his head. Try as I might to reassure him, I realized in a moment what was happening. The old acid bummer, which can get started at the drop of a hat and feed off just about anything, was feeding off that little disagreement Snoopy had with Paul over the short lid. There's an amplification component included in every dose of acid. It can increase the vibrancy of colour and the level appreciation of music and art, or it can do what it was doing to Snoopy, turn something small into something big, and make a bad thing worse. And Snoopy was already the sensitive type, to begin with.

"Snoop," I'll try again, I thought, "it's the acid. That's what's doing this. Remember? We took the acid. Everything's all right. Don't worry."

Suddenly, he smiled a smile of relief. "Oh, the acid. I forgot." He was trying to climb up the anchor chain, to the boat.

I reached out to give him a hand up. "Hey, man, let's go back inside the club and listen to music, O.K.? Let's go have fun."

A wave of scepticism crossed his face, and he turned to look at Skip and Paul, standing in the doorway. Then scepticism turned to horror and his eyes grew big. "No, I really don't want to go back in there." The acid had sucked him back down to where the anchor met the ocean floor. I knew we had to leave.

I took him by the arm and led him gently to his car. "Come on, Snoop. Give me your keys,

I'll drive us home." He handed me the keys to his new Corvette and climbed in the passenger seat. I got in and fired it up. As we pulled out of the parking lot I looked back at Skip and Paul and sort of shrugged and waved good-bye. Snoopy watched me suspiciously out of the corner of his eye. I turned onto Sunset, then headed up Vine to Franklin. I took a half-smoked joint from the ashtray, lit it and passed it to him. East on Franklin and then left on Beechwood. No cops. No problems.

On the way up Durand, Snoopy began to relax a little. Passing the joint back to me, he smiled, "Yeah, Michael, I don't know what was wrong with me back there, man. Too high, I guess. I really thought they were going to kill me." He laughed long and hard and, for a second, I figured everything was going to be O.K. But then he stopped laughing. Glancing over, I saw the look again. Desperation. Horror. It was sucking him back down. "But they were going to kill me, you know. If we had stayed there they would have."

It was coming in waves. The acid would grab him then let him go. It would drag him under then let him up for a quick breath of air. I tried one more time. "Remember, the acid, Snoop. It's not real." But it was too late. It had him for good this time.

I pulled into the driveway of our house and, as we got out of the car and I unlocked the big double front doors, he kept asking, "Aren't you on this trip with me, Michael? We're on it together, right?"

I finally gave up, "Yeah, Snoop, I'm on this trip with you. Don't worry. I won't let 'em kill you." We went in and sat down on the couch and tried to relax. I reached over to where we kept the dope container on the coffee table and started to roll a joint. A song by Odetta was playing softly on the easy listening FM station we always tuned to. I remember her voice was so soothing and beautiful and high. It was real peaceful. "This'll work," I thought. But in spite of the apparent mood of tranquillity, I could sense that all was not yet well with Snoopy. For one thing, he hadn't said a word for a while, and he was looking all around at the interior of our living room like he didn't recognize the place. Occasionally, he would lift his eyebrows and shake his head from side to side, and his lips would move, ever so slightly, like he was engaged in his own private conversation with himself. If I tried to talk to him, he would only smile a little and nod, as if in agreement, but he wasn't really listening. The acid monster had him by the ying-yang.

Without warning, he set the joint down in the ashtray, stood up and walked over to the top of the staircase. He took a couple of steps down and then, looking over at me, eyes big as saucers, he hopped back up the stairs, like he had burned his feet. He stayed for a minute in the foyer, as if glued to the floor, twisting and turning, gazing longingly down the stairs, then at the front doors. He agonized. He was torn. He had to get out. But which way? Down the stairs, to the safety of his bedroom, or through the doors to the freedom of the outside? Finally, he broke loose from the psychological grip of the linoleum and burst violently through the front doors, running off down the street and disappearing into the darkness.

I walked over and closed the front doors. I was alone. Odetta's voice began to waver. The pitch began to go low, then high, like if you rest your finger gently on the edge of an LP, and then release it as the record goes round and round on the turntable. The situation was beginning to get to me. I mean, I was on acid, too.

As I sat on the couch, I lit the roach and tried to laugh it off. "Hey, what is this? Am I ever gonna have a trip where somebody isn't crying because he can't have a glass of milk, or going into a standing coma, or freaking out and thinking people are about to kill him? It's not supposed to be this way every time, is it? Or is it? Maybe if I do this often enough, someday I'll take it with some friends and we'll all have a good time and, at the end, everybody will still be happy." Someday – but not today. I was becoming a little depressed, sitting there all alone in the middle of the night. Wide-awake. Odetta's voice continued its transformation into a growling, satanic menace.

"I don't have to listen to this," I thought. As I stood up to turn the stereo off I caught a quick glimpse of a figure, lurking outside on the deck. He stared back at me. Red eyes, hairy body, fangs: The Wolfman! My adrenaline surged. I reached over to lock the sliding glass door. At the exact same moment, the creature extended his hand toward the door as well. I suddenly realized it might be necessary to wrestle the sliding door from his grasp, so I took a step closer to get better leverage. He took a step. Wait a minute! I was watching my own reflection in the door. The Wolfman was me! "Here we go," I thought. "I better get a grip on myself, or before I know it, Snoopy and I will be racing each other down the street."

The phone rang and, grateful for the opportunity to talk to another human being, I picked it up. A friendly female voice asked, "Michael? Is everything all right?" It was Ronnie Haran, LOVE's manager. What an angel. Did she call out of the blue or was she telepathic?

"No, Ronnie, everything is not all right."

"You want me to come over?" she asked, concerned.

Relief coursed through my body. "Yeah, come over."

"I'll be right there." We hung up. Ronnie lived in Malibu, maybe half an hour from our house. It was around 3 a.m., so I knew she couldn't get there before 3:30. Still, it was comforting to know that she was on the way. Because, despite of being physically petite (and beautiful and feminine), mentally and psychologically, Ronnie was strong as a bull. She would know what to do. She would take control and make things all better. Ronnie to the rescue. Oh, boy.

Almost as soon as my phone hit the cradle, it rang again. "Michael?"

"Snoop, where are you? What are you doing?"

"Hey, Michael, can you come get me? I'm in a phone booth across the street from The Hullabaloo."

"How'd you get all the way down there?"

"I ran. Come get me."

I climbed in my Porsche and wound my way down Durand, onto Beechwood, through the deserted streets of East Hollywood, down Franklin, left on Vine to Sunset, then over to The Hullabaloo. A good four or five miles at least. And Snoopy ran it. I activated my windshield wipers and rolled my window down. A light rain was falling, and the traffic lights and lights from the closed business reflected off the wet asphalt. The air smelled cool and clean and fresh.

I spotted him standing near the phone booth, like he said, so I pulled a U-turn and slowed to a stop by the curb. I stole a glance at the Hullabaloo parking lot, strange and empty of the humanity that had filled it only a few hours before. He opened the door and got in and we slapped each other five and laughed, and headed off in the direction of home. "Let's drive around for a little while and unwind before we go to the house, O.K.?" he asked. So we drove through the streets of Hollywood and just listened to the radio and talked. "I'm not on the bummer, anymore, honest. I don't know why that happens, but it usually does. I guess I just can't take acid. I hope I didn't ruin your trip."

Actually, except for the drained feeling you have near the end, the acid had pretty much worn off, and emotionally, things were getting back to normal. "Don't worry about it, Snoop," I reassured him, "but what do you mean, 'It usually does?'"

As we turned onto Durand, he gazed out the car window. "I mean, I've never had a good trip. I always go on a bummer. Every time."

"Well, then, why do you take it?"

He shook his head. "Because there's no reason I shouldn't be able to. Everybody else does. Besides, I always think the next time will be my first good one."

"What happened tonight," I asked him, "I mean, after we got home from the Hullabaloo?"

"I was feeling O.K. for a while, but after I took a couple of hits of weed I saw the walls began to breathe. It felt like they were breathing all the air out of the room. I couldn't catch my breath, so I decided to go downstairs to my bedroom and get some rest, but the red carpet turned into a whirlpool of blood, and when I stepped on it, I burned my feet. So, I thought I would go outside and maybe go for a walk, but the doors talked to me and said, 'Oh, no, you're not coming out this way.' I looked over at you and you looked..."

"What did I do? What did I look like?" I asked him.

Snoopy glanced down and shook his head. "I don't want to talk about that part any more."

As I rounded the last corner and approached our house, I noticed a car in our driveway. Ronnie. I had forgotten all about Ronnie.

I pulled in next to where she was parked and got out. "Hi, Ronnie. Thanks for coming over. I guess everything's O.K., now," I said. She didn't get upset, when I told her that she had essentially wasted her time coming all the way out from the beach, it was just the effects of an acid bummer, and that I hadn't even been polite enough to give her a call back right away to save her the trip. I felt guilty as hell. She just told me she was happy everything was O.K., and she started her car and went home, back to Malibu. A half-hour drive at four in the morning. Talk about a good sport. Looking back, I still can't figure out what a person as calm and cool as Ronnie was doing in the music business in the first place.

But, personally, I always felt Snoopy's problem taking acid was rooted in his sensitive nature, and for having been yelled at for so long by the other guys in the group because they thought he was such a lousy drummer. Which he wasn't. Even after I joined the band and the pressure was off, and he could just kick back and play keyboards like he was trained to do, it was too late. The constant ridicule had done irreparable damage to his self-image.

The very next weekend, The Everly Brothers were scheduled to appear at The Hullabaloo and LOVE didn't have a gig, so Snoopy and I made definite plans to go see them. We arrived in time for the first set, around a quarter to ten, and Skip met us at the front door. "Hurry up, they'll be starting in about fifteen minutes," he waved us in and pointed to the far door. "We saved you guys a good spot in the orchestra section. Paul'll show you where." Then he went back to taking tickets.

But when we got inside, it was real hot, what with the hundreds of sweating bodies all over the place and the poor ventilation, so I told Paul, "Hold on a second, man, Snoopy and I are going to get something to drink." We started walking in the direction of the snack bar. Paul caught up with us halfway: "Michael, don't drink the Coke, man. Skip and I were mixing up the Coke syrup down in the basement, and Skip told me he needed to take a piss, so I said, 'Why don't you just piss in the Coke?' – you know? just kidding – and he said, 'Maybe I will.' I told him he didn't have the guts. Before I could stop him, he took a leak in the Coke syrup. So, don't drink the Coke. Skip pissed in it. Everything else is O.K." Then he walked away.

I thought, "Thanks a lot for the info, man." I mean, I wasn't going to order a Coke anyway.

"Orange Crush, please," I told the girl behind the counter. Snoopy ordered an Orange Crush, too. I wondered if they mixed the Orange Crush next to the Coke, but it was too late to worry too hard about it, I guess.

We walked in just as the P.A. boomed, "Ladies and gentlemen, The Everly Brothers." The usual two-thirds full house welcomed them enthusiastically, the curtain rose and the stage revolved The Everlys and their band into position. Working off one microphone, they did all their hits – 'Bird Dog', 'Wake Up Little Susie', 'Devoted To You' – a full hour, nothing but great hits, and each one sounded just like a digitally remixed version of the original recording, but live. And no mistakes. Every instrument was perfectly in tune and their group was totally in balance. No one instrument was louder or softer than it was supposed to be. And the Everlys sang like that's what they were born to do. Which they were.

I know, technically The Everly Brothers started out as a "country" act, and maybe they never quite lost that twang, but they were one of the best things to happen to rock'n'roll. Period. And their level of professionalism was unsurpassed. They moved from song to song like clockwork, a finely tuned, two-stroke engine, pausing from time to time long enough only to take an occasional sip of Coke.

Like I said, LOVE played The Hullabaloo too, right after we debuted *Da Capo* at The Whisky. The date was marred by an unusual situation: just before the first set we were in the dressing room, going over the sequence of songs we would play and tuning guitars, when an Elektra rep paid us a visit.

"Hey, guys, the album came out great," he gushed. "You looking forward to the tour?" He was real upbeat. "You know, I don't think I mentioned this before, but we've arranged for a film crew to be here tonight to get some footage. We'd like to use it to promote the group and the new sound. We feel it'll help get us exposure and help sell the album in places where you haven't gotten any airplay yet." A chill descended.

Arthur, who had been sitting on a stool in the corner, quietly playing his harmonica, suddenly stopped and looked up. "Film crew?"

"Yeah, But it'll just be during the first set. Ignore 'em. Pretend they're not there. They'll be gone before you know it." He reached for the doorknob, "See you after the show." And he left.

In a little while, the stage manager rapped on the door and yelled, "Ten minutes." We gathered up everything we needed to carry and headed toward the back stage entrance. The amps and drums were already in place, so everybody just plugged in and got ready.

The stage began to revolve and the curtain started to rise. "Ladies and gentleman, LOVE!" Arthur counted it off, "One, two, three, four" and we launched into '7 and 7 Is':

"Baroom. Baroom, baroom, baroom..." Heavy piece of music. A symphonic tornado with words. It got everybody's juices flowing, that's why we usually started with it. Johnny played such a powerful blues progression at the end. A few more songs went by and then, in the middle of 'Revelation', I noticed one of the film crew guys had moved to the centre aisle, right in the middle, where he couldn't be ignored, in front of Arthur. Arthur was looking at him, giving him the bad eye, like he was saying, "Move, I don't want you there, man. You're bothering me." But the guy didn't get it, and he just kept filming away. So, in a minute, Arthur's patience evaporated and he just seemed to decide, "O.K., that's it," and he kind of nonchalantly strolled slowly over, bent down and then grabbed his camera away from him, momentarily holding it aloft over his head, like a prize.

The film crew guy was outraged. His complexion was flushed and he began hollering and motioning for Arthur to give him his camera back, but Arthur just took it over to the back of the stage and shoved it under some of the equipment bags that were stored where the audience couldn't see them. The rest of us kept playing as if nothing had happened. After the set was over, somebody came backstage and retrieved the camera. I never heard any more about the publicity film, though. I think the other guys in the crew stopped filming and packed up and left when they saw what happened to their buddy's camera.

I always felt that the hair problem had something to do with that. Once every couple of weeks, Arthur would disappear for a few hours and take a run over to the west side of L.A. to a beauty shop where they performed miracles with hair. He would sit in a chair and the beautician would put the curlers in and then squirt the straightening solution on the rolled-up locks. When they were finished preparing the treatment, he would sit under the hair dryer for about twenty minutes, then they would be all done and his hair would look real nifty.

But, after we'd recorded *Da Capo* and just before we embarked on our shamefully limited promotional tour, Arthur decided he had had just about enough running back and forth to the west side. It was kind of expensive. He figured, "Shit, anybody can put straightening solution and curlers in hair," so he went and bought the stuff at a local beauty supply shop in Hollywood and set about doing the thing himself. He didn't have a professional hair dryer so he decided to put some music on his stereo, smoke a little hash, stretch out on the couch for a while, relax and let his hair dry by itself. And he fell asleep... for a couple of hours.

So, he wakes up with a start, runs into the bathroom and very gently begins removing the curlers. Of course, the hair comes out with them, unevenly and in chunks, because the straightening solution is only supposed to stay in for twenty minutes. Not two hours.

A few nights later we debuted the album at The Whisky and, soon after that, at The Hullabaloo. Arthur wore a navy watch cap: it was black, like hair, and had a fuzzy consistency like hair and didn't look too bad, actually. But I think Arthur might have been a little self-conscious because he had the altercation with the camera dude. He was too pissed off for no reason otherwise.

The morning after that show, Johnny woke up so sick with the flu, we knew he wouldn't be able to play our second night at The Hullabaloo. Arthur called a meeting and asked, "What do you want to do? We can either not play at all or maybe find somebody who knows our songs to fill in. Michael, what about Randy? You think he might be willing to do it?"

After the meeting, I gave Randy a call and he said, "Sure." So, we got together an hour or so before the gig to go over the arrangements.

The first set went smoothly until we got to something that Randy took a solo on. I don't remember what, probably the John Lee Hooker thing, I guess. In the middle of the solo, Randy started gettin' down: he dropped to his knees, closed his eyes and started wailing. The crowd liked it, and Bryan thought it was cool and nodded his head – Kenny, too: they began playing riffs that complimented what Randy was playing. It was a great solo. Early heavy-metal soul. Randy was knockin' 'em dead.

Meanwhile, Arthur was whacking on his tambourine with his back to the action. When he turned around and saw what was going on, he did a real exaggerated double-take. Then he looked out at the audience and, laughing, walked over and took Bryan's guitar away from him and started picking the small strings, way up high on the fretboard. Not taking a solo, though. Just making noise. Then, he dropped down on his knees, like Randy had done, and, a second later, grinning, Arthur rolled over on his back.

Arthur had a reputation for almost super-human coolness. He could do no wrong. Everyone, fans and fellow bandmembers alike, recognized his extraordinary talent. He was different. An aura of calm, quiet power surrounded him. Bigger than life, he was special and creative and, somehow, he seemed better than other "regular" human beings. More capable. Everyone looked up to him and respected him, and feared him. What I'm saying is, he projected a hell of an image. He didn't have to put anybody down.

The audience had to have been a little confused and disappointed. "What's he doing?" They must have been asking themselves. And, of course, it made the whole group look bad. I mean, here my old bandmate had come in to help us out, but when he started having a little too much fun, and sounding a little too good, he had to be put in his place in front of seven or eight hundred people, or whatever the place held. Bryan, Kenny and I just kept playing the song. "All part of the act, folks."

When all this was happening, Randy just looked the other way and pretended not to notice, but after the set, backstage, he asked me, "Hey, what was Arthur's problem? Was he pissed off at me about something?"

"I don't know, man," I shrugged. I guess maybe he thought you shouldn't have kneeled down. Whatever, don't worry about it."

Randy shook his head and walked away. "I won't."

Chapter Ten

Hanging With Snoop

AFTER THE second night of the Hullabaloo gig, Snoopy and I were driving up Beechwood, on the way home. When I turned left on Durand, the headlights of the car in back of us did too. I noticed it right away because that almost never happened. Not many people lived up there, really. When we rounded the first hairpin turn, the other car got momentarily hung up, and had to see-saw back and forth a couple of times to continue; second hairpin, same thing. "Hey, Snoop, better put the joint away," I told him. "Somebody's following us."

He placed the ember end of the joint against his tongue to extinguish it, then he tucked what remained in his mouth, to be ready, if he had to swallow it. "Can you see if it's a cop?"

I shook my head. "Naw, all I can see is headlights. It looks like a sedan, though. Could be a narc."

We approached the house and pulled into the driveway. As I turned off the ignition, the sedan slowed to a stop in back of my car, effectively blocking me in. "Uh, oh," I thought. But as we got out, I heard giggles. I looked over to see if I could catch a glimpse of the occupants. It was a car full of girls, maybe fifteen or sixteen years old. Laughing nervously, the driver turned off the engine and headlights and they got out and walked over to where Snoopy and I stood by my car.

"Hi," she said. "We followed you guys all the way from the Hullabaloo. Aren't you Michael and Snoopy?" They giggled some more.

"Yeah," I answered. "I'm Michael and that's Snoopy. Who are you?" More giggles. Frankly, I was so happy they weren't the Man, I was ready to like them, whoever they were. But they all introduced themselves and told us they had our records and went to all our concerts. They were our fans.

One of them turned to Snoop. "Why do they call you Snoopy? Snoopy's a cute name." Giggles. She had a crush on Snoop.

He put his arm around her shoulder. "I'll tell you why, because I want to know what's going on all the time. I want the answers. I'm interested. I want to know everything. Especially about girls. The more I know about girls, the better I like it. Someday I'm gonna get a job as a private detective and all I'm gonna investigate is girls. It'll be my specialty, my life's work." They giggled.

"Do your moms and dads know where you are, right now?" I asked. "You could get me and Snoop in big trouble, hanging around here this time of night. Unless, of course, you all are twenty-one. If you're twenty-one, then it's cool." Giggles.

"No," the driver admitted, reluctantly, "we're not twenty-one. We'll leave, but can we come back sometime, like next Saturday? We'll clean your house for you and do your laundry, and your dishes, O.K.?"

"Yeah," I told them, "but only in the daytime. Don't come over at night any more." I mean, we had to be a little bit careful here. They don't call 'em "jailbait" for nothing.

"We'll be back on Saturday," they promised, piling back into their car. Then, backing over the curb and almost taking out our mailbox, they turned around and headed back down Durand. "Bye!" they yelled through the window, waving as they left. They were happy girls.

I looked at Snoop. "They were really young, man." Then, as we unlocked the front door and went inside, I asked him, "By the way, how did you really get the name?"

"Well, when I was a baby, I used to crawl around and get into things, you know, my mom's purse, kitchen cabinets, wastebaskets, anything I could reach. So my mom started calling me 'Snoopy,' and it stuck."

"Oh," and I let it drop. Still, it left unanswered exactly how it came about. The emotional reference point, I mean. Was it, a loving "pet name"? Or was it more, "Hey! If I catch you snooping around in my purse one more time, I'm gonna permanently change your name to 'Snoopy'. Would you like that?"

His real name was Alban. And he did have good acid trips, sometimes. One day I caught him climbing in over his terrace railing to get to his bedroom, and he was with his regular girlfriend, Linda. They had taken acid a few hours earlier and they were laughing and dirty and they were covered with great big ticks from rolling around in the canyon sagebrush, and they didn't even care. The bottom line is, when Snoopy took acid, I think it was real important for him to be in a controlled mental environment. Like hanging around home with somebody that was crazy about him. Which Linda was.

The morning after the Hullabaloo bummer, I asked him, "Snoop, when you have a bad trip, what do you think is going to happen? What exactly are you scared of?"

He looked off in the distance. "It's not 'scared of', it's 'terrified of'. It's insanity and death, all rolled up into one gigantic fear ball, then multiplied a thousand times. And the danger is imminent. When I come down, I always think, 'That was stupid,' but like the dread you wake up with in the middle of the night, it's beyond reason, and like a nightmare, it seems so real." Then he told me, "Last week I took some acid with Arthur and Kenny, and they went in the other room for something. When they did, when I couldn't see them anymore, I thought Arthur had killed Kenny with a knife. So, I snuck out the front door and ran down Laurel Canyon for help, because I knew Arthur would be coming after me, next."

I mean, sometimes I thought I saw cockroaches or spiders that weren't really there, or maybe sensed slight modifications of audio-reality, like the night I misheard Odetta singing in a scary voice, but that was about the limit of my hallucinations. Snoopy's bummers bordered on the unique. The monumental. The outrageous. All about death and insanity and unspecified horror, and then magnified to unimaginable proportions, they were of championship status. Nobody had bummers as bad as his. Snoop was the bummer king.

The following Saturday at 11 a.m. sharp, the doorbell rang. I went upstairs to answer it.

"Hi, Michael. We've come to clean your house." It was the five underage girls that had followed us home from the Hullabaloo.

But, right away I asked 'em, "Hey, do your parents know you're up here?" Because I wasn't going to let them stay, otherwise.

"Oh, yeah, they know. It's O.K. Honest."

I opened the door wide. "Come on in." They had a bunch of cleaning junk with them, like rags and Windex, and they got right to work dusting and washing dishes and cleaning. So, Snoop and I rolled a couple of joints and took some chairs out on the terrace and smoked and talked for a while and pretty much did our own thing. We didn't hang out with them at all. In a few minutes, one of the girls opened the sliding glass door, "Where's your laundry detergent?" she asked. Later, I heard the washing machine going downstairs.

"These girls mean business," I told Snoop.

After they left, Snoopy and I went down to the bedrooms and all our clean clothes were folded and stacked, and the windows and bathrooms were clean. They had done a great job. It got to be a regular thing. Every Saturday we weren't on the road, they came over and cleaned and hung out and listened to the stereo, and then they would go home. That was their entertainment, I guess, so Snoopy and I began to leave admission passes for them at places we played in the L.A. area to pay them for the work. Places that didn't serve alcohol, anyway.

After a few months of the free maid service, Snoopy and I were on our way home one day, stuck behind a slow moving Lincoln Continental, wondering, "What is this person doing on Durand?" Predictably, she was getting hung up for about thirty seconds every time she tried to navigate a hairpin. Back and forth, back and forth. "Where is she going?" I asked Snoop impatiently.

Bryan's shot of me arriving for practice in the parking lot of The Whisky after the release of *Da Capo*

Suddenly, she pulled over and stopped right in front of our house. As we got out of my car, she got out of hers and approached us. The woman was in her late thirties, hair neatly coifed, elegant, beautiful, nice jewellery... She was – how shall I say? – "well-to-do" looking. Rich.

She reached out to shake hands and smiled, "Are you Michael and Snoopy?"

"Yes," we answered, taking turns shaking her hand.

"I feel like I know you two, already. My daughter has your pictures and your albums, and even your telephone number and address, pasted all over the walls in her room. That's how I knew where to find you."

She stopped smiling. "Jody didn't come home last night, and she hasn't called home today, but her dad and I aren't really worried, yet. You know kids. She probably spent the night at one of her friend's house and simply neglected to tell us. We know she's O.K. But, nevertheless, it passed through my mind that she's been spending a lot of time up here at your house, and she and her friends are completely infatuated with your rock group. I can't help but wonder... she's not here, is she?"

"No, Ma'am, certainly not, absolutely..." On and on for about a minute.

"Because, if I thought for one moment she was," the lady interrupted, "I would have the police back here in a heartbeat, you know? You guys wouldn't even have time to hide your dope. I'll tell you something else, my husband is an attorney. We have friends who work in the District Attorney's office. If you know what's good for you, you'll be mighty careful in the future about letting little fourteen and fifteen-year-old girls use your house as a hangout." Then, she turned and walked back to her car, got in and drove away. Of course, as she was leaving, Snoop and I were following her and reassuring her, in no uncertain terms, that she had nothing to worry about from us, and that, although her daughter's visits to our house with her friends were innocent in nature, she wouldn't be allowed back under any circumstances. Things like that. Because we didn't want her to go get the man. But, she wasn't really interested in what we had to say. She had delivered the message most effectively. That's all.

From then on, Snoopy and I did our own cleaning and laundry and stuff.

The almost-bad scene became a non-issue several weeks later, when the group left town to begin a promotional tour across the western U.S. First stop, Dallas, Texas. Elektra's distribution was good in this area, so the first album and '7 and 7 Is' had been big hits. It was all set up for the group to arrive at Love Field (the airport), be greeted by the Mayor and a few other local dignitaries, and be presented with the key to the city. Photographers with the *Dallas Morning News* would be there to get some shots for the paper. A rock station had worked hard to promote the arrival and the concert, so a few thousand fans would be waiting to greet us when we landed, as well. It was a real big deal. Red-carpet treatment.

So, at the appointed hour, our plane landed. A high school marching band on the tarmac played its rendition of 'My Little Red Book' and the crowd started cheering. The cabin door swung open and all the passengers began to disembark. Everybody but us, that is: we weren't on the plane. We had missed the flight. I mean, we showed up a couple of hours later but naturally, by then, the marching band had left and most of the fans had gone home. I don't think the guy who gave us the key to the city was even the Mayor. At least, he didn't look like a Mayor. He looked more like an aide. But the photographer got a shot of it anyway.

We made the plane on time for our next stop on the tour, though, Las Vegas' Teenbeat Club. A large recreation centre-type place, probably held a couple of thousand people, tops. A driver met us at the airport and led us out to where the limo was parked near luggage claim.

"Welcome to Vegas, fellas. Anything you need, let me know. I'll be taking you to where you're staying, and then later, around eight, I'll be back to pick you up and take you over

Publicity photo for the 'My Little Red Book' single

to the club." He grabbed our bags and began loading them into the trunk, while a locally hired equipment dude put our instruments into his van. It had been arranged for them to be taken right over to the Teenbeat Club where our equipment manager, Neil, was waiting to set everything up.

Arthur opened the passenger side door wide and held it for Johnny. "Here you go, Echols. You can sit shotgun, if you want." But Johnny didn't budge from his place on the sidewalk several feet away. He eyed Arthur suspiciously. He had fallen for this too many times. We all had. It was an old trick and one of Arthur's favourites. He would offer you shotgun, then, when you sat down, Arthur would sit down on the edge of the passenger seat and scoot in and close the door after him, crowding you over next to the driver. And there you'd be with the shittiest seat in the limo and he would have shotgun as usual. This time, Johnny had a plan.

"Yeah, thanks Arthur. Don't mind if I do." Johnny strode purposefully over to the open door, climbed in and, sitting right on the edge and not giving an inch, grabbed the door handle away from Arthur. "Let go of that door, motherfucker," he yelled, trying mightily to pull it away from Arthur, but Arthur wouldn't let go. So, they wrestled with each other for a few seconds and, finally, Arthur sort of got in and sat down on Johnny's lap and closed the door.

"Hey, man!" Johnny yelled, immediately sliding out from under Arthur's butt and over next to the limo driver, where he belonged. The limo pulled away from the curb and began to manoeuvre its way through traffic. Arthur had won again. As usual.

The driver took us to the Sands Motel. Not "The Sands Hotel and Casino", just the Sands Motel. Different place, altogether. After we checked in and got something to eat, we hailed a cab and paid a visit to The Teenbeat Club. We wanted to make sure the instruments had gotten there safely and do a sound check. It was cavernous and the echo was bad, because there were no people there to absorb the notes, but it made us feel better to go there and look things over, anyway. Then, we went back to the motel to relax for a while before the gig.

In Vegas, you don't have to go to a casino to gamble. Slot machines are everywhere. Supermarkets, gas stations, airport, you name it. The fact is, Nevada wants your money. The ones at the airport get me. In theory, you can fly into Vegas, sit down at a slot machine near the boarding area, lose all the money you brought with you and turn around and fly home broke. Immediately. Without even leaving the airport. Or you could arrive in town, have a great time, win a lot of money, and then, just before you board the plane for the flight home, you could sit down at a slot machine for one last pull and... well, you can guess the rest. That's how they have it figured. They get you coming and going.

But, according to state law, each group of machines have to be monitored by an employee of the business where they're located, because if a state gambling official observes a minor gambling, the business can be fined or even lose it's gambling licence permanently. And in Nevada, that's the kiss of death.

When we got back to the motel, as we were passing through the lobby, Bryan removed his wallet and walked over to the registration desk. "Come on, Michael. Let's play the slots for a while." He handed the clerk a ten-dollar bill and I handed her a ten and she looked at us for a moment, then gave us each a roll of quarters. We sat down at the end of a line of machines and began to play. But it was only a matter of seconds before a security guard seated on a stool at the other end of the line, got up and walked over to where we were playing.

"I'll have to see some I.D., fellas." So, I showed him my driver's licence and he looked at it and looked at me to see if the picture matched and, when he was satisfied, he handed it back. Then he reached out for Bryan's but Bryan, ignoring the guard's request, just continued feeding quarters and pulling the handle. "Your I.D., sir?" he repeated.

"I don't have it with me," Bryan responded, matter-of-factly," I think it's up in the room. I'll show it to you later." He kept playing. Suddenly, he won a little jackpot.

"I'll have to see the I.D. now, sir. Right now." And he placed his hand over Bryan's, so that he couldn't collect his winnings.

"All right! All right! Just let me stand up, will ya?" The guard grabbed Bryan's arm and helped him to his feet, but when he did, Bryan reached out with his other hand to gather in the jackpot.

The guard pulled him away. "You can't collect until I see the I.D., buddy."

Bryan yanked his arm from the guard's grasp and walked toward the elevator. "Come on, Michael. Let's go get my I.D. so I can prove to this dude that I'm twenty-one."

After we were safely on the elevator and the doors closed behind us, I asked him, "So, do you really have any I.D., or were you bullshittin'?"

Bryan rubbed his arm where the guard had held him. "Of course I don't have any I.D. You know I won't be twenty-one for a couple of months. But as soon as that motherfucker is off duty I'm gonna come right back down here and play slots, I.D. or no I.D. You watch me."

Around eight, we all met in the lobby to leave for the gig. Arthur counted heads. "You guys got everything, right? Let's not have any slip-ups this time, O.K.?"

So, we all went out the front doors and got into the limo, which was waiting, like the driver said it would be, and drove off in the direction of The Teenbeat Club. As the clear, dry desert air passed by the open limo window, Tjay took his soprano sax out of its case and began running through some arpeggio-type crap the way reed players have to, to warm up properly. At a stoplight, a man and his wife looked over at us from their car and smiled and nodded. Arthur pulled a Coke bottle out from under his leather coat and drank from it.

He coughed once and handed it to me. "Here, Michael. Take a hit. I dumped a jug of meth in it back at the hotel. You ought to get a pretty good buzz from two or three swallows. Should last all night, in fact."

The initial bitterness was overwhelming, but I drank some anyway, then I passed it to Snoopy. "Here you go, Snoop," I rasped. He drank, then coughed once and passed it to Bryan, who took a swig, and choked.

"How many jugs did you say you put in it, man?"

"Just one," Arthur answered. He removed the hash pipe from his pocket, packed it and fired it up.

The Coke bottle made the rounds, from Bryan, to Kenny, to Johnny, to Tjay, then, finally back to Arthur, who finished it. I don't know. It tasted like straight meth, with maybe a tablespoon of Coke mixed in for flavour. Real bad. Not enough Coke.

When we got to the club, the second billed act was on and the place looked to be filled to capacity. Not very many long-haired dudes, though. Vegas had a reputation for being hardcore straight back then. Not a good place to be a hippie. And if you were hip, not a good idea to advertise it. The penalties for drug possession in Nevada were outrageous. The legal atmosphere was very much Conservative Republican.

We made our way to the dressing room and sat around and smoked and waited for the other group to finish their set. After a while, a stagehand came back and told us it was time, and we went out and played. That's all I remember about the gig – except that, as friends, we were all still getting along, and musically we had an excellent night. The *Da Capo* material was fresh and we had been playing regularly, so everything went well and the crowd liked us.

At the end of the second set, I was hanging out with Snoopy over by the side of the stage, signing autographs and talking to some of the people who had come to see us play, when somebody said, "Here, sign this, will you?" I looked up and a guy was holding out a Zig-Zag. Then several of his buddies started laughing. "Hey, better yet," he said under his breath, "we just scored some good weed. Why don't you and Snoop come on over to my place and help us break into it? My car's out back."

I looked at Snoopy and he was nodding and smiling. Then we both glanced over to where Arthur and Bryan were sitting at a table, wrapped up in a conversation with the local D.J. who had promoted the concert. Most of the fans had left. Kenny and Johnny and Tjay were headed to the exit to catch a cab back to The Sands. I said, "Sure, man. Let's go."

Once we got out to the parking lot and into the car, the guy fished a joint from the ashtray and fired it up. As we pulled out of the lot and headed in the direction of his pad, he passed the joint to Snoopy and then he began to tell us a little about himself.

"You guys know what I do? For a living, I mean? I'm a professional comedian. I work the casino hotel show rooms. I open for the big name acts, like Elvis and Ann-Margaret and Wayne Newton. You know, I warm up the audience." His buddies were giving him a hard time and telling him he wasn't that funny but you could tell he was. He was hip, too, but he had the square appearance you had to have back in the sixties to get that kind of gig anywhere, especially in Vegas. He told us he lived with his wife and baby in an apartment complex not too far from the strip. She was a showgirl.

When we got to his pad it was late, around one a.m., and his wife and baby were asleep, of course. So, our host turned the stereo on low and one of his buddies took out a baggy and papers and started to roll pinwheelers. And, naturally, we were polite and spoke in soft tones so as to not wake the wife and baby. In other words, in the beginning we had appropriately quiet conversation. But after about the third joint, it was as if a switch had been tripped inside his head. Our host started to tell us a story about something that had happened at the casino one night, when suddenly he got up out of his chair and walked over and turned the stereo up a little, and then he was off and running. He didn't sit back down again the whole time we were there. He jumped from one subject to another, doing improvisational commentary on whatever happened to cross his mind. He was doing his act.

After about fifteen minutes everybody was laughing real hard and making more noise than we intended and, sure enough, from the back bedroom, we heard the baby start to cry. He stopped. "Uh, Oh. I think I might have..."

We heard the door open and footsteps pounding down the hall and then his wife charged into the living room. She stood momentarily, hair in curlers, fists at her sides, glaring threateningly at the comedian. "You woke the baby up, dipshit! I have to be at rehearsal in five hours! Haven't we talked about this before?"... Like we weren't there.

He kept stammering, "But, honey... but, honey..." but honey wouldn't let him get a word in edgeways until he said, "But, honey, they were just leaving."

She looked at us for the first time and snorted, "All righty!" Then she turned and went back into the bedroom with the crying baby. The mood darkened a little.

Our host looked at us, apologetically. "Well, guys, sorry. I guess it's time I have to give you a ride back to your hotel." Snoop and I were embarrassed for him.

"Hey, man. Don't worry about it." I got up off my temporary home on the couch. "Snoop and I had a hella good time, honest." I put the joint back down in the ashtray. "Thanks for the invite, and the weed." We all stumbled out to the apartment complex parking lot, piled back into his car, everybody high as a kite, and he took Snoop and me back over to The Sands.

Even though it was around 2 or 3 a.m. when the dude dropped us off, Snoop and I were pretty wide awake, and we still had a good buzz going from the meth, so we decided to walk across the street to one of the big casinos and hang out for a while. It was real noisy and crowded. Jackpot bells were going off all over the place and the folks standing at the craps tables were cheering in unison every time somebody hit their number. No matter how hard you tried, you couldn't help bumping into people when you tried to move from point A to point B. I looked around and wondered, "Who are these people? Don't they have jobs?" They didn't look like professional gamblers, exactly, or as if they were on vacation or anything. They looked more like local residents. Normal folks.

I saw one lady dressed in her house slippers and a wrinkled muumuu, sitting at a dollar slot machine feeding in what could have been her and her husband's life savings, three bucks at a time. Three bucks, pull. Three bucks, pull. No jackpot, wave good-bye to the money. No apparent big deal.

A guy wearing greasy mechanic's overalls, emblazoned with the Texaco Star, sat at a blackjack table in back of a beer bottle and a couple of hundred dollars in chips. There was an empty stool on either side of him. Snoopy nodded at the table. "Want to give it a try, Michael?"

"I guess," I shrugged. "You know how to play?"

"She deals you cards until you tell her to stop. The object is to come as close to the number 'twenty-one' as possible, without going over. What else is there to know?" He sat down on one stool, I sat down on the other, we each gave the dealer-lady fifty dollars; then she placed some chips in front of each of us and welcomed me and Snoop to the table.

First hand, she dealt me two face cards and went bust herself, trying for twenty-one, so I won. So did Snoop. Next hand, she gave me a fourteen to start, and I went bust trying to get closer. But I could see out of the corner of my eye, and around the mechanic, that Snoop was gathering in chips. He won. In fact, every time I looked his way, he was raking in chips and placing them in a neat little stack in front of him. For the next fifteen or twenty minutes, I won and lost and won and lost in streaks, like you usually do when you gamble, so I was in the middle of breaking even, when Snoop got up off his stool, crammed all his chips in his pockets, walked around and tapped me on the shoulder. "Ready to go, Michael?"

"Yeah, sure, man." I picked up my chips and we started off in the direction of the cashier's cage to turn our chips back into money, which is something the casinos dearly hate to see you do. In fact, if you walk out the door with any of the money you came in with at all, it hurts their feelings a little. That's what somebody told me once. But on the way out, Snoop had an expression on his face like the cat that ate the canary. When we got out on the sidewalk, he punched me in the arm. "Michael, man, I killed 'em! Look, I won three hundred bucks!" He took the money out of his pocket and waved it in my face.

I looked around, "Put that away, fool. You want to get rolled?" He shoved the wad back in his pocket and we walked back across the street to The Sands.

As we opened the door and walked in, the walls of the darkened room virtually pulsated from the illumination of the small red light on the telephone, signalling we had gotten a call. I picked up the receiver and hit the Play Message button.

"Hey, it's me. You guys call my room as soon as you get in!" Click. It was Arthur, and he sounded hot.

"Come on, Snoop. Let's go!" Arthur's room was only a few doors down the hall and I figured it was better to do this in person. About a second and a half after I knocked on his door, Arthur jerked it open like he had been waiting for us.

"Well, nice of you guys to come back to the hotel." His voice dripped with sarcasm. "I appreciate it. I do!" Then he exploded. "What's wrong with you two? Don't you know I've been worried sick? I was beginning to think I was going to have to call the Musicians' Union and line up a couple of replacements for tomorrow night's gig. My imagination was working overtime, man. Were you guys dead? Had you been busted? This is Vegas, you know. The authorities here don't enjoy people like us even being in town. They're lookin' forward to busting us! They train for it!" He was all shook up. But in a situation like this, I thought it was better to tell the truth and be done with it..

"Hey, sorry, man. We didn't think it was any big deal. We just accepted an invitation to go over to a dude's apartment and smoke some weed, for a little while, that's all," I shrugged.

He smiled and shook his head. "Oh, is that all? Is that all? That dude could have been the man, motherfucker! You guys could be sitting in a jail cell right now!" So, he went on and on for a while about how Snoop and I should have let him know where we were going when we left the club, and that we didn't have any regard for the other guys in the group, and how would we like it if it was him who had disappeared.

For the last two or three minutes of the lecture, Snoopy and I had been nodding and inching our way over to the door and saying, "Yeah, you're right, man, it won't happen again," until finally I had managed to get close enough to rest my hand on the knob. So, when Arthur began to wind down, and started repeating himself and saying, "And, and..." followed by long pauses, I went ahead and turned it and swung the door open.

Snoopy and I stepped through the doorway, and into the hall. "O.K., Arthur, we get the picture. Really," I said, with as much sincerity as I could muster. "We'll let you know where we're going, next time, I promise. Come on, Snoop. Let's hit the hay." Snoopy and I started to make our way down the hall.

"There better not be a 'next time,' motherfuckers," he yelled after us. Then he slammed his door closed. Funny thing is, from the time he started his tirade, I had been in the grip of a powerful deja vu. Like, I had gotten a lecture an awful lot like this one before, several times, a long time ago. But where? Then it hit me. Arthur would have made somebody a great mom.

"Arthur shouldn't have drunk so much of that meth," I told Snoop as I unlocked the door to the room. "He'll be up all night."

Suddenly our attention was diverted to another commotion, further down the hall.

"Open the door, Traci. We know you're in there with Bryan." Several girls were standing outside Bryan's door, banging on it. "Traci! Come on out, or we're gonna go call your parents!" More banging, but no sign of life from inside. "We're going to the pay phone to make the call, right now!" Nobody made a move. I mean, they were obviously worried about what was going on behind that closed door but their concern for the safety of their friend was being offset by their lack of desire to get the girl in serious trouble with her folks. So, they were just bluffing about making the call, but they weren't about to walk away anytime soon, either.

Even though it looked like Bryan was trying as hard as he could to manufacture considerable trouble for himself, Snoopy and I just shrugged and left it alone and went into our room.

"Bryan's nuts," Snoopy mumbled, closing the door behind us.

Next day around eleven, Snoopy and I found ourselves standing next to Bryan, waiting for the elevator.

The temptation was too great. "Hey, uh, Bryan, you were taking a little bit of a chance last night, weren't you?" I asked him. "But, as long as you seem to have gotten away with it, how was she?" The elevator doors opened and we all stepped inside.

He turned and stared straight ahead at the closing doors, expressionless. "A little toothy on the downstroke. You guys want to play some slots with me when we get downstairs? I was in the lobby earlier and that jerk security dude wasn't anywhere around, so, if the coast is still clear, I'm gonna play. Who wants to play with me?" About that time the doors opened and, sure enough, no security guard in sight.

Snoopy shook his head. "Not me. I'm hungry." He headed off in the direction of the coffee shop.

"I'll play, for a while," I told him. We dug some quarters from our pockets, sat down on a couple of empty stools and started feeding the machines.

The lady at the registration desk leaned over and yelled around the corner into a back room, "Bert, that kid's back." Bert the missing security guard emerged almost immediately from the back room. He was straightening his tie and his clothes were rumpled, like he might have been catching a few winks, but he was wide-awake now.

He marched right over to where Bryan sat and extended his hand. "I'll need to see that I.D. now, sir."

Bryan kept putting quarters in the slot and pulling the handle, virtually ignoring Bert. "Wait a minute," he said finally, not looking away from the machine. But Bert meant business, this time.

He placed both hands on Bryan's shoulders, from behind, and pulled him off the stool.

"No, now!" Then, the wrestling match was on again. Bert lost his hold on Bryan's shoulders when he stood up, then Bryan knocked over a stool. I grabbed my quarters and moved back to give them room. Bert took Bryan in a bear hug. "Give up, buddy, you can't win!"

Bryan struggled to free himself. "Let go of me, man. I'm gonna call the police!" They knocked over another stool.

"Go ahead, hippie. You're the one breaking the law. You're gambling and you're not twenty-one." They continued hugging and dancing around, for a while, falling against slot machines, knocking over a few more stools, but Bert was older, tougher and bigger, and he had the situation under control in no time.

Bryan was exhausted. Red in the face, he held his hands up, "All right, all right!" Bert let go, and Bryan gathered himself and, tucking his shirt back into his pants, turned to me. "Come on, Michael. Let's get out of this dump and go get some breakfast. I'm tired of gambling, anyway." Then he calmly strolled off down the hall toward the coffee shop, as if nothing had happened.

I think the spectre of public confrontation, or even humiliation, divides the people of the world into two distinct categories: those who can't stand it, who avoid it like the plague, and those who seem fascinated by it to the extent of actually courting it. Bryan courted it.

That night, we went back to The Teenbeat Club to play our second, and final, night of the gig. During the first break, a girl I recognized as one of the group gathered outside Bryan's motel room door the night before approached me at the snack bar.

"Traci's grounded because of last night, you know. She didn't get home until six in the morning. We just told her parents we were out driving around because we didn't want to get Bryan in trouble. She's only fourteen, you know. Her dad's a cop."

Musically, the second night in Vegas went like the first. Really well. The fact that right after we finished recording *Da Capo* we went on tour to promote it, meant that we knew the material and were in practice, which is key in sounding good. Everywhere we played, the audiences responded favourably to the jazz-orchestral rock of *Da Capo* just as they did to the harder, folk rock stuff off the first album. They even liked the John Lee Hooker jam, 'Revelation' A.K.A. 'Nineteen Minutes of Aimless Meandering'. They liked the drum solo, too.

Snoopy once told me, "After the first time Arthur saw you play with The Sons of Adam, the next day he told us, 'I just saw a guy play who's better than Conka,' which blew our minds, because until that time Arthur always said nobody was better than Conka. He was the best, before he got strung out.

The fact was, Conka was an incredibly gifted solo drummer. His solos were legendary. But that's not all he could do, he was a great all around drummer, as well. It's just that he was known for his solos. I think what must have happened was, when I agreed to join up, Arthur said to himself, "All right! Now we can start playing 'John Lee Hooker' again!" – because, with Snoopy on drums, they didn't play it. But what Arthur overlooked was, in the early days, when Conka was the drummer and LOVE played four or five sets a night, the jam was an important cog in the repertoire. It served a purpose, because it was so long and the group didn't have that big a song list. But over time, 'John Lee Hooker' lost a lot of its value. The kinds of performances the group played after I became the drummer were much shorter. Maybe, two forty-five minute sets a night, and now we had a lot of songs. We didn't really need it, anymore. Frankly, it only got in the way of us playing the shorter, more popular cuts from the albums, the songs the people came to hear. Besides, like I said before, I never got off on all that solo crap, anyway. On record or onstage, I like music best when everybody plays together. Drums are a foundation instrument, that's all. That's their job. Watching somebody take a drum solo is like watching somebody balance a bowling ball on the end of his nose. Impressive? Hell, yes. Enjoyable? Whatever. But then again, I never saw Conka play one.

Chapter Eleven

On The Road

AFTER LAS VEGAS, we were booked into a large, "Over 21" type place in Cleveland. It was a long plane ride and, as usual, we smoked and passed the hash pipe all the way there, no problem. On the first night of another two-night gig, we walked in the front door of the club about an hour before we were to start playing. The group sharing the bill with us was on stage and they were cookin' and sounding good, but right away we noticed there weren't many people in the audience. It was practically empty. The club manager came over and greeted us and introduced himself, and he was real friendly and personable, so none of us had the heart to ask him why the place was so dead.

"Hey, guys, there's a nice quiet booth for you, right over there." He jerked his thumb in the general direction of the back corner. "Go have a seat and I'll send a girl over in a minute to take your order. You can have a couple of drinks on the house while you're waiting for your set to start." Then he walked over to the bar and began talking to the bartender. We all sat down at the booth he directed us to, one of those large circular jobs that accommodate seven or eight people. Without hesitation, Arthur pulled the hash pipe out of his jacket pocket, loaded it and fired it up.

"What's with this place, man?" He passed the pipe to Kenny. "Elektra's got good distribution in Cleveland, I know our records have gotten radio airplay, they told me they've been plugging the gig. I don't get it. Where is everybody?"

The waitress came over and quickly sat on the edge of the booth seat, next to Arthur. "Fellas, the manager wants me to tell you to put that stuff away, now. You know, last night the narcs made a big bust here. They took away the band and most of the patrons. This place is hot, you have to be really, really careful."

Arthur looked at her with an expression of feigned concern. "Wow, you say all this happened just last night, huh?" She nodded. He tapped the old hash ashes out of the pipe bowl, repacked it with fresh and lit it again. Then, laughing and choking back a cough, he passed it to me. "Well, if that bust took place here just last night, then tonight we should be pretty safe, don't you think?" Then he laughed again, long and hard. Arthur was not into being careful. No reason to be. Getting busted was something that only happened to other people. He wasn't afraid.

Arthur was blessed with an athlete's optimism, the kind that makes you feel you can come back and win even if you're down by a lot of points. One day before a rehearsal at the Whisky, when we were preparing for the tour, I found out why. I was the first one there, setting up my drums on stage and a guy came in and looked around and asked me, "Arthur around?"

I looked up. "No, he's not here yet, but stick around, he'll be here in a minute." And I went back to setting up. When I did, the guy grabbed a chair at a table near the stage and struck up a conversation; and he began to tell me a little about Arthur when he was in high school.

"Yeah, man, we were on the basketball team together. Arthur was All League. He was a hell of an athlete. Team Captain. If we got down, he wouldn't let us give up. He'd yell at you and stay on your ass, too, if he didn't think you were doin' your best. Most people he went to school with didn't even know he was into music. They thought of him as an athlete only." So, Arthur's high school buddy hung out for a while longer and then he said he had to go take care of some business but he would be back later, and he left. But after that, a lot of what had confused me about the heavy handed approach Arthur took to heading up a rock band, started to make more sense. He had implemented this "team sport" concept of leadership into his "musical boss" role. He thought of himself as our "coach", and of business associates as "the other team".

I mean, in sports, like anything else, it helps to be talented, and you have to work hard to be good enough to succeed, but a really good athlete has to possess a variety of tools to win, especially in basketball, because on the court it's a series of situations matching five individual players from one team against five on the other. You know, there's a lot of "one on one". On any given day, it can be a very personal, psychological confrontation. Basketball isn't just a game of putting the ball through the hoop. You have to cause the other guy to miss his shot, as well, take him out of his game. Spoil his rhythm. Sometimes, you might have to mislead the opposition, fake him out, make him think you're going to do one thing, then do something else. You might have to intimidate him, stare him down, make him think you're going to kick his ass, after the game. Ridicule him, embarrass him, rattle him enough to raise self-doubt. Threaten him. Get into his head. Do anything you have to do to cause a momentary lapse in concentration, because that moment can be the key to victory. Deception, force, intimidation. All critical elements in the "Swiss Army Knife" approach to winning. A variety of blades.

Arthur didn't have to go to extraordinary lengths to achieve the status he needed. His talent gave him the upper hand. His songs were imaginative and articulate. He was an awesome physical presence on stage. People already respected and admired him – for his ability to create beautiful and exciting music, not because they knew he could make them look a fool or beat 'em up. But it was almost as if that ability to win by any means was something that he had worked so hard at for so many years, and he was so good at it, the blades were so sharp, that he liked to use those skills on a regular basis just to keep them from getting rusty. It seemed he wanted, more than anything, to remain totally able to do whatever was necessary to win. To be capable. To find the pruno. To be powerful.

A few days after we returned to L.A. from the *Da Capo* tour, I caught Snoopy playing Blackjack with himself at the dining room table.

"Michael, how much did you bring home with you, man?" Without looking up, he gathered the cards together, assembling them into a neat little stack, tapping them down one way, and then the other. Then, he began shuffling them like the experienced card players do. The fancy shuffle.

I took a potato out of the cupboard, wrapped it in foil and placed it in the oven. "You want a baked potato, Snoop? I'm gonna make myself a steak and a baked potato. You want one?"

"How much money, man?"

"I don't know. Five grand, I guess. Why?"

He continued shuffling absent-mindedly, all the while staring down at the cards. "I thought you might like to play a little '21' just to pass the time. For money, of course."

He was transparent as hell. He was trying to sucker me. "I don't know, Snoop. What if you lose? Sometimes money breaks up friendships." I wrapped another potato in aluminium foil and placed it in the oven, next to mine. Then, I sat down in the chair opposite Snoop and fired up the pipe.

Suddenly, he looked me in the eye, and his voice cracked with excitement. "Michael, man, I can't lose. I've got a system. Remember Vegas? I don't think I lost one hand all night. If you'll let me try my system out on you, I promise we'll stop after you lose a hundred. You can afford a hundred bucks, can't you? Who knows? You might win." Without waiting for an answer, he slid the deck over to my side of the table for me to cut.

"What's your system?" I tapped the cards, and pushed the deck back to Snoopy, signalling him to deal.

"Five bucks a hand, just like in Vegas. You deal every hand." He smiled.

I couldn't believe what I was hearing. "Ahem. Snoop, if I deal, the odds are in my favour. That's why in Vegas the house usually wins. Remember? The player receiving the deal has to try to come close to twenty-one first, and that's how you go bust and lose. Half the time, the dealer doesn't have to do anything to win except stand there with his arms folded and give the sucker a card when he says, 'hit me,' and wait."

But he was adamant. "I don't care. That's how I won in Vegas and that was against professionals, so I'm not worried about playing the same system against you. Besides, even if you're right and it's a bad system and I lose, all I have here is a hundred bucks. I'm safe. A hundred bucks is all I can lose, right? Deal the cards."

So, I dealt him a face card and a four of clubs and he went bust on the next card. Next hand, I dealt him another face card and a five of diamonds. "Hit me," he said confidently. Bust, again. On and on. His hundred was gone in about ten or fifteen minutes.

"Snoop, I..." That's as far as I got before he jumped up and headed for the front door, pausing only momentarily to grab his keys off the counter on the way out.

He pointed his finger at me. "Don't go anyplace, man. I'm going to my mom's house to get another hundred. I'll be right back, O.K.?" Then he stormed out the door. In a few seconds, I heard his car start up and peel off down the street, and before long, he was back, waving a fresh hundred as he closed the door behind him. "Now, let's try that again."

For the next fifteen minutes, I dealt and he lost. When the second hundred was gone, Snoopy leaned back in his chair and took a deep breath. "I don't get it. What happened?" He stared off into space, stunned.

I handed him the deck of cards. "I'll tell you what happened. In Vegas, you were lucky. That's all." I stood up and walked back into the kitchen. Opening the oven door I removed a hot pad from a hook and squeezed one of the baked potatoes. "Hey, Snoop, your potato's almost ready. You want a steak?" No answer. He was pissed.

By this time, San Francisco had become the group's home away from home, I guess, because we played there almost as often as we played in L.A. Usually at The Fillmore. The first time, Bill Graham was handling the introductions. He said, "And now, here they are from L.A., 'The Love!'" It was a natural mistake. All the bands back then had "The" incorporated into their names: The Beatles, The Rolling Stones, The Kinks... Everybody except us. We weren't a bunch of things, like beatles or rolling stones or kinks or animals. We were a concept. Arthur came up with that, naturally. After we finished the set, Arthur cornered Bill Graham backstage, "Hey, man," he scowled, "the name of the band isn't 'The Love'. It's just LOVE, O.K.? Correct that, when you introduce us for the next set." Then, Arthur turned and walked slowly away, shaking his head, like "How could you be so stupid?" The Father of The Fillmore just stood there for a moment, mouth open, as if recovering from a punch in the gut.

But come the introduction for the second set, "Folks, I had it wrong, the first time. Let's hear it for one of the truly great bands to come out of L.A. in a long, long time: LOVE." So, he corrected himself and it went off without a hitch, the second time around. Bill was even a pretty good sport about it, considering the rude and condescending way he had been treated.

Sometimes, on our trips up the coast, we played the Avalon Ballroom. Other times, after Chet and Bill split, we played an old converted ice rink called Winterland. The only memorable concert we played there would come much later, in April of 1968 after the release of the group's third album, *Forever Changes*. We appeared with The Staple Singers and jazz great, Roland Kirk. LOVE had top billing, then The Staples, then Roland Kirk because then, as now, you were given billing status based on popularity, not talent. People that went to Winterland and Fillmore concerts only listened to mainstream stuff, anyway. Not jazz. Ninety percent of the audience had probably never even heard of Roland Kirk.

When he was introduced for his set, Roland was led out from behind the curtain by an assistant. He was short and stocky and he was wearing dark glasses and he walked with unsure steps, because he was blind. The guy that helped him to the microphone reached down and removed his sax from its stand and placed it in Roland's right hand. Then, he took his left, and extended it out to the microphone, to show him where it was. Roland nodded, and his backup group, piano, bass, drums and trumpet broke into the intro to their first number.

You knew as soon as they played the first few notes, it was going to be special. It was almost as if Roland was trying to educate this audience of rock fans. His solos were flowing and powerful and sophisticated and they lifted the audience up and showed them how good music could be. It was stuff the likes of which many of them had never seen or heard before. It was different. Halfway through the first number, his man brought out a second sax and put it in the sax stand. While he held and played the first sax with his right hand, Roland reached down and removed the second sax with his left hand. Then he placed the mouthpiece of the second sax in the left corner of his mouth and began to play both saxes, simultaneously.

We were standing in the wings and Arthur and I just looked at each other. It wasn't simply what he was doing: it was more that he did it so perfectly. An orchestrated duet with himself, so complicated he had to have had two brains working. It was beautiful and moving. He played his heart out. He was third billing.

Whenever we flew up for a weekend gig, the group always stayed at The Richelieu Hotel, downtown. It was really old, with black-and-white TVs in all the rooms and heated by those big iron radiators you see in B-movies. The beds looked as if they had been purchased at a YMCA garage sale. It was straight out of the 1930s.

The elevator had to be manually operated by a professional operator, a little old man in a tattered uniform who sat on a wooden stool, on duty, near as I could tell, night and day, waiting for somebody to come along who needed to go up to their room. The elevator was activated by grasping the handle of a large crank and rotating it back and forth, several times, which sounded a series of bells designed to attract the attention of people standing around in the lobby who might want to go up or down. Only there was never anybody else around but us. It's like, when we were there, we never once, that I can remember, saw any other people in the lobby or the halls or the restroom or anywhere, for that matter. No other customers, I mean. Just the old dude working the elevator and the guy at the registration desk and us. That's all.

And, although he looked like he had to have been cranking that elevator mechanism for a good twenty or thirty years, the old dude was surprisingly inept at it. That is, he wasn't any good. He didn't have the knack of stopping the elevator right at floor level, so that when he would stop the car and open the doors, it was always just a little higher or lower than it was supposed to be. But instead of tapping the crank handle a couple of times to fix it, like he could have, he would just nod at the discrepancy and say, "Watch your step." Like, "That's it. Take it or leave it." Not that big a deal, really, but I think it began to stick in Bryan's craw some, that the old dude didn't try a little harder to get it right. He thought it was disrespectful, or something.

So, a few weeks after we got back home from Cleveland, the group had booked a two-nighter at The Fillmore and then the following weekend in Reno. As usual, we flew up and, as usual, we stayed at The Richelieu. Around one a.m. the first night, we got back to the hotel and the old dude was at the controls. We all got on the elevator and it was a pretty tight squeeze, because there were still seven of us and Bryan and Johnny and Kenny had their instruments. The operator swung the crank back and forth and the bells sounded, then he closed the doors and we started up. When we reached our floor, he opened the doors back up and, naturally it was way off. About two inches below where it should have been. "Watch your step," the old dude rasped.

Bryan was the last one to get on, so he was standing closest to the doors. As he stepped over the threshold, he tripped – on purpose. The old man's eyes widened and, rising off his operator's chair, he made a desperate grab for Bryan's arm, but it was too late. The old man winced and Bryan executed a real exaggerated pratfall, going down hard, all the way on his face, dropping his guitar case. The impact caused the strings to vibrate and it made a real loud, "Bronggg" sound, and rolled several feet away. For a few moments, Bryan stayed down on the hall floor, motionless, then he began to rise slowly to his hands and knees, shaking his head, as though stunned. The rest of us stepped over the threshold, off the elevator, around Bryan and walked down the hall to our rooms. Nobody said a word.

The hotel had a pretty good coffee shop downstairs, and when we ate there nobody else was ever in the coffee shop either, except us and the waitress and the cook, who we never saw, of course. Come to think of it, maybe we never saw anybody else because we were always doing our business in the middle of the night. Could be. Whatever, I think maybe The Richelieu Hotel was located in a small corner of San Francisco called The Twilight Zone.

For a while, Chet Helms and Bill Graham had a working relationship, of sorts, but there came a time, around early to mid-1967, when they broke off their partnership and Chet no longer operated out of the Fillmore at all. It didn't really make a whole lot of difference to the groups, I suppose, except that, from then on, when we played the Fillmore, it was usually for Bill Graham and when we played concerts put together by Chet's Family Dog production company, it was nearly always over at Winterland. Actually, there was one more small difference: their personalities. Chet was one of the coolest, calmest individuals in the business of concert production.

He never got upset about anything, therefore playing concerts for Chet at Winterland was always a peaceful, enjoyable experience. And Bill Graham? Well, he was nervous and high-strung and always worried sick about something. When you played a concert for Bill, you could expect some kind of trouble. He thrived on it. It there was none around, he manufactured some. He gave new and deeper meaning to the word "uptight." When you were in the same room with him, you wanted to go over and put your arm around his shoulder and say, "Hey, Bill, settle down, damnit, please. It'll be O.K., honest it will." But that wouldn't have done any good. He didn't want to relax or calm down. He liked being uptight. It was his destiny.

After the final performance of these two nights at the Fillmore, Snoopy and Kenny had helped me pack up my drums and we were waiting near the front door for our equipment manager, Neil, to bring the van around, so we could load everything up. The plan was for us and our limo and the equipment van to leave that very night from the Fillmore, and drive to Reno for the next gig. While we waited for the van, we talked with the fans and signed posters that they took from a stack of maybe four or five hundred, sitting on a large wooden table next to the office.

In a few minutes, Snoopy glanced up and pointed through the glass door. "Neil's here, man." Then, he picked up one of the equipment cases and headed toward the van.

"Hold on, Snoop. I'm going to grab a couple of posters." I walked over to the table and took two posters from the top of the stack. Out of the corner of my eye, I saw the office door abruptly swing open.

"What do you think you're doing?" Bill Graham stood in the doorway, with his hands on his hips.

I held up the two posters.

"Did you ever hear of asking?"

Just then, a guy I recognized as the assistant stage-manager approached him from behind and touched his arm. "Uh, Bill..."

"Wait a minute, Jack!" he yelled over his shoulder, "I'm making a point, here." Then, turning to me again, "You people pay for a ticket to come in and hear the groups and you think you own the place, right? Well, ask for a poster and maybe I'll let you have one."

I put the posters back on the stack. "Forget it." I turned and walked out the front door and joined Kenny and Johnny and Snoopy in the limo, idling at the curb. "Jeez, I saw that Michael. What a nitwit," Kenny marvelled. "What's his problem?"

"I don't know, man. Lot of overhead, I guess. Let's smoke while we wait for the other guys." As I rolled a number, I saw Arthur and Bryan headed to the limo followed by Bill Graham in a dead run, rolling up a couple of posters and securing them together with a rubber band. When he got to the limo, he stuck them through the window to me.

"Sorry, Michael. I didn't recognize you. No hard feelings?"

I took the posters. "No, Bill. No hard feelings." He smiled and shook my hand and walked back into the building. Arthur and Bryan climbed in, and the limo and the equipment van drove off in tandem toward Reno.

Our equipment manager, Neil, was soft-spoken and lovable and gentle and never got mad about anything. Not the kind of person you would expect to be put in charge of transporting and setting up equipment for a rock band. He was probably a little too low-key for the job, I guess, but he more than earned his pay by settling arguments and keeping the peace.

One day, after *Da Capo* had been completed, before I had met Neil, Kenny and I had taken a run over to Wallich's Music City, to pick up bass strings. When we walked in, he said, "Wait 'til you see what they have on display. It'll blow your mind." We made our way to the instrumental section, near the back of the store, and as we approached the counter, he pointed to a large cardboard display standing next to the cash register. "Check it out," he said, grinning.

It was the modelling-assignment advertisement photo I had done with my old bass player in The Sons of Adam, Mike Port about six months earlier. We were standing in a field of yellow wildflowers in a vacant lot on the outskirts of Palos Verdes with two other guys we didn't know. "The Beasts of the Field make it big with a Leslie," the caption proclaimed. Like we were a band and we made the big time because we used Leslie speakers. Mike and I had our hands resting on the Leslie and we looked like we meant business. The night before the shoot, Mike and I were leaving The Eating Affair across the street from The Whisky and a guy jogged up to us and asked us if we wanted to make a hundred bucks each, the next day, and we said, "Yeah," and we did the ad. A few months later, one of those cardboard stand-ups was on display in every music store in the US and Canada. Thousands of them. I still have one in a drawer someplace.

Anyway, a lot of aspiring musicians probably thought we were a real band, "The Beasts of the Field", but it was just made up. I don't think Mike and I ever even spoke to those two other guys, because the shoot only lasted about twenty minutes.

Kenny laughed, "I was in here with Bryan, and he saw that picture and he said, 'Michael's only been in the band a month and he's already playing with somebody else.'"

After we left the store, on the way out to the parking lot, Kenny asked me, "Have you ever met our equipment manager, Neil? We'll be going on tour pretty soon, I may as well take you over and introduce you to the guy that'll be setting up your drums every night."

Pretend group, "Beasts of the Field": Leslie Speaker ad with Sons of Adam bassist Mike Port and myself standing with two guys we didn't know.

On The Road 107

When we got to Neil's house, we parked at the curb, on the street, at the bottom of a long staircase leading up to the front door. It was one of those places typical to Laurel Canyon; hard to see, shrouded in trees and bushes, the surroundings provided a natural visual barricade to unwanted visitors. A few moments after Kenny rang the doorbell, a voice answered from inside, "Be right there." Then, the door opened.

A dude with long greasy-black hair who looked to be in his mid-thirties smiled and ushered us in and gave Kenny a one-armed hug. "Hey, man, what's happenin'?" Then, turning to me, "This is Michael, right? Welcome to the group, man." A large, white Alaskan malamute trotted out from a back room and started licking my hand. "Meet Tundra. Everywhere I go, he goes. Except when we're on the road."

If it's true that dogs take on the personality of their masters then it was definitely the case with Neil and Tundra. They were both happy and friendly. Tundra took up residence at Neil's feet and while we sat on the couch, he began trying to shake paws with me, first the right, then the left. Over and over. I shook Tundra's paw and scratched him behind the ears while Neil and Kenny discussed the specifics of the schedule of the upcoming tour.

And as they talked, I began to notice something I hadn't picked up on immediately. Neil was doing everything with his right hand, holding his left at an unnatural, perpendicular angle to the ground. Looking closer, I realized Neil had a complete outfit balanced precariously on the back of his left hand, the needle fully inserted into a vein; a cloudy mixture of brown heroin and blood filled the eyedropper syringe.

I came to learn that Neil was born and raised in Hollywood. In high school, he was one of a large number of young people who were introduced to hard drugs, and to whom heroin held no real element of fear. But at the same time, he became experienced enough to know that there's absolutely no way to tell the potency of a drug, until you try it. All drugs start out relatively pure, but every time a shipment is sold, especially if it's a powder drug, like heroin or cocaine, the new owner steps on it. How much? You can't know until you try it. And, if you underestimate the potency, even just a little, there can be problems.

Unfortunately, most people who shoot heroin, enjoy the initial surge, so, traditionally, the accepted way to get the most out of the high is to stick the needle into a major vein and inject the drug over the span of maybe ten seconds, then wait for the rush. And, of course, that's the most dangerous way, because if the drug hasn't changed hands very many times, or if the previous owners were conscientious and tried to be nice and only stepped on it a little, well, the rush can escort you right into the grave. That's the reason there are so many overdose deaths. Like I said, you don't know how strong a drug is until you use it.

So, Neil developed a system that would enable him to get a rush, albeit a slow one, and still not take a chance of killing himself. He would just put the spike of the outfit containing the smack, into the vein on the back of his hand, then go about his business, using only somewhere between slight and moderate care to keep it from falling off its perch. That way, the stuff could seep slowly into his system and do its job, safely and effectively. And if he felt himself start to get too high, he could simply yank the needle out and save the rest until later. Pretty good system, really. I mean, he had to do a lot of things with one hand, but he did everything pretty good, that way. In fact, most of the things a person has to do around the house can be done with one hand, if you use a little imagination. Answer the phone? One hand. Fix your dog's dinner one handed? Sure, no big deal. But even though he was real matter-of-fact and nonchalant about doing it around other people, the procedure looked unusual as hell to the unsuspecting eye.

All in all, Neil was relatively industrious. That is to say, a lot of people who juggle an addiction lie around in bed all day, watching TV and sucking on a popsicle. Neil held down two jobs and led an active social life. When he wasn't managing our equipment, he worked at a men's clothing store on La Cienega, The London Fog. Neil's boss was even cool enough to let him bring Tundra with him to work everyday, so it was a real nice set-up.

Neil's friends and customers were from all walks of the entertainment business. One day I was in his shop, buying a sweater, and Tundra was over in the corner, taking it easy, when a big, rugged looking dude came in with a couple of little kids in tow. Neil walked right over, "Hey, Charlie, what's happenin'?"

He gave Neil a friendly hug. "Hey, Neil, nothin' much. What's happenin' with you, my friend?" And while they talked, I just browsed and looked at sweaters. But, right away, the two little kids started getting into everything, pulling clothes off the racks and chasing each other around and trying to play with Tundra, who was ignoring them. Once in a while, their dad would pause in the conversation, and turn around and tell them to behave, but as soon as he went back to talking to Neil, they would do something else bad. Sure enough, in a minute, his kids pulled a big box of pins that store employees used for marking alterations, down off the counter and they spilled all over the floor. A couple of thousand of them, at least. Charlie smacked himself in the forehead with the flat of his hand.

"Oh, my God! I'm sorry, Neil." Then, glaring at his two sons, "O.K., you guys are really in trouble, now!" But they just squealed and laughed and kept chasing each other around the store while Charlie got down on his hands and knees and started picking up the pins and putting them carefully back in the pin box. He wasn't really mad, because they were only about four and five years old, but he was probably a little embarrassed.

While the dad was engrossed in picking up pins, Neil made eye contact and signalled me to come over, which I did. "Michael, say hello to my friend, Charlie. He's an actor. Charlie, this is Michael. He's the drummer in the LOVE group. I manage their equipment when they're touring."

Bracing himself on the floor with his left hand, he smiled and extended his right hand up to me. "Charlie Bronson."

I don't think Neil needed the money he made selling men's clothing or managing our equipment. He seemed to be financially comfortable. It's more likely, he realized it wouldn't be healthy for him to sit around his house all day with that outfit balanced on the back of his hand, so he made up his mind to be with people and challenge the theoretical limitations of his addiction. Did a damn fine job of it, too, 'til about a year and a half later when he got hold of some stuff that was so pure that not even his surefire system would save him, and he overdosed and died. Friends told me at first Tundra wouldn't let the paramedics in to get Neil's body. Tundra stood over him, growling and bearing his teeth at anyone who tried to come near, then, after they finally left with Neil, Tundra started howling. He howled all night long.

Three and a half hours after leaving The Fillmore, in San Francisco, we arrived in Reno. The limo pulled over to the curb in front of the hotel and Neil stopped alongside and rolled down his window. "Hey, I'm gonna go ahead and take the equipment over and set it up. The building manager said he'd wait there for us and I don't want the instruments to stay out in the van while we're sleeping." As the rest of us got out of the limo and made our way into the hotel lobby to check in and get some shut-eye, Neil drove off in the direction of the Memorial Auditorium. It was about an hour before daybreak, and the cold, dry desert air cut through our lungs like a knife. So, we said our good-byes to the limo driver and broke up into two's, and went up to the rooms to grab a few hours sleep.

Around noon, we met in the coffee shop downstairs for breakfast and then caught a couple of cabs over to the Reno Memorial Auditorium, an old, red brick building, circa 1945. The van was parked near the rear entrance. When we got inside, Neil was directing a couple of local dudes who had been hired special for this gig, on where to set everything up.

"No, man," he was telling one of his helpers, "the bass amp has to go over on the left, next to the drum riser." He looked over at us and shook his head as if to say, "I told 'em where to put the stuff a while ago, but people don't listen." Neil was, like, "in charge."

Arthur gestured to a hallway, "Let's go check out the dressing rooms while they're finishing up." We walked down a long row of doors until we reached one with a faded star stencilled on it, then we went inside and sat in metal folding chairs with padded seats and backs and Johnny took his guitar out of its case and Kenny his bass, and they both plugged into the small tune-up amp that adorned almost every dressing room I was ever in. Then, Arthur took his harp out of his jacket pocket, and I reached for a pair of sticks that rested in the accessory case that Neil had stashed there, and I started pounding on the pad of one of the folding chairs, and Kenny joined in, then Johnny, and we jammed for a little while. It was some of the best music we ever played together. No audience, no recording equipment, no pressure, no egos.

After a few minutes, one of the stagehands opened the dressing room door and came in. He was nodding along with the beat and grinning and, when we stopped and looked at him, he told us, "Neil said to tell you guys everything is set up and ready to go for tonight. You can come on in and check it out whenever you're ready. By the way, anything the group needs while you're here, be sure and let me or one of the other guys know, like if you're hungry or something, tell us. We'll run out and get it." He turned to Arthur, "Hey, Arthur, I have all your solos memorized." He held up a small harmonica. "I play harp, too."

Arthur leaned forward, feigning interest, "Really? You do? Tell me, have you been studying long? I mean, seriously, we might need somebody to fill in from time to time. Could you get away, if we needed you?" Without waiting for an answer, he rose from his chair and walked to the other side of the room and stood with his back to us, his body convulsing with silent laughter.

The stagehand looked suddenly uncomfortable, "Well, I don't exactly study, or anything. I just listen to records. Anyway, your stuff's all set up." And he left, closing the door after him.

When he had left the dressing room, Arthur wheeled around and began staggering in circles, "HAAW, HAAW, HAAW! Did you hear that? 'I have all your solos memorized,' he says. That cracks me up! Like he could play my shit." Then, guffawing mightily, holding his sides and bent over double, he collapsed back down onto the folding chair.

Bryan, who had been quietly running over a guitar part, stopped picking. "You didn't have to be so rude to the cat, Arthur. He's a fan, you know."

Suddenly, Arthur quit laughing and gave Bryan the glare. "Hey, I don't care who he was, man. I really don't, so just mind your own fuckin' business. All right?" Bryan had sort of spoiled Arthur's good time, rained on his parade a little, and he didn't like to be told who he could or couldn't laugh at by anybody.

Late that night after the gig, I left with Bryan through the rear stage exit. As we looked around for a cab, I asked him, "What's Arthur's trip? How can he ridicule somebody like that, I mean, right to his face. Does he actually think it's funny to belittle other people and try to make them look stupid? Nobody else was laughing, so what's the point?" Bryan shook his head.

"I don't know, Michael. He gets off on it, that's all I know. Arthur's been like that as long as I've known him. It's like, that's his entertainment. It pumps him up. It makes him happy, so I just humour him, usually. But tonight was different. I mean, the stagehand dude was so defenceless, I had to say something. It's kind of embarrassing for the group when that kind of stuff gets around. I hate to think what it makes us look like. Hey, there's a cab." The driver saw us flag him down and pulled over to the curb and stopped. Bryan opened a rear door and got in and I slid in after him.

As the driver pulled away from the curb, he introduced himself. "Hi, fellas, I'm Larry. Where to?" We gave him the name of the hotel and he drove off in that direction, but later during the ride, as we sat at a red light, his eyes hit the rear view mirror mounted on the windshield. "Hey, I know a really classy whorehouse just outside the city limits. You guys want me to take you there? I will. If I turn right here, we're on our way."

"No, that's all right," I told him. "Thanks anyhow, though. Just take us to the hotel."

Bryan whacked me on the leg with the back of his hand. "Hey, Michael, let's go! What else do we have to do? Turn right, Larry." Larry turned the cab right and accelerated out onto 395.

"You guys won't be sorry. These girls are beautiful. And clean!" He smiled.

I couldn't believe it. "Get outta here, Bryan. We don't have to go to a whorehouse. What's wrong with you?"

Bryan gazed out the window of the cab at the passing desert night, the blackness lit only by moon and stars. "I don't know. It's something to do. It's different. That's all."

"Yeah, well it's a little too different, to suit me. I'm just along for the ride on this one, O.K.? I'll have a beer, or something, while you do your thing."

The cab driver, Larry, overheard me. "Oh, you'll change your mind when you see these girls, buddy. They're gorgeous!" We drove south on 395 for about another ten minutes. Suddenly, Larry said, "Hey, we're here!" He turned off the main highway onto a small dirt road marked by a wooden sign, made purposefully to look rustic and weather-beaten. "AUNT CANDY'S KITTEN RANCH," the sign said. We travelled another hundred yards and came to a mobile home compound surrounded by a chain link fence, topped with barbed wire. The cab driver slowed to a stop near an intercom and rolled his window down.

"Customers, Candy." The compound gate opened and Larry accelerated. Then, looking over his shoulder at us, he smiled. "I come here all the time. Get it?" He drove over to the largest of the trailers and parked in front. The three of us got out of the cab and climbed the small stairs leading to the front door marked, "Entrance".

"Come on in, guys. I'll introduce you to everybody." Larry opened the door and we stepped inside. An acrid, pungent odour of stale perfume and perspiration filled the room. The girls were lounging around in their nighties and see-through lingerie and panty-and-bra outfits, sitting on lazy boys and a big sofa, watching TV and talking; but as soon as one of them noticed us, she announced in a loud voice, "Company!" and they all put out their cigarettes and jumped up and stood in an inspection line. A large woman in a housedress came out of the back room and gave Larry an enthusiastic hug.

"Hey, babe. Welcome back. Brought us some fresh blood, huh?" Larry nodded. "These two don't look like the cowboys you usually bring in here. Where'd you find these hippies?" Then, she turned to us. "What about all that 'free love' I'm always hearing about? Why don't you boys go get some of that?"

"The free love is back at the hotel," I told her. "We decided to come over here and pay for it for no particular reason."

"These boys aren't hippies," Larry interjected. "They're musicians. They make a lot of money."

Candy smiled and put her fat arms around our waists. "Come on into the bar and have a drink first." Then, as she led us into an adjoining room, she looked back over at the line of girls. "Sit down, ladies. They'll be right with you, shortly," she laughed. I guess she thought if she got us liquored up, a little bit, we might spend more. So she took us into the bar and sat us down on a couple of barstools and Bryan and I each ordered a beer. Then, Aunt Candy left us, saying she would be right back. Country muzak played through speakers located in both rooms.

I took a sip of beer. "Hey, Bryan. Can I ask you a question?" He shrugged. "What are we doing here?"

Bryan studied the giant western-theme mural that hung on the wall, in back of the bar. Men on horseback, rounding up steers and kicking up a lot of dust at sunset. "Michael, haven't you ever wanted to go to a whorehouse?"

"Yeah, sure," I told him, "when I was a kid. But now that I'm all grown up, I find that it's not necessary."

He squinted, "I used to want to go to a whorehouse, too, and now we're at one, don't you see? Some men live their whole lives dreaming of going to a place like this and we're here, man! A new experience! It's different, it's unique. Enjoy it!" He drained his glass and ordered another beer.

When the bartender went to fetch the beer, I tapped Bryan on the knee and leaned closer to him. "Hey, man," I said softly, "have you taken a good look at these girls? They appear to be a little on the hard side, don't you think?" He picked up his fresh glass of beer and, taking a sip, swivelled on his stool and squinted through the doorway into the other room at the girls, now slouched back down in their lazy-boys and overstuffed sofa, smoking and watching TV. He swivelled back and scrutinized the mural hanging over the bar, once again.

Aunt Candy waddled back into the bar, "What's the deal?" she asked, impatiently. "Did you fellas come here to get laid or drink beer? Let's get this show on the road. Whaddayasay?"

When I looked at Bryan, I could see he was thinking things over, pondering the situation, as it were. In the first place, he didn't like to be pushed. In the second place, yeah, the girls were kind of hard looking. In the third place, we didn't have to give anybody any money to go to a whorehouse. I mean we were already at a whorehouse. We had been to the whorehouse and now it was time to go back to the hotel.

Bryan dabbed the beer from his moustache with a cocktail napkin and stood up. "Well, Michael, we have to get going. Where's Larry?"

Bryan had a lotta, lotta nerve, an unquenchable curiosity, and an irrepressible need to explore the depths of the human psyche. He probably would have yelled, "Fire!" in a convalescent hospital, just to watch a wheelchair race.

Chapter Twelve

Downtime

FOR SIX MONTHS following the recording of *Da Capo*, the group did a good job of promoting the album with live appearances throughout the western United States, but there were still weeks during which we did absolutely nothing. By March of '67, Snoopy had acquired a steady girlfriend so a lot more of my free time was spent hanging out with Kenny at his house on Lookout Mountain, in the Canyon. Kenny had bought a used XKE that was in such bad shape, it would have to have been classified as a "restoration project". The car was painted yellow and had several small dents and scrapes along the side, which was a job for the body shop later, but in the meantime, there were a bunch of simple things that had to be taken care of that he could do himself. Replace the spark plugs and distributor cap and rotor, new shocks, battery, hoses, windshield wipers, stuff like that. So, every day that the group didn't have a rehearsal scheduled, I would wake up around eleven and go over to Kenny's house and help him work on the Jaguar.

One morning, while I was getting ready to leave my house to grab breakfast, the phone rang. It was Kenny, and he was all excited. "Michael, hurry up. I've got a huge radiator leak. I need you to follow me down to the shop. I already called the guy. He's expecting us and I told him I'd be right over."

Lookout Mountain is a funny street. Like most Canyon roads, it's pretty steep and winding, and when it was built, the area was relatively remote. I guess in the beginning, visitors could drive right up to where they were going and park in front on the street, next to the curb; but as the population of the area rose, the street had to be widened, and suddenly there was no longer any room to park in front of the houses at all. Travel access to the houses shifted from the front to the rear. So, even though the fronts of the houses face the main drag, access to the front doors to the homes is from around back. You can't park in front at all anymore, because there's no room on the street. In fact, if you even slow down, like if you're looking for an address, you have a real good chance of getting bulldozed by the car following you. You have to drive at a pretty good clip, past your destination address, all the way to the end of the block, and then pull around back and park in the alley, next to the garbage cans. So, on this day, when I turned onto Kenny's alley, I was greeted by a river of green radiator coolant coming my way. It was everywhere. The Jag had its hood up and Kenny was leaning over into the engine compartment wrapping the crack in the radiator with duct tape. He waved me over.

"When I start it up, the anti-freeze is gonna spew all over the place, even with the tape on it. But it's cool, the guy at the shop says it's O.K. as long as we take it right there. It won't damage the engine and the radiator's already shot, so let's go." He topped off the anti-freeze level and put the cap back on. Then he climbed in and turned the ignition and, of course, as soon as he did the Jag started leaking like a sieve, but, real quick, Kenny pulled a U-turn and headed off down the alley, then left on Lookout Mountain and lickety-split on down to the shop. It was on a side street in the heart of Hollywood, someplace.

As soon as we parked in front, Kenny shut his car down and naturally it continued leaking radiator coolant out onto the sidewalk, because of all the pressure it had built up, and a guy wearing a big smile and a name patch that read "Dale" came out of the office wiping his hands on one of those pink garage towels that all the mechanics use. He extended his freshly cleaned right hand to Kenny. "Hi, I'm Dale. You're Kenny, right? Pop the hood and let's check the damage."

After poking the crack in the housing a few times with a screwdriver, he removed his head from under the hood. "This radiator's original equipment. Probably should be replaced. Jaguar makes shitty radiators. New one will run about two bills. You'll want to replace the thermostat, too. It's only another twenty-five bucks."

So, he got the O.K. from Kenny to do the work and told us to come back in a couple of hours and the job should be all finished. Kenny and I decided to get something to eat over at Hamburger Hamlet on Sunset, then we drove over to Wallich's Music City to look at a new bass amp and buy new strings, then to Neal's to hang out and smoke dope, for a bit, and before long, it was time to go get the Jag.

I parked in front of the shop. We were met by Dale, emerging from the office, wiping his hands on the pink towel again.

"She's all set." He opened the hood and proudly displayed the brand new radiator he had installed in the Jag. "Climb in and fire it up."

Kenny started the engine and it purred like a kitten and there were no leaks anywhere. After Kenny went into the office to settle up, he came back out smiling, "Park your car, Michael. I have to make a run to Pep Boys. Ride with me and check out the Jag. You've never been in it." So, we went to Pep Boys and bought some stuff and we drove on back to the radiator shop to pick up my car, and then I followed Kenny to his house, just to make certain the Jag didn't spew another leak on the way up the hill.

When we got there, Arthur was sitting in his black Porsche, waiting for us. As we pulled up and parked in the alley behind him, he got out of his car and approached us. "Hey, Michael, Snoopy told me you were over here. I have to talk to you guys about something. Let's go inside." His mood was sombre.

"Yeah, sure," Kenny said. He turned and reached over the garbage cans and opened the gate, then we walked down the stairs to his front door and went into the living room. Kenny turned on his stereo, and then sat down to roll a joint.

Arthur began to pace back and forth. "The material Bryan and I wrote for the next album is orchestrated to be played by a five man group with strings and horns. That's all. There's no need for Snoopy and Tjay to stay with the group as regular members any more. I guess they're gonna have to go. It's probably my place to tell Snoop but can one of you guys tell Tjay?"

"Yeah," I volunteered, "I'll do it. I'll do it right now and get it over with." I took one hit off the joint and walked out the front door and back up the stairs to begin the short journey to Tjay's house. He only lived around the corner from Kenny, so I figured I might as well just walk over, to give myself time to compose a little speech, something that wouldn't be hurtful. Tjay was a nice guy and a talented musician. On the way there, it suddenly occurred to me that we had joined the group at the same time, and now, only a few months later, he was being fazed out.

But, even though Tjay and I had the *Da Capo* album and the time-line connection, we never really hung out together at all. I mean, I had been to his pad a couple of times with Kenny to smoke dope, but it was mostly him and Johnny. We only interacted at rehearsals and gigs. So, when he answered the door and saw me standing there, I think he knew something was up. Like, some kind of negative group business bullshit.

"Hey, Michael. Come on in, man." As soon as he closed the door behind me, Tjay's pet monkey, Train, descended from his T-bar perch in the corner of the room and raced across the floor to greet me, arms extended in the universal sign toddlers use when they want to be picked up. I reached down and Train grabbed my index fingers and, pulling himself up my arm, the monkey climbed up onto my right shoulder, where he sat triumphantly, suddenly the tallest man in the room.

Tjay walked over and carefully plucked Train off my shoulder. "Better let me take him, Michael. Sometimes he bites even when he's happy. Actually, sometimes he bites because he's happy. The excitement factor, you know?" Tjay returned the monkey to the T-bar perch in the corner and handed him a piece of banana. Tjay motioned for me to sit down. I didn't waste any time with small talk. I got right to it and told him about Arthur's plans for the new album. It was hard to be the bearer of such bad news.

When I finished what I had to say, he studied the floor. "Yeah, I thought it might be just a one album deal, but that's O.K." He scratched his beard and looked up, forcing a thin smile. "It's not like I've wasted my time, or anything. I've been playing music for more years than I can count. I have a lot of friends and ex-bandmates in the business, and frankly I've been looking forward to getting back to playing more pure jazz, not the hybrid stuff that LOVE plays. That's where my heart is."

Tjay stood and walked over to a bureau. Then he picked up a small gold frame and held it in his hand, gazing down at the photograph. "I guess the thing I'm most grateful for is the 'one percent group membership' recording contracts you and I signed when we joined, Michael. I never told any of you guys this but I have a little girl. She lives with her mom. I made up my mind to put that one percent into a special fund just for her. All of it. And I won't touch it. Then, I will have done something for her. Something valuable and important to help take care of her someday and show her I love her. See?" He handed me the frame. It was a picture of Tjay's little girl. She was about four or five years old and she was laughing, like kids do when they're little and uninhibited, and without a worry in the world. Her hair was dark, like Tjay's, and kind of messy, as if she had been interrupted while she was playing to stop and pose briefly for the snapshot.

"She's beautiful, man." I gave him back the picture.

Tjay gently returned the frame to its place on the bureau. "A few weeks ago, I asked Arthur when the group could expect to start getting our recording percentage royalties, so I could get that account for my daughter set up. He told me there was a few more thousand bucks owed to Elektra on the recording debt and, as soon as that was paid off from album sales, we would all start getting our checks every quarter for as long as the album sells. And, hey, *Da Capo* could sell for a long time, right?"

I nodded, "Sure it could."

We talked for a while about his plans for the future and about his little girl and pretty soon I said, "Well, Tjay, I have to get going." We shook hands and wished each other "good luck," and I told him we'd be seeing each other around, and I left.

Walking back down Kenny's alley, toward his house I noticed he was bent over the front fender with his head under the hood, still tinkering, but when he saw me coming, he leaned out and slammed the hood closed. Then he began to put the tools back in the toolbox. "How'd he take it?" he wanted to know.

"Tjay'll be all right. He's got other stuff going," I told him. Kenny cleaned up, then we went inside and fired up the hash pipe and listened to some music.

We'd only played a couple of songs, when there was a knock on the door. "Oh, jeez. That's my neighbour. My stereo's too loud, again." I mean, Kenny had gone to a lot of trouble and expense to have the interior of his living room covered with studio grade acoustic tile, even the ceiling, but when he cranked his stereo up, some of the sound always managed to leak out a little bit, anyhow. And it was a pretty quiet neighbourhood.

Kenny set the pipe down and walked quickly over and turned the volume down, then he went to the door and opened it. The neighbour had been over to complain about the stereo before when I was there, several times. A thin, bald dude with only a ridge of hair around the perimeter, dark moustache and a very baritone-professional voice. He was a character actor in several hundred films. No exaggeration. He played the record-label partner of Elvis' love interest in *Jailhouse Rock*, for one. I swear, he's in about one out of every ten movies you see on AMC. Almost.

"Excuse me, but I'm trying to take a nap and your stereo is keeping me awake again," he resonated. "I wonder if you can turn it down." He always said the same thing, like it was scripted.

"Oh, I'm sorry. Yeah, I'll turn it down," Kenny mumbled. Then he closed the door. Kenny was always polite to the neighbour. I mean, he never gave him a ration of shit or anything, because of all the drugs he kept in the house. It was sort of an unspoken deal they had. "You turn the stereo down, like a good boy when I ask you, and I won't tell the police about all the drugs you and your friends use."

Because it's common knowledge, if you're breaking the law, you have to be careful, an angry neighbour can get you sent to prison. So, Kenny was usually a pretty good sport about the stereo, but this time he came back shaking his head. "Man, that guy pisses me off. His dog barks all the time when he's gone and I never complain. It bugs the hell out of me, too."

"You say, the dog only barks when he's gone?" I asked him.

"Yeah, why?"

"Well, the dog's just never been trained properly, that's all. Didn't you bust out Johnny's window with a BB gun, one time?"

Kenny smiled, "It's still busted, too. Johnny never got it fixed."

"And doesn't your window look right out over that dude's back yard?"

The thing is, dogs usually bark for bullshit reasons, anyway. A dog is supposed to bark when a burglar is climbing over the fence or something, but when do they bark? They bark whenever they feel like it, and for entertainment, most of the time, to maybe get a conversation started with some other dog down the block. And they get away with all that racket because their owners are too lazy or too busy or too gone to tell them to shutup. That's why I didn't feel guilty or anything. About the plan.

A few hours later, the character actor woke up from his nap and Kenny and I saw his Corvette drive past his house and down the hill on the way to the studio. So nobody was home. Right away the dog started up.

"BOW, WOW, WOW, WOW!" On and on. I looked out the window into the neighbour's back yard and a big German shepherd was prancing around like he owned the place. Which, in a manner of speaking, he did. "BOW, WOW, WOW, WOW, WOW, WOW!" Louder, this time. Really irritating.

"Go get the BB gun, Kenny. You have to take some of the wind out of this dude's sails, that's all. Now's the time to do it."

Kenny took the BB gun out of his closet and positioned himself at the window, resting the barrel on the sill. "BOW, WOW..."

"POP!!" Kenny nailed him in the butt. The dog yelped and jumped about two feet straight up into the air, turning at the apex to look at the spot where Kenny shot him, like "What the hell was that?! Did I get stung by a bee or something? That makes me want to bark some more! BOW!"

"POP!!" Kenny nailed him again, in the same spot. The dog shut up and tried to hide under the deck, except his butt was sticking out a little bit. Just enough. "POP!!" One more time to really drive the point home. The dog whimpered and tried desperately to scoot further under the deck.

I placed my hand on Kenny's arm. "That's enough, man. In psychology, that's called 'conditioning'. You just conditioned your subject to avoid barking." After that, Kenny told me, whenever his owner left or if a cat got into the yard or if another dog barked somewhere, the German shepherd would just hunker down under the deck and stare at Kenny's window with a real guilty look on his mug. Because he was thinking about it.

Around six, Kenny and I were back outside, fooling around with his Jaguar again when we heard a car coming down the alley. It was Arthur's black Porsche. He pulled over and stopped next to where we were working and when he got out of his car, he looked kind of sad and upset.

"What's happening, man?" I asked him.

"I hope I don't have another day like today for a long time. I can't handle it." He took his hash pipe out and packed it. "Let's go in and smoke. I got some new blonde Afghan. It's pretty good." So, Kenny and Arthur and I went inside and listened to music and smoked the pipe for a while.

Finally, Arthur asked me, "How did Tjay take it, man? He O.K.?"

"Yeah, he's got plans to do other things." I told him. "How about Snoop?" Arthur shook his head.

"I guess he's all right. Snoop's been with us for a long time. It had to be done, though. I had no choice, man. We can't afford to carry those guys around on our backs another day, you know? I've booked studio time in June, so we have to start rehearsals for the new album right now. We got to get rollin'. Snoopy and Tjay would've just been excess baggage." Arthur removed a vial of coke from his shirt pocket and poured six lines out onto a copy of *Downbeat*, then he did his two and handed the tooter to Kenny. Kenny did his, then handed it to me.

After I did mine, I stood up. "Well, I'm gonna go home and check on Snoop. I'll see you guys later." I took one last hit off the hash pipe and then I left.

Driving up Beechwood, I passed Snoopy's girlfriend going the other way. Her face was all red, like she might have been crying. When I got to the house and opened the front door, I saw that Snoop had most of his stuff all packed and ready to move out. "Well, Michael, it was nice being your roommate, man. I'm outta here."

"Wait a minute, Snoop. Don't move. Stick around. This is still your house, too." Frankly, this whole turn of events had been so sudden and unexpected, I hadn't had time to think this far in advance. What about my living arrangement? If Snoopy was going to move out, I would be here alone. That wouldn't be any fun. The Beechwood pad was a pretty big house and I needed a roommate if I was going to stay in it.

As he continued gathering his belongings, he shook his head. "I can't live here, Michael. Not on the money I'll be making from now on. Linda and I have a place picked out down in the flats. A duplex. Fortunately, the landlord said we could move in tonight. As soon as Arthur gave me the bad news, I got right on the phone and called a buddy of mine I knew was looking for a new drummer, so I have a gig already lined up with another group. I start playing with those guys tomorrow night. He'll be here in a minute, in fact. He has a van and he's helping me move to the new pad. Really, man, I never felt comfortable on keyboards, anyhow. I'll be glad to get back on drums. Everything's cool. Don't worry about me." He began to stack his clothes and his equipment over by the front door.

A van pulled up to the curb, Snoop turned and shook my hand. "Take it easy, Michael. By the way, I hear Johnny's looking for a new place to live, so there you go. You're all set. He called a little while ago, and I told him to call back later, when I knew you'd be here."

Snoopy's new bandmate came in and he introduced us, and I helped them load his stuff into the van and then he was gone. Just like that.

A few hours later, I got that call from Johnny. We talked about the rehearsal schedule for the new album. Then he told me he had to move out of his house, and I told him Snoopy's old room was his if he wanted it. So, the group membership number was reduced from seven to five, and our lead guitarist, Johnny Echols, became my new roommate.

Johnny had around twelve or fifteen guitars, acoustic Spanish, acoustic American, twelve-string, six-string, single-neck, double-neck, everything. He was one of the top guitarists in Hollywood playing with a name group, so some of those guitars were on open-ended promotional loan from manufacturers seeking the group's endorsement. Meaning, they didn't really care if they got them back or not. He usually kept a small amp in his room and spent a lot of time tinkering and practicing, experimenting and fooling around, or just listening to his stereo. Johnny had a reel-to-reel tape deck that he used to record the results of those experiments, and to aid in the self-hypnosis ritual he performed nightly, around three in the morning.

He had made a tape of himself playing some really soft acoustic stuff and then he over-dubbed himself saying, "You will listen to MY VOICE, MY VOICE... You will relax and your mind will peter off into infinity..." or something like that. Whatever it was, it must have worked because every day he always looked like he had been sleeping the night before. Anyway, as soon as he moved in, he got settled into his new bedroom, with his guitars and his tape and everything, and we got along real good. Except Johnny still didn't have a car.

A car is a funny thing. To some people, a car is a very important gizmo in their lives. It can stroke your ego. It can be a big part of your identity and serve your lust for spontaneity. It can take you as far as you want to go, as fast as you want to go, wherever you want to go, with musical accompaniment. A person can test the limits of his ability, or just cruise. And the visual effect of a car, the design, is nothing less than art manifested in utility. A car is alternately exciting and soothing.

A car is beautiful. It's so powerful, but you have power over it. It can be an influential component to your mental well-being. When you're not with it, like if it's somewhere in a strange parking lot, you hope it's O.K. and that nobody else is touching it or scratching the paint. You wax it, you change the oil and give it a tune up yourself, if you know how, and you don't even mind laying down on the ground and getting dirty and greasy because it's fun. Having a great car is a lot like being in love, only better, because if you suddenly decide you're tired of it, you can sell the thing and buy a newer, better, faster car without feeling guilt, like you would if you dumped your girlfriend. After all, it's just a hunk of metal and rubber. It has no feelings.

Or: a car is just a way to get from one place to another. A lot like riding the bus, but it's smaller and you have to steer. That was Johnny. He hated the responsibility that comes with owning a car: the insurance, the driver's licence, stopping to buy gas, dealing with traffic, all that business. He thought of a car only as a liability, a financial burden. So, when his Jaguar sedan got itself towed away from in front of Arthur's pad, he said to himself, "Fine, I don't really care. I'll just get a ride from now on."

As soon as Johnny became my roommate, I became his ride – which was O.K., actually, because we were good friends and bandmates and went to all the same places. Besides, I have serious doubts as to whether or not Johnny could have supported a car long term, even if he had wanted to. He never had any money. He made the same money as the rest of the guys in the group but he didn't like hanging on to it. If we went up to play a two-night gig at The Fillmore, we usually got paid for the first night as soon as we went backstage after the second set, sometimes a grand or two apiece. On the way back to the hotel, Johnny would buy some dope and maybe take a few friends out to eat. Then, the next day he would wake up and go shopping, buy a new leather coat, maybe some boots or a new guitar to add to his collection. By late afternoon, the money he had made the night before would be gone. And after the second night's performance, it would start all over again. Before the group went to the airport to fly home the next day, all the money he had earned that weekend had oftentimes dwindled to zero.

As Johnny's guitar style was free-spirited, so was his philosophy of money management. I guess, because our basic living expenses (rent, utilities, etc.) in addition to a weekly allowance of several hundred dollars each were covered through Schlessinger and Tabor, we had all developed a false sense of financial security and, with it, a tendency to regard our concert money as "extra cash". Nevertheless, the rest of us always came home with most of what we had earned on the tour. Not Johnny. He literally spent his like he was trying to get rid of it. It was almost as if he had no use for money itself, just what it would buy. That concept of putting something away for a "rainy day" had no place in Johnny's life at all. Funny thing is, each and every one of us had every reason to believe that rainy day might come. And soon. Because, while Arthur and Bryan put those finishing touches on the songs that would appear on *Forever Changes*, our performance schedule became sporadic, at best. We went from travelling and playing almost every weekend, to every other week, then only one weekend out of three. *Da Capo* was still on the *Billboard* album charts somewhere, still deserving promotion, but, somehow, we couldn't fit performances into our schedule.

The thing is, everybody knows, once a rock group has a fanbase, the formula to perpetuate success isn't complicated. You record the music, then you have to play as often as possible, in as many places as possible, as soon as possible, to help sell the records. In the words of the old farming axiom, "You got to make hay while the sun shines." But this next album was different. It had to be recorded on its own schedule. The touring and performing would have to wait.

During this period of relative inactivity, there was one scenario that played itself out over and over. My phone rings. "Hey, Michael, this is Humble Harve. Are you guys busy on the sixteenth of July? I'd like to book the group into the Santa Monica Civic. The Doors will accept second billing. What do you say?"

"Well, I say have you spoken to Arthur? He does all the booking, you know."

Suddenly, gloom would permeate the telephonic atmosphere. "Yeah, I mentioned it to him a couple of weeks ago, but he didn't seem too interested. I thought maybe if you talked to him... You know what, man? LOVE is a hard act to book!"

"Sorry, Harve, but we're getting ready to record a new album. There's nothing I can do." And Johnny and Kenny and I would spend the sixteenth sitting on our butts, getting high and waiting for Arthur and Bryan to hurry up and finish writing the *Forever Changes* album. In the beginning, these phone calls bothered me a little, but after a while I got used to it. Still, it seemed like our timing was off, as if we were letting something slip away. Sometimes I found myself thinking back to that conversation I had with Arthur, before *Da Capo* when he told me how he looked forward to retirement.

Before long, rehearsals started to pick up to meet the deadline for the recording dates set for the *Forever Changes* album. It had become apparent from the outset that the orchestration on the new album was going to be intricate, and the guitar parts especially difficult. The charts on the new material would require more technical skills than any of us had previously been forced to display. Much harder than what was demanded on *Da Capo*. Concentration would be a key element. But after so many months of relative inactivity, we were all a little out of practice, and because of the nature of the work we had to do, mistakes were more glaring. It was difficult stuff.

In retrospect, it probably would have helped us sharpen our skills if we could have played this material live, in front of an audience a few times, to get comfortable and fine tune out all the mistakes, and get us used to the concept of a deadline. Then, when we got into the studio, all the energy we were having to put into bearing down and trying real hard not to make a mistake could have been channelled into exploring the limits of our ability and riding the groove. But if we had played the tunes in public, the content of *Forever Changes* wouldn't have been a "secret" anymore, so I don't know. What I do know is that we were behind schedule and we weren't approaching the recording of the album in the right frame of mind. The bottom line is, time was short and the parts were still a long way from where they needed to be.

The recording of music is a very exacting blend of science and art. There are a lot of things you can get away with on stage that you could never get by with in the studio. Most of the crowd at a concert wouldn't notice the occasional wrong note or muffed pattern, but on record the listener will hear that note or that pattern over and over, every time he listens to the cut, so if somebody hits a bad one, it's "take two" – or twenty, or one hundred. You can't let it go. And studio time is expensive, so you've got to hurry up and get it right. Once you're in the studio, you can't dilly-dally.

We began to worry a little.

As we packed our instruments up after the final rehearsal before the *Forever Changes* sessions were to begin, Arthur walked into the room loading the hash pipe. "Don't anybody leave. Ronnie's on her way over to take the picture for the liner note side of the album, right now. We're gonna use my back deck."

So, we sat and smoked and listened to music for a while. Before long, Ronnie arrived. Johnny put on his white Cossack hat and lit a fresh joint, and we all strolled out onto the back deck.

"You guys stand over there against the far railing," Ronnie directed. "That's where the light's the best." Johnny turned inward, toward the rest of us and placed his hands together, as if in prayer. As I stepped back, my foot brushed against a white Mexican-style vase, containing a bouquet of dead flowers. It fell over and broke in half. Arthur looked down then he bent over and picked up the two halves. Grasping the top half of the vase with the dead flowers by the handle in one hand and the bottom half in the other, he looked up at Ronnie, "Take the picture."

Chapter Thirteen

The Trouble With Cars

A FEW DAYS before we went into the studio, I was sitting on the couch upstairs, drinking a cup of coffee and listening to a McCoy Tyner album, when I heard Johnny coming up the stairs. I looked up. "Hey, Johnny, what's going on?"

"Well, Michael, I'll tell you, man, I want to buy another car, but I don't feel like going out shopping for one at a used car lot, or anything. Do you know somebody that has a car for sale?"

"I don't know, let me think for a minute." I remembered that I had run into my old band mate, Jac, from The Sons of Adam, a couple of weeks before, and he had mentioned to me that his new group was doing so well, he was about to buy a new car and dump the '58 T-Bird he had owned for the last year. I debated back and forth with myself whether or not it was wise for me to put myself in the middle of this thing, but, against my better judgment, I eventually went ahead and gave Jac's number to Johnny, and they set up a meeting so Johnny could give it the once over.

Later that afternoon, Johnny and I piled into my car for what I assumed would be the last ride I, or anybody else, would have to give him, ever, over to Jac's house; and on the way down the hill, I told him, "Look, man, I really don't know anything about the shape this car's in. It used to be O.K. but Jac's had it a long time and he's not exactly a car buff, so check it out pretty good, before you give him any money. How much does he want, by the way?"

Johnny stared straight ahead. "Three hundred bucks. You think it's worth it?"

I shook my head. "I have absolutely no idea, man. That's for you to decide. Even when I was in The Sons of Adam, I never rode in that car. This is your transaction."

I had ridden shotgun in Jac's old car before, the one he had before the T-Bird, only twice, and twice was two times too many. Jac was an awful driver. Too aggressive. No skill. To top it off, Jac had worked as a cab driver in Baltimore, before he and Randy and Mike had moved west, and during that time he had picked up this frightening habit that big city cab drivers routinely use to help them manoeuvre through heavy traffic. It's called "making a place where there isn't one."

What he would do, if he wanted to change lanes, was abruptly jerk the wheel in the direction of the lane he wanted to move into without even looking over there first at all. THEN, he would nonchalantly look over his shoulder, and casually change lanes. Because, after the horn-honking had stopped and the other cars that had been there were finished swerving to avoid a collision, there would always be plenty of room for him to get over, no problem. So Jac always carried lots of toilet paper for his passengers. I mean, it's a dangerous move that's most effectively performed in a vehicle like a cab because their bright yellow colour gives them a high level of visibility – and other drivers expect that kind of thing from cab drivers. But I guess you can do it in any car you want, as long as you don't mind picking up a few scratches and getting flipped off all the time. That's why I never rode with Jac.

Johnny and I pulled up in front of Jac's house. The T-Bird was parked in the driveway, looking as well as could be expected. Jac saw us arrive and came outside. When we got out of the Porsche, Jac and Johnny talked about the car and then he told us about his new band. After a little while, Johnny drove the T-Bird around the block a few times. When he got back, he had a smile on his face and he said he was satisfied with the condition of the car and he and Jac went inside to exchange the money for the pink slip.

The irony of the situation was palpable. Here, the lead guitarist from my group, LOVE, a band which had already earned the respect of its peers in the recording industry, not to mention an international following of fans, was, from financial necessity, about to buy an old, beat-up piece of junk from my ex-band mate, Jac, to use as his only source of transportation. I mean, we hadn't played a paying gig in so long, we were all running out of money, for Christ's sake.

Before they went inside, I said my goodbyes to Jac and told Johnny I'd see him back at the house. Then I left to run a couple of errands.

Heading up Durand, I noticed a familiar face in my rear-view mirror. It was Snoopy. He had a couple of girls crowded into his two-seat red Corvette, they were smiling big, holding up a fat joint and pointing up the road. I nodded and signalled for him to follow me. When we arrived at the house, Snoop pulled into his old parking place in the carport, next to my Porsche, they all piled out of his Corvette, the girls fired up the weed and we just stood around in the carport for a while, talking over old times and catching up on new ones.

"My new group's doing good, Michael. Shit, man, I don't make nearly as much per gig when I play with these guys, of course, but we work all the time and the money's decent." Snoopy looked calm and happy and everything seemed peaceful in his life. "I can't afford a house like this one, anymore, but I've got a nice pad down on Gardner I like. I hear you guys are ready to go back into the studio. How's it going?"

"Aw, everything's cool."

But as we hung around out front in the carport, talking and smoking and horsing around with the girls, I became aware of some sort of auditory disturbance way off in the distance, a clanking sound, mixed in with an unending series of small explosions. As we broke off our conversation and looked in the direction of the approaching noise, a plume of smoke belched, still several blocks away, but the thing was heading, without question, toward us.

"What is it?" one of the girls asked, with a hint of concern.

I knew what it was even before I saw it coming around the corner. It was Johnny's new T-Bird, barrelling full bore up Durand, like a runaway calliope. Obviously something important had gone wrong after he left Jac's house but, instead of pulling over to the curb and stopping to address the problem, like he should have, he decided to try and make it home. No matter what. A move suicidal for the T-Bird, because Durand was a challenge for any car, even one in excellent running order – which, obviously, the T-Bird wasn't. At least, not anymore. As we all looked on in disbelief at the mechanical nightmare gallumping toward us, it slowed to a crawl and Johnny leaned his head out of the driver's side window.

"Get your God damned car out of my space, Snoopy!" he screamed, waving his arm as if to say, "Hurry up!" And with good reason. The T-Bird was only seconds from shutting down, permanently.

"Well, nice seeing you again, Michael. We're down at The Brave New World. Come see us, man," Snoopy said, making a game stab at a polite goodbye. Then they quickly piled into the Corvette and roared off. Johnny nursed the short-timer, lurching and hissing, into the carport. He turned off what was left of the motor, got out and, without bothering to close the car door, went into the house and, I assume, down the stairs to his bedroom to lie down for a while. On his way in, he gave me a look that said, "Thanks a lot, Michael. I really needed that." I followed him inside to offer support.

See? I knew I'd get the blame if something went wrong. Never get involved in a car transaction between friends. I couldn't believe it, really. Johnny hadn't even made it home from buying it, without the thing breaking down. What are the odds of that happening?

About a half-hour later, when I went back out to check on the T-Bird, several small funnels of steam were still rising from around the perimeter of the closed hood, and there were puddles of yellow and pink and brown fluid on the carport floor. A bad smell filled the air. It was dead. In a few minutes, Johnny emerged from his bedroom lugging the reel-to-reel tape recorder he used to listen to his self-hypnosis tape. "Michael, give me a ride down to the pawn shop so I can hock this thing, will you?"

The next day, Johnny and I pushed the T-Bird out into the street, so it could be ticketed and towed and, eventually, taken to city impound where I assume it was squished. Of course, Johnny never filed the change of ownership, so Jac was probably stuck with the towing fee.

A few days later, the group had a photo shoot, which was scheduled to take place in Laurel Canyon, with Bill Harvey, the photographer Elektra contracted to do most of their stuff. We had all agreed to meet up in front of Arthur's old pad on Brier, then walk up a little dirt path to a remote spot on the side of a hill.

It seemed like everything was scheduled at one p.m., and today was no exception, so you know, we were there at the appointed time, me and Arthur and Kenny and Johnny and Bill Harvey... but no Bryan. He was late, as usual, and after we stood there a while, making casual conversation and ignoring the obvious, Arthur finally started going off, "You know what man?.. That motherfucker Bryan doesn't give a shit about anything, you know? He doesn't care about this group at all!," and the rest of us were saying stuff like, "Yeah, you're right, man," which only added fuel to the flames, of course, like when the congregation shouts, "Preach, preacher!"

Bill Harvey excused himself, "Well, he'll probably be here in a minute. I'll go ahead and get my equipment ready and load my cameras," and he walked over to his car and opened the trunk and started fiddling with things.

"You know what we should do?," Arthur continued, "We should fire his ass! Bryan doesn't even belong in this band!" We all continued murmuring, but a little less enthusiastically, still offering support to Arthur's diatribe, but saying things now more like, "Well, I guess..." and kind of trailing off, figuring Arthur would cool down when Bryan finally arrived, like he always did.

Sure enough, in a couple of minutes, Bryan's car made the turn onto Brier and pulled up in back of my Porsche. He got out, checked his hair in the side-view mirror and walked over to where we were standing. "Hi guys," he said.

Arthur was ready for him. "Hey look Bryan, we've all been talking, man, and we think it would be best if you weren't in this band anymore, right fellas?" He looked around at us for what he thought was the agreed upon and pre-arranged affirmation.

But Johnny and Kenny and I were all of the same unspoken mind... although Bryan could be insufferable and arrogant at times, he was, after all, a valuable member of the group, and we were much better with him than we would ever be without him, so we all began to say things like, "Well, I don't know, man..., you know, he's here now, so let's just go ahead and do the shoot."

Arthur's eyes widened, "Oh, well, hey thanks motherfuckers!" He was mad and humiliated because he ventured way out on the limb and we all kind of chopped it out from under him. "Come on and let's go take the pictures, then!" and he stalked off and up the little dirt path, with us following apologetically behind.

When we got to the place on the side of the hill, Bill Harvey kind of positioned us, then, Arthur said, "So, are you ready, Bill?" and when Bill replied he was, Arthur says, "OK, hold on a minute." Then, he started taking off his clothes, until he was finally standing there all barefoot and naked except for a black bathing suit. Then he said, "OK, go ahead."

Bill slowly and deliberately set his camera down on the ground, then folded his arms across his chest, "Hey Arthur, Jac doesn't want any pictures of the band with you in a bathing suit. It's a waste of time and film for me to take pictures with you in a bathing suit. I'm not taking any pictures until you put your clothes back on." But eventually he did take a roll or two, because it was kind of a Mexican stand-off and Arthur usually won those things.

Chapter Fourteen

Forever Changes

IN JUNE of 1967, the group was scheduled to finally make its way into the studio to begin recording *Forever Changes*. On the first day, as Johnny and I gathered our equipment and made final preparations, there was an unexpected knock at the front door. When I opened it, Arthur brushed his way past me, announcing, "I'll give Echols a lift." He looked around. "Where's he at?" I heard Johnny's bedroom door open and close and then he emerged at the bottom of the stairs, carrying a guitar case.

"Let's go, man." Johnny slapped Arthur five and they headed out the front door. "See you down there, Michael," Arthur yelled over his shoulder. Then, they climbed into Arthur's black Porsche and drove off in the direction of Sunset Sound.

It had been decided early on that Johnny, Bryan, Kenny and I would lay down the basic tracks of all the songs, then studio musicians, strings and horns would be added, and finally the vocals. Something else was decided, as well. The Elektra execs who had made visits to RCA during the recording of *Da Capo* thought it might be a good idea to keep a second recording unit rolling continuously to capture the humorous interplay and verbal barbs that were always such an entertaining part of LOVE sessions. For posterity.

But there were serious problems from the outset. On the first day, as we prepared to lay down the first instrumental cut, with everybody in position behind the baffles and ready to go, Johnny and Bryan couldn't get their guitars in tune. They tried and tried, but no dice. Eventually, somebody went out and got one of those electronic guitar tuner-uppers and brought it back to Sunset Sound. Arthur, having no instrumental responsibility, was sitting in the booth with the engineer, occasionally flipping the switch to make verbal contact with Johnny, Kenny, Bryan and me. Sarcastic chit-chat, I think it was.

"It's probably those new strings we put on, Johnny," Bryan volunteered. But as they worked feverishly to hurry and tune up, Arthur was yammering over the booth microphone, engaging in what was supposed to be "humorous interplay", but it wasn't making it. Nobody was responding. The verbal barbs were mean spirited and inappropriate, and they made the others in the studio uncomfortable. Even at this early stage, we realized that the constantly rolling conversational tape was a barrier to cohesive creativity. It was erecting a wall between us, and it was something else to worry about. We couldn't relax and play the music because, as long as the tape rolled, we felt an unspoken responsibility to be funny. We wanted to get rid of it, but like HAL in the movie, *2001: A Space Odyssey*, the tape seemed to have a life of its own. Nobody knew how to shut it off, diplomatically, because to stop it now was to admit that had been a bad idea in the first place, so on it rolled.

After Johnny and Bryan had tuned up, we launched into the first take on Daily Planet. But after only a few bars, Arthur's voice came in over the studio speakers,"Hold it, hold it!" We stopped playing. "Let's try it again." The mic was left open and you could hear somebody in there talking something over with somebody else. Then finally: "Let's try it one more time, guys." So we did. But the next take was shut down prematurely as well. Same with the third and fourth.

"Let's take a fifteen-minute break, fellas," the voice in the booth said. So Johnny and Kenny and Bryan and I all went out into the hall, where the Coke machine was, and got Cokes. Then we kind of stood around in an uncomfortable silence, nobody saying a word. I had a clear shot through the little glass window in the studio door and, looking back into the booth, I could see Arthur and the Elektra exec and the engineer, all huddling up, apparently trying to come to some kind of decision that would resolve the problem. Bryan and Johnny wandered off down the hall to discuss the guitar difficulties, Bryan gesturing on an imaginary fretboard, Johnny nodding.

I looked away from the big powwow in the booth and took a sip of my Coke. "Kenny, what do you think, man? We gonna be able to get it in time?"

He shook his head. "Uh-uh. We should have seen this coming, man. We haven't been practising hard, like we should have."

He had that right. As far as I could tell, Johnny and Kenny and Bryan and I hadn't spent a lot of time going over our parts on our own at all. We were all relying on the time we spent at group rehearsals to get to where we needed to be musically to record the album. Problem was, there just wasn't a sense of urgency at these rehearsals. We got high too much. Even during the final rehearsals, just before the group went in to record the album, it didn't sound like it should have. We simply figured that, when we got into the studio, it would all come together. We were wrong.

I guess the thing that should be understood about drugs is that they don't necessarily spell the end of a productive and successful career. A habit isn't exactly the kiss of death, but it's awfully close. Not enough of the stuff, you're nervous and jittery; too much and you're a tick slow. So, it's real important to get the right balance, a near impossibility considering all the variables. But a lot of great musicians have been able to juggle the habit and career without losing their balance and falling into the toilet. The bottom line was, it was beginning to look like we weren't going to be able to pull this thing off right away.

Arthur and the Elektra rep had finished their discussion and somebody leaned out into the hall and said, "O.K., let's come on back in and try it one more time." So, we settled back in, Bryan counted it off and we slid into the beginning of 'Daily Planet'. Almost immediately, somebody made a mistake.

Arthur's voice came in over the music, loud and clear. "All right, that's it. Stop." We ground to a halt as Arthur exited the control booth. He was followed by a beleaguered company rep. "O.K., gather around, we gotta have a meeting." We all climbed out from behind our baffles and walked over to where Arthur was standing. "Look, we've been talking." He nodded to the rep. "This could go on forever, so here's what we decided. Elektra's willing to pay to hire studio cats to come in here and lay down, not just the string and horn tracks, but the foundation tracks as well. Everything. It could save us a lot of money in the long run, and it's not like you four won't be on the record, because we all have vocal parts, and there'll be some instrumental overdubs on a lot of the cuts, which you guys will do. What do you say?"

Incredibly, Bryan, Johnny and Kenny started shaking their heads and saying things like "Well, maybe you're right, man" and "Yeah, maybe it would be better." I just had to walk away. This is what it had come to? Give up? So quick?

"It's settled, then," Arthur concluded. "The studio cats'll be here tomorrow, but you guys be here too. Elektra wants your input on the kind of stuff we want these dudes to play. It's still gonna be our album."

Oh yeah, right. But during this little conversation, I had watched a veil of doom lift from the faces of the group's members: a reprieve, a stay of execution! Everybody tried to look disappointed, as if to say, "Well, hey, we could have nailed it if you had just given us a little more time." In a way, that probably would have been correct because, in the world of the recording industry, four takes is nothing. To cut and run after four takes is jumping the gun a little. But our expressions said most of us didn't want "take five". We were off the hook. We weren't gonna have to sweat and cry and worry and practice real hard to get our parts right, after all. And, even on a simplistic level, I could see Arthur's perspective, too.

Because, there was another agenda at work here. And, with a little creative planning, this latest turn of events might speed things up somewhat. Simply put, for what it's worth, Arthur was the most important dude in the group. So much so, that it was really unfair for the band to have a name that didn't reflect the individual talent and the recognition he so richly deserved. Actually, instead of "LOVE", it should more appropriately be known as "Arthur Lee and LOVE" – like "? and The Mysterians" and "Rosie and The Originals" and "Tommy James and The Shondells". Or better yet, no "LOVE" at all. Forget the "LOVE". Maybe someday it should be just "Arthur Lee". Yeah. A solo career. Everybody in the group had begun to realize that's what Arthur coveted. It was no secret.

Of course he was the most important dude in the band. So what? Let's all acknowledge that little fact and get on with the business at hand. Making records and touring. It was self-destructive and a complete waste of time and energy for us to get into a "Who's the most important member?" purse fight. "You're the most important guy, absolutely. Take the title, it's yours." I don't know, maybe if I had been Arthur, I would have felt the same way. I mean, everybody's selfish to some extent. The problem was LOVE, the group, had another prolific singer-songwriter as a member who was just starting to come into his own. His work had begun to rival anything Arthur had ever done, in originality and artistic beauty; and even though Bryan Maclean had a wealth of material to contribute to the current album, he had been told, in no uncertain terms, that he would be limited to two songs per album from now on. That was the new rule. Like it or don't like it. Arthur was having a hard time holding Bryan back, and he knew he probably wouldn't be able to do it for much longer.

Arthur was feeling the heat. He was starting to look over his shoulder. He was still the main guy, all right, but I think, in his mind, not by much and maybe not for long, if he didn't keep a tight rein on things, given the current trend. This latest exercise in strategy might help him buy some time and put a little distance between himself and Bryan, as well as between him and the group. Kill two birds with one stone, so to speak.

The next day when we got to the studio, it was pretty damn crowded, what with studio cats, producers, Elektra reps, engineers and us, the odd pigs in the litter. Everybody was all set up and ready to go when we got there. Right away Arthur and the company rep called us over and asked me and the other band members what we thought should be played during a certain segment of a certain song – you know, to make us feel needed. It was a joke. But, nevertheless, I was kind of curious to see how long they would take to knock out the first track.

I looked across the studio and swallowed hard. They had brought in Jim Gordon to play the drums. I suppose if he was good enough to tour with the Everly Brothers, he was good enough to do the LOVE sessions. As a matter of fact, the last time I had seen Jim Gordon, he was onstage at the Hullabaloo Club with the Everlys, taking a big swig of that Coke my friend Skip had helped prepare down in the basement. But he saw me come into the studio and he waved me over behind the drum baffles and introduced himself. We talked drums for a few minutes, and he asked me what kinds of riffs I thought he should use, and stuff like that. He was cool. The bass player they brought in to replace Kenny was a woman,

Carol Kaye; but while she and Kenny were sitting there, going through her part on 'Daily Planet', and Kenny was showing her what he thought she should play to give it the "LOVE sound", Arthur overheard and said, "Shit, Kenny, what you're playing sounds pretty good. You go ahead and play the bass part on this tune, and we'll give her a guitar part to play instead." So they bumped Carol over to guitar. She plays that opening, "Daing, ding ga ding-ding, ga ding, diang ding ga ding-ding, ga ding..." and Kenny plays the bass part.

But the studio people (plus Kenny) didn't exactly get it right on the first take either, and after the fourth or fifth take Carol started complaining that the sliding up and down the fretboard necessary to play the part was getting to her fingers. You know, because she wasn't really used to the guitar, and bass strings are nice and big and soft, and guitar strings aren't. They're skinnier.

"Let's try and get it on this next one, O.K.?," she said between takes. "This part's hurting my fingers." I guess they weren't really trying to get it before she piped-up, because sure enough the very next take was a keeper, which was a good thing. She was getting pretty aggravated.

But, truth be told, as clean and technically correct as the track sounded, and in spite of the studio people being, in most respects, better musicians than Johnny and Kenny and Bryan and I, when they were through and we listened to the results over the studio monitors, it sounded like plastic. Another day at the office. It stunk, really. So, later on, after we all went home and several hours had passed, I wasn't even shocked when the phone rang and it was the Elektra rep who had been present at the session.

"Michael, I'm calling all the guys in the group personally to talk over something real important. Tell Johnny to pick up the extension, will you?" After I yelled down and Johnny joined us on the line, the rep explained, "Look, I just spoke with Bryan and Kenny and Arthur and I told them what I'm about to tell you guys. Elektra signed LOVE to a four-album deal because we were convinced you guys had a special sound that the record-buying public would appreciate. That crap we heard today was about as far from what we had in mind as I can possibly imagine. The fans won't like it. What we want, at this point, is for the group to take as much time as it needs to get it together and come back into the studio and record this thing right. O.K.? Not studio musicians. The band. LOVE. We're willing to wait. You guys tell us when you're ready. This idea Arthur came up with about the studio musicians taking over recording the foundation tracks isn't going to fly. It's gonna have to be you guys, all right?" And we hung up, me and Johnny and the rep.

That was it. No giving up. No sneaking out the back door. Just us and hard work, as much as it was going to take to get it right. I could almost feel everybody suck it up. That night, at home, Johnny began to woodshed the guitar parts that had been giving him difficulty. For the next few weeks, I heard the unmistakable sounds of him practicing for hours on end in his bedroom. And I could hear him getting it, the licks coming together and sounding good.

I set my drums up in my own bedroom and began going over the basic rhythms and the fills, all the parts I had written, track by track, until I could play them without a hint of a flub. Then, one morning, I was sitting at the breakfast table, drinking coffee, and Johnny came pounding up the stairs and made his way over to the coffee maker and poured himself a cup. He sat down in the chair across from me, blew into the cup, across the surface of the coffee to cool it a little, then took a sip.

"Hey, I think I'm ready, Michael. In fact, I know I'm ready. You ready?"

I nodded, "You bet." Then Johnny just reached over and picked up the phone and called Bryan and Kenny and said, "You guys got your shit together? O.K. then, what are we waiting for? Let's go in and do it." So, Arthur rebooked studio time, and we went on back down to Sunset Sound, and Johnny and Bryan and Kenny and I knocked the tracks out, one by one, just like we were supposed to do, as a group.

The first order of business when we came back into the studio, was for us to lay down a new instrumental track to 'Andmoreagain', which the studio people had recorded as well, so we did. Elektra kept the lone testament to the presence of the studio musicians, the instrumental track to 'Daily Planet'. Then, we recorded the instrumental tracks to 'Live and Let Live', 'The Good Humor Man, He Sees Everything Like this', 'You Set The Scene', 'Bummer In The Summer', Bryan's story of the sage advice offered by, the 'Old Man', then right down the line. The next day, when Johnny came in to add the acoustic guitar part on 'Andmoreagain' to the foundation Kenny and Bryan and I had already recorded, I added some drum fills to Jim Gordon's track on 'Daily Planet,' as well..

Elektra publicity shot for the *Forever Changes* line-up

After all the instrumentals were down, we came back in and recorded the vocal tracks. A few months earlier, when Bryan was showing Arthur 'Alone Again Or', Arthur had said, "Yeah, that's a good tune. What do you call it?" and Bryan said, "I don't know yet. I thought I might call it, 'Alone Again,'...or..." and Arthur said, "Yeah, that's good, call it 'Alone Again Or'." Predicated instrumentally, on a theme written by the Russian composer Prokofiev, and decorated with a flamenco edge, it was, of course, a song about a guy who's been left alone and he loves being with people. Loneliness or solitude... perspective is reality. Arthur, Bryan and I sang three part harmony off of one omnidirectional microphone set up in the middle of the studio. I sang the low harmony part.

'Old Man' and 'Alone Again Or'. Those were the two songs Bryan was allowed.

Arthur's songs seemed to be, most often, based on his observations of our society and the world in which we live... be it the brutality of war, ambulance sirens filling the Los Angeles airwaves and dying, or simply the conversations of people walking briskly between Clark and Hilldale, ("Hello, how are you and how have you been?")... and his conclusions based on those observations. But then again, sometimes his songs were, "...just about some chick," as he was prone to patiently explain, to those who would dare interrogate him. One of the few exceptions was, 'The Good Humor Man, He Sees Everything Like This'.

What happened was, just before we started the early rehearsals for *Forever Changes*, Bryan took to wearing a white dress suit almost all the time when he was out in public, like the one Colonel Sanders, the KFC guy, wore; and in the South, they call those all-white suits, "Ice Cream Suits", because they're all white, like vanilla ice cream, and Arthur thought it was funny. So, whenever Arthur would encounter Bryan wearing that white suit, he would always say, in a loud voice for all to hear, "Hey, Bryan's wearing his ice cream suit again. Haw, haw!" It was more or less, a running joke, with Bryan as the butt. You get it, right? The Good Humor ice cream man? You know him... he's the guy in the little Good Humor ice cream truck that makes the rounds in most American neighbourhoods in the summertime? He usually wears a white suit, as well.

Then, Arthur also regularly gave Bryan a hard time about the lyrics to his songs, like 'Orange Skies', and 'Softly To Me', lyrics referencing, "Orange skies, carnivals and cotton candy and you", and, "...orange, sugar chocolate and cinnamon and lovely things...". "Why do you always have to write about happy shit?!," he would demand rhetorically. Arthur felt like Bryan's lyrics didn't really fit the character of the band. He was like embarrassed by them, I think, because they weren't badass enough, or, at all. They were the opposite of badass, actually.

So, anyway, the lyrics of Arthur's tune, 'The Good Humor Man, He Sees Everything Like This', his song about, "...little girls wearing pigtails in the morning," and hummingbirds humming, particularly when combined with the title itself, was a relatively transparent critique of... well, like I said, an observation and a conclusion, as usual, but not of the world or society in general; of Bryan, it was, and of the way he "sees everything". So I guess it's not really an exception after all, but merely a slight adjustment in the target.

I mean that's just my take. Arthur and I never sat down and had a heart-to-heart about 'Good Humor Man', but if it walks like a duck it usually is.

On, 'The Red Telephone' I sang the "Ahhh"s, the "sha, la, la, la, la, la,"s, and on the line, "...paint, me," when everybody says a different colour, I said, "white." Cool part, huh?

After we laid down the first instrumental, we all gathered in the control booth to listen to the overall sound and check the product. As far as I knew, this was Arthur's first attempt at producing a record and every time I glanced up through the booth window, he had been standing over the engineer's shoulder, gesturing, kind of telling him what to do. They didn't seem to be communicating too well, so I made a mental note to pay close attention and listen with a critical ear to the drum mix to make certain I didn't get lost in the shuffle. Sure enough, as soon as the engineer cued up the playback, after only a few bars, I could hear the mix on the drums wasn't right – and not just the drums: other things were wrong with the overall sound as well. Things were slightly out of balance and muddy. But I didn't want to say anything right away because I knew the mix was Arthur's baby and I didn't want to embarrass him in front of the engineer and the company rep so, later, I took him aside out in the hall and told him, "Listen, Arthur, the mix on the drums is too thin, not enough presence. Check it out."

Elektra's pre-release *Forever Changes* billboard, over the Liquor Locker on Sunset. Fall of '67

    Before I could get to the other issues, Arthur looked off in the distance and threw up his hands in disgust, "Man, that's exactly what's wrong with this group! You're looking out for yourself, Kenny's telling me the volume on the bass needs to be up, it's every man for himself!" He turned and walked back into the studio, shaking his head. And he never re-evaluated the mix, at all. Never even gave it a second listen, just to see if maybe I was right. Which I was.

    "So, that's the way it is, huh?" I thought. "After all this time, just hurry through it?" I mean, the bad mix was so obvious, I figured Arthur would most certainly notice it on his own, sometime before production wrapped up, so I left it alone after that. I thought, "Maybe he was just a little resentful that it was me that noticed it instead of him. Maybe, when the time is right and nobody's looking, he'll correct the thing." But several months later, on the very day the album was due to be released, when it was too late to fix it, my worst fears were realized when Arthur approached me at a rehearsal.

    "Hey, uh, Michael," he began, self-consciously, "I just wanted to tell you, that you were right about the mix. We'll get it right on the next album though, O.K. man?" But his affirmation that he had screwed up lacked any tone of remorse. No apology, or anything. Not even a simple, "Sorry for being such a know-it-all."

    "Yeah, sure, Arthur. Next album."

    We were through recording *Forever Changes* in September of 1967 and a release date was set for December. Elektra had arranged for a billboard ad for the group, and the album, to go up at a high profile location on Sunset, right where it meets Laurel Canyon Boulevard, the heart of the strip.

    The day the ad was to be erected, my phone rang. "Michael," it was Bryan, "Come pick me up and let's go check out the billboard, man. A friend of mine just told me it's up." Actually, at that point, none of us had seen the proposed album cover design, which we knew to be the same as the billboard and I was curious to see what they had come up with. I hopped in my car and picked up Bryan, and we drove down Laurel Canyon. As soon as we turned right on Sunset, there it was.

    "Watch for the third coming of LOVE", the caption read. The artist, Bob Pepper, had taken the portrait stills of us, shot by Bill Harvey at Terry Melcher's house, and drawn them in a kind of psychedelic caricature, arranging them so that together they formed an organic heart. My face was right in the middle. Lime green. Red hair.

    "Hey," Bryan complained, "he put you in the middle." But then, "Uh oh, we've been busted. That dude caught us cruising past our own billboard." Bryan jerked his thumb in the direction of a guy in another Porsche, which had slowed to a crawl next to us.

The stranger was making eye contact and pointing to the billboard and nodding and smiling and giving us the thumbs up. "Let's get out of here." Bryan sounded miffed. "My picture doesn't look like me, at all. I don't like it."

A few weeks after the billboard went up, the group began preparations for a few short tours to promote the album. Most of the tour rehearsals were held at Arthur's new house in Laurel Canyon, a house located at the tip top of Kirkwood, up a single-lane dirt road, all by itself, actually. No other houses within a mile or so, in the middle of the Hollywood Hills. Off the deck, stretched a view of Los Angeles, clear to the ocean. There was a large, circular fireplace in the centre of the living room, bordered by an indoor-outdoor pool. The property was so unusual, it had been used as the set for most of the first Peter Fonda/Dennis Hopper collaboration, *The Trip*.

I think the plot of the movie was, more or less, they take some acid and spend a lot of time "tripping" around Arthur's house. Sounds pretty shallow but, in the mid-sixties, audiences were horny for any entertainment involving psychedelic drugs; so *The Trip* eventually became a "cult classic". The only specific thing I remember about the film, is that, at some point, Peter Fonda starts freaking out and he runs over to the utility closet, near the front door, crawls inside, closes the door and hides from the acid monster. The same one Snoopy was always trying to escape.

Arthur kept all Self's dog food in Peter Fonda's utility closet. You know, those big twenty-five pound bags of Purina? When I told Arthur about the scene in *The Trip* where Peter Fonda hides in Self's food closet, he said, "Yeah, I hide in that closet myself sometimes."

One day, when I was the first to arrive for a rehearsal, Arthur yelled out from the bedroom, "There's some hash on the table, Michael, help yourself. I'll be out in a minute." I sat down on the couch and reached for the hash pipe. Then, noticing a small book Arthur had left laying out, I absent-mindedly picked it up and looked at it. *How To Write A Song*, the cover read.

"No shame in hitting an occasional flat spot in the creative process," I thought, firing up the pipe. "Arthur must use this for a jump-start when he gets stuck. 'Writer's block' and all." Hey, no doubt about it. Writing is a heavy burden but, nonetheless, one Arthur had chosen to carry, so I didn't mind giving him the needle a little bit when he walked back into the room.

"What's this, man?" I asked, tossing the book back onto the table.

Arthur moved quickly over to where the book lay, retrieved it, and threw it in a drawer. "It's not mine," he answered impatiently. "Somebody left it over here."

Arthur took his black Gibson out of its case and began tuning up, "I think I hear Bryan. Let him in, will you, Michael?"

I opened the front door and, sure enough, there stood Bryan holding his guitar case in one hand and a big bag in the other. Like, a grocery bag. He walked in and set the grocery bag on the kitchen counter and pulled out a six-pack of beer. Yanking one free from its brothers, he popped it open and took a long swig.

"Hey, Michael, you want a beer?" He opened his guitar case and removed his guitar and started tuning up.

"I don't know," I answered. "Maybe in a little while. I have to finish setting up my drums." I wasn't in the mood for a beer, actually, but I didn't want to seem rude. Arthur had re-entered the room and was staring at Bryan chugging the beer. Finishing the beer, actually. Bryan was one of those people who can drink a whole six-pack all by themselves. Crumpling the empty can, Bryan threw it in the trash, then asked, "Want a beer, Arthur?"

Arthur snorted indignantly, "No, I don't want a beer. What's the matter with you, man? Why are you bringing that stuff around here? I thought you had been putting on weight, lately. Is that it? The beer?" Arthur's tone was disapproving and condescending, like, "We're a drug band, fool, not a beer band. You trying to blow the image? What if somebody finds out that you're drinking beer? Our reputation'll be tarnished."

"I don't know," Bryan responded, "I like beer. It tastes good and on days like today, when it's hot and I'm about to sing, it makes my throat feel good."

You could see Arthur, kind of thinking that one over. Maybe Bryan had a point. "All right," Arthur finally decided, "One beer each rehearsal. That's all. One. Now get the rest of those beers out of my house. Take 'em back out to your car. You've had your one for today." Sieg Heil.

But, ever the gamesman, Bryan had a plan. The next day, when he arrived for rehearsal, he was nursing beer from one of those enormous German mugs, steins, whatever... It held three beers at least; but Bryan wore a nonchalant expression, like, "What are you looking at? You said 'one', this is my one." But Arthur made him go pour it out, anyway.

Chapter Fifteen

Kenny's Pad

AFTER *Forever Changes* was completed, I accepted an offer to move in with Kenny into a spare bedroom of a house he was renting in Laurel Canyon. The Beechwood house had come completely furnished, with kitchen utensils, beds, couches, stereo, everything, so I didn't have any furniture to move, just small stuff. Kenny came over and gave me a hand with my clothes, my drums, my bedroom stereo, and we did the move to his pad in a couple of trips in our cars.

Whereas the house on Durand was located in the hills above East Hollywood, a more or less, upscale residential neighbourhood, Laurel Canyon, where Bryan, Kenny and Arthur lived, was positioned above West Hollywood, where the clubs operated. Where the action was, as they say, thereby attracting a larger population of music and movie industry professionals. Kenny and I had always gotten along, and we hit it off as housemates right from the beginning, just as Johnny and I had. He was usually happy and upbeat and he was a neat and clean freak, like me.

Kenny had recently moved out of his house on Lookout Mountain and into a new pad on Kirkwood. It was well laid out for two people and it was canyonesque, and came completely furnished, like the house on Durand. It had a gas fed fireplace that we always kept going at night, and in the morning the heat from the fireplace flame was perfect for shag-drying your hair after a shower.

The stereo always played music by Charlie Parker, John Coltrane and Tito Puente... I don't think Kenny owned any rock'n'roll records, at all. If he did, he didn't play them when I was there. But, more than anything else, the thing that we shared was a profound interest in – a passion for – cars. Talking about cars, restoring and working on them, doing stuff that didn't even need to be done, like the easy stuff that you usually pay other people to do for you but you can do yourself if you're interested. After I moved in, our nightly schedule included rolling a couple of joints and taking them down to our garage where we worked until the early morning hours.

Kenny had spent the last six months restoring his Jaguar to mint condition. The original mustard-yellow had been covered by a high-gloss jetblack lacquer, and the small dents and surface rust had been removed. Cracked white-walls had been replaced by new Pirelli radials and the standard wheels by tuned spokes. Even though, in 1967, the car was still only four or five years old, it had been neglected by the first owner almost past the point of no return, beyond the possibility of restoration. But Kenny had brought it all the way back. It would eventually be better than brand new, actually. Much better. I mean, my Porsche was a great-looking car in excellent condition, but Kenny's Jaguar was special, pristine, immaculate. It literally glistened. Every time we took it into Hollywood, heads turned and we were recognized.

One typical night, about a month after I moved in, I was in the bedroom, cleaning my drums, when Kenny opened the door and poked his head in. "I'm going downstairs to work on my car, you coming?"

I threw the rag down and put the top back on the cleaning solution, "Yeah, man, I'll be right there."

We had only been in the garage a few minutes, when, out of the corner of my eye, I caught a car rolling to a stop in front of the house. It was an E-Type Jaguar, like Kenny's, but all beat-up, with little dents and rusty paint and primer spots. It looked a bit like Kenny's Jag had when he first bought it. The front bumper hung crooked, like the driver had recently hit something. A tall dude crawled out of the Jag and approached us. "Excuse me, fellas, but I wonder if you could help me? I'm trying to find Stanley Hills Drive. Would either of you know where it is?"

There was something really familiar about the driver of the beat-up Jag. The voice, so professional and resonant. The walk. I had seen this guy someplace before. "Sure," Kenny offered, "You're on the wrong street. This is Kirkwood, and Stanley Hills is off Lookout Mountain. Go back down to Laurel Canyon and turn left, it's the next street up."

He smiled, "Thanks a lot, I never would have found it." Before he left, he pointed to Kenny's black Jag. "That sure is a nice Jaguar you have there." Kenny nodded, and the stranger climbed back in his car and drove away.

Kenny picked up the container of wax and wiped some out onto a towel, "Poor Charlton Heston: he led the chosen people to the Promised Land but he can't find Stanley Hills Drive."

Suddenly, a Fiat came screaming up Kirkwood and the driver, a kid who looked to be about seventeen, gave Kenny and me a big wave, then pulled into a driveway several houses up the street. In a few minutes, the unmistakable strains of the group's second album *Da Capo* filled the air. It wasn't the first time we had heard our music played over a speaker that seemed to be set up to serve the neighbourhood, but we had never been able to figure out exactly where it was coming from. "Hey, that must be the fan who always plays our albums when we're hanging around outside," I said to Kenny.

"Yeah," he responded, "he likes The Doors, too. The kid plays their albums night and day, real loud. Maybe it's Jac Holzman's nephew, you think?" He went back to waxing the Jag.

Our next-door neighbour was a real cute girl named Karen. She did a lot of gardening, so I saw her working out in her front yard almost every day, and we often stopped and talked. I learned, early on, she had a job as a secretary for somebody at Capitol, and she lived alone.

One day as I backed out of my driveway, she waved me over. I pulled up next to the curb and leaned over and rolled down the passenger side window. "Hi, Karen, what's up?"

She seemed worried and nervous. "Michael, I'm having a little problem with my new neighbour on the other side, that strange guy, David."

"What kind of a problem?"

"Well, I don't know him, or anything, except to say 'Hi', but lately I've caught him watching me through the window, and occasionally he does it when I'm sunbathing in the back yard, but, you know, from his own house. I'm beginning to wonder if he's a 'peeping Tom'. He's not sneaking around in the bushes or anything, but it's starting to make me feel self-conscious, like I'm a prisoner in my own home. I think I'll have a talk with him the next time it happens. I guess I just wanted somebody else to know what was going on, in case there's trouble, God forbid, but I really think if I just confront him and embarrass him a little, he might stop."

I told her I would try and keep an eye on the situation, and to let me know if there was anything I could do to help, and I drove away. I knew what she meant about David being strange. He was a big beefy dude with a crew cut and a faraway look in his eye. Once, when he first moved in, I saw him out front, just sitting in a lawn chair, smiling, for no apparent reason, so I went over and introduced myself and we talked for a while.

"I was just discharged from the Marines," he had said, "and I didn't have anyplace to go so I came here." I remember thinking at the time, he seemed so lonely and pitiful, and nice enough, but big. In fact, he looked really out of place in Laurel Canyon. David was one of those guys that, if you were walking through a real tough neighbourhood, the kind of neighbourhood where you could get your butt kicked, you would want to be walking with David. Except that, actually, he seemed a lot like that Disney character, Lambert the Lion, who thought he was a sheep. Even though he was a little off, he seemed, more or less, incapable of doing anybody actual harm.

But, sure enough, a few days later, Kenny and I heard a female voice yelling something from outside. When we went to the front window, we could see that Karen had David cornered. She was shaking her index finger in his face and giving him the business about the staring routine. David appeared absolutely petrified. "Well, that's the end of that," I said, "I don't think we'll be hearing any more about David looking where he shouldn't be looking," and Kenny and I went back to the joint we were smoking. But we could hear that the kid up the street, the Elektra fan, had his stereo cranked up during this little confrontation. He was playing a Doors album, again.

The next time I saw David, I had stepped outside to tie up my dog, Bristol, so he could watch traffic as dogs like to. David was digging in his front yard so I thought, "That's good, no lasting emotional damage from the chewing-out he got from Karen" – by the time she had finished yelling at him, he had looked pretty hurt, and he was a nice guy, after all. When he saw me, he stopped digging and he waved and smiled, "Hi, Mike, how's it goin'?" He put the shovel down and began walking my way; the closer he got, the more apparent it was that he had something all over his face. Bruises and abrasions, things like that. And one eye was swollen shut.

"David, what happened to your face, man?"

"Well, I think you know, there's some pretty weird people around here, don't you? I mean, bad people."

"You better believe it," I said, "but who, exactly do you mean?"

He signalled for me to follow him into his house, "Come on in, man, I want to play a record for you." So we went into his house, where I had never been before, and he put on the first Doors album. "Listen to this song." He cued up the song that had been the background music for the confrontation when Karen chewed him out. "The other day, I was outside talking to Karen and somebody started playing this song and I realized The Doors had recorded a whole album of stuff making fun of my thing with Karen, because we like each other, you know. Listen to the words."

So, I did. But, of course, they had absolutely nothing to do with him or Karen. I played along, though. "I don't know, David, I'm not sure I hear the words you're talking about. Point 'em out to me."

"Right there! Right there, they are!" he yelled periodically. "Listen, Michael, the son of a bitches are ridiculing me, man!" His face got red and his brow furrowed as he stood, pointing to the stereo, like I had asked him to do.

"But, how did you get the cuts on your face?" My curiosity was starting to get the better of me.

He reached over and turned down the volume on his stereo. "Well, after I realized what they had done, I thought I should go on down to Elektra and have a talk with Jim Morrison and those guys, to set 'em straight. When I got there, the only guy in The Doors I could find was that piano player, Ray Manzarek, so I walked up to him and I said, 'What are you guys doing to me, man!?' and I punched him a couple of times in the face. Popped him pretty good, too. Sounded like I might've broke something."

I couldn't believe what I was hearing.

He continued, "All the women in the office, the secretaries and the receptionist, started screaming and Ray fell on the floor and he was thrashing around begging me not to hit him again and he was bleeding real bad, so I figured it was a good time to get out of there. And I did."

"But how'd you get the cuts?" I wanted to know the rest of the story.

He smiled self-consciously through split lips, "That's when I made a mistake. After I had walked a few blocks, I started feeling bad about busting Ray up and I went back to apologize. I thought it was the right thing to do under the circumstances. As soon as I opened the door to the studio, somebody yelled, 'There he is!' A bunch of guys jumped me and I don't remember anything after that until I woke up on the sidewalk."

What you have to remember about Disney's Lambert the Lion is that, at the end of the story, he lost his temper and the ferocious lion personality took over, and he put the hurt on the wolf that had been terrorizing the flock. Just like Lambert, David had simply remembered, for a moment, he was a lion and not a lamb.

The following morning, bright and early, there came a tremendous banging and pounding on our front door. I heard Kenny yell, "Who is it?" as he rousted himself out of bed.

"It's Billy!" A voice responded. Billy was a fellow musician, who had made his mark earlier in the decade as a founding member of a highly successful surf band but had not, as yet, been able to make a successful transition to the new rock. He was still struggling to find a niche. He and his wife Sarah lived in a house about a half a block from Kenny and I. Sarah was what you might call "voluptuous". She had the long hair and full lips and great big knockers that caused most men to stare shamelessly when she walked down the street. When Billy was out of town, she was known to frequent Hollywood clubs like The Whisky with her girlfriends, and to drink a lot. About a week earlier, Billy had mentioned that he had a temporary gig coming up with Sky Saxon and The Seeds for a short tour up the West Coast.

Like The Doors, The Seeds didn't have a bass player. In the studio and in small clubs, the keyboard bass did a semi-adequate job of filling in the low end but, in a large venue, it sounded shallow. Therefore, Sky had decided to experiment with carrying a bass player for live performances for a while, to see if he liked it. The problem was, this was an era during which the individual members of the groups got practically as much recognition as the lead singers, and Sky wasn't real sure that he wanted to add the bass player, permanently. So, he came up with a plan.

"Sky wants me to wear something over my head when I'm onstage, like a hood," Billy told us. "I'll be billed as 'The Mystery Bass Player'. People won't know who I am for a long time, and it'll cause controversy because all The Seeds' fans will wonder, 'Who the hell is this guy?' And then one night onstage we'll take off the hood and Sky will introduce me as the newest member of the group. The fans'll talk about it and the critics will write about it, see? It'll be good publicity. A good way to break me into the group." That's what he had said. So, for the past several days, Billy had been out on this tour with a hood over his head and now, evidently, he was back. Knocking on our door at seven a.m.

I heard Kenny padding down the hall in the direction of the front door, "All right, all right, I'm coming," he mumbled. I figured, "I may as well get up, too, and see what the noise is all about." So I went into the living room and turned on the stereo and started to roll a joint.

When Kenny opened the door, Billy kind of stumbled through it. Kenny had to grab him by the arm to keep him from falling. He was totally distraught and his eyes were red, like he had been crying. "Do you guys know what just happened? I wasn't scheduled to get home 'til tomorrow, you know? But the last gig cancelled and we flew back a day early. Well, I just walked in my house and found some dude in bed with Sarah, asleep. It was so dark in there, at first I thought it was one of Sarah's girlfriends, you know, spending the night to keep her company while I was gone, but then I realized, 'No, man, it's a guy!' And like, he didn't wake up, right away, but Sarah did. She saw me standing next to the bed and real quick, jumped up and told me to be quiet and took me out to the living room, because she figured I was about to start yelling. Which I was. But then, I thought, 'To hell with this bitch!' I just went and got my gun out of the drawer of the bedside table, man. I was gonna blow the motherfucker's head off. But then, about that time, the dude woke up and he realized what was happening, and he saw me with the gun, so he jumped up and grabbed his pants and ran out the door. The whole time he was yelling, 'Don't shoot me! Don't shoot me!' Like, he was begging me and all, so I didn't shoot him." Then, Billy started crying, again.

"When did all this happen, man?" we asked him.

"About five minutes ago, man! Do you guys think I should forgive her? I can't live without her. I'm gonna forgive her," he announced, with determination. "I'm goin' home right now and tell her I forgive her." In a flash, he turned and ran out the front door and down the stairs and was gone.

"That's sad, man. I'm going to make some coffee." I fired up the joint and handed it to Kenny and went into the kitchen. Kenny put Tito Puente on to lighten the mood. Billy was back in about fifteen minutes, crying even harder than before. He staggered in, holding a half-empty bottle of bourbon.

"She doesn't want me to forgive her, she's gonna leave me! She already has her clothes packed and she told me she's going to move in with that guy I caught her with. His name is Roger, for Christ's sake!" Billy spent the next half-hour or so stumbling around our pad, crying, taking an occasional swig of the bourbon and saying how he couldn't live without Sarah.

Every so often, when one of us could get a word in edgeways, Kenny or I would interject words of encouragement: "Don't worry, man. You'll find somebody else" and "Hey, Billy, things'll look better tomorrow. She'll probably change her mind when she's had time to think things over, anyway. You wait and see." But everything we said, just seemed to make things worse, not better. He was miserable, inconsolable, despondent. He just kept staggering around in circles and moaning and groaning until, finally, he wandered into the kitchen and flopped down face first on the floor. "Boom!" I know it sounds mean, but Kenny and I ignored it, because by this time Billy's act had started to get a little old. I mean, we felt sorry for him and all but enough was enough. Get over it, man.

After the Tito Puente record was through playing, and we had finished smoking the number, I looked over at Kenny and said, "Well, you wanna go check on our guest?" When we entered the kitchen, Billy was laying on the floor unconscious in the centre of a pool of bourbon, still clutching the empty bottle. "You grab his feet, man, I'll get his arms." We picked him up and carried him over and threw him on the couch, so he could sleep it off.

He never did get that permanent gig with The Seeds, either. And Sarah didn't change her mind. She moved in with the new dude, who turned out to be a pretty nice guy, actually. Sarah introduced us once. He was a concert promoter or something. I used to run into him from time to time at restaurants and clubs on The Strip. We always exchanged pleasantries, our common ground being Sarah. One day, several months after the incident with Billy, I saw the new dude, Roger, walk into the Hamburger Hamlet with another girl, not Sarah.

I waved and he came over to my table. "Hey, Michael, I'm not with Sarah anymore." He smiled, sarcastically. "You won't believe what happened. I came home early one night and caught her in bed with somebody else, a sixteen-year-old kid! You know the first thing I thought? I should have known: if she would be unfaithful to Billy, she would be unfaithful to me, too."

Chapter Sixteen

Daisy and The Bear

SOMETIMES, I guess because of their geographical proximity, the Hollywood scene kind of leaked over into the Beverly Hills scene. In the fall of 1967, while the group continued to rehearse for the tours we would soon take to promote *Forever Changes*, Bryan and I began hanging out at a small, private club on Rodeo called The Daisy.

It was owned by Jack Hansen and his wife, Sally, and was the type of place where, any night of the week, you would find yourself sitting next to the top celebrities in movies and TV, mostly. Not the music business, too much. Johnny Carson and Ed McMahon came in a lot, just the two of them, and sat at a table and drank and cracked each other up, non-stop. Dick Smothers was there just about every night.

Once, when we heard loud voices coming from the direction of the foyer-entrance, Bryan and I grabbed our drinks and strolled over to where we could hear a little better. There wasn't really a lot to do at The Daisy, so eavesdropping was a favourite pastime of everybody in the club. And, because it was recorded music, not a live band, you could usually hear stuff pretty good if you wanted to. But, in this case, Bryan and I didn't have to try too hard.

"What the hell is the matter with you, Maurice?" Dickie shouted at the doorman. I told you not to tell my wife I was here, if she called, didn't I?"

Maurice tried to apologize, "But Mr. Smothers, I'm sorry, sir, I didn't realize it was your wife. It'll never happen again, I assure you."

However, the damage had been done and Dick was not accepting the apology by any means. In fact, he continued to berate poor Maurice for several more minutes in front of everybody before finally, mercifully, ending it and walking away in disgust.

Aaron Spelling and his beautiful young wife were there quite a bit, too. She had an unusual habit. If Aaron had to go to the bathroom, she would get up from her seat and follow him, a step or two behind, and then she would stop at the bathroom door and wait for him to finish – "standing guard", as it were; when he came out, she would escort him back to his seat. It was like she was afraid that if she let him go alone, he might not come back out. Like he might crawl through the bathroom window and run away. Or, maybe, another woman might intercept him on his way back to the table and drag him off someplace. She did it every time. Everybody used to poke each other and point and snicker, but Aaron didn't mind. I think he was kind of proud that his woman was so jealous, or protective or worried. Whatever, it looked odd as hell.

Bryan and I used to get free booze at The Daisy. The bartender was a LOVE fan and he used to pour us straight shots of tequila and serve them to us in coffee cups, because coffee was complimentary. Anybody that saw us sitting at the bar, getting drunk on the tequila (like the guy who had to purchase the booze for the club), would have thought Bryan and I were just drinking the complimentary coffee, so no big deal. But actually we were getting high as kites and drunk as skunks for free.

Off the foyer of The Daisy was a pool room; on the wall near the entrance to the pool room hung a framed photograph of a shit-eatin' grinning Jack Hansen surrounded by ten or twelve Playboy bunnies. "Playboy's Man of the Year", the caption read. 1965 or 1966, I don't remember. Bryan and I spent a lot of time in that pool room because, even though there were two or three tables, we were nearly always the only ones in there playing pool. So, it was a peaceful way to get away from the noise in the main room, where the regular members liked to hang out and float from table to table and make deals and hobnob.

One night, after Bryan and I had drunk just about all the "coffee" we could handle, we went into the poolroom to get away from the crowd. When we had been playing for a few minutes, a gnarly-faced dude with a big nose and a gravely voice, poked his head in and asked Bryan and me: "You guys want to play some Eight Ball?" It was ex-Dodger manager, Leo Durocher, famous for, among other things, being responsible for the expression, "Nice guys finish last." I recognized him because, when he walked into the club, somebody at another table had said, "Hey, look, it's Leo Durocher." I think I probably would have recognized him anyway. His face is so... unique.

We said, "Sure, we'll play you, man." So, he yelled for his buddy to come on in. Then, Leo and Bryan lagged to see who would shoot first. Leo won the break lag and I racked the balls up and then Leo started to run the table. After a few shots, Bryan and I and Leo's partner all found seats up against the wall and just kind of sat there, holding our cues and watching the show. He played like a pool legend, not the "Gas House Gang" baseball legend he was, banging in the balls seemingly without even looking at what he was doing. Never took more than a second to line up a shot. He couldn't miss.

In 1918, when Leo was a thirteen-year-old kid, he made enough money hustling pool to wear what was, at that time, expensive $75 custom-made suits. By the late sixties, he hadn't lost a thing.

I was glad Bryan and I were drunk. As George C. Scott said in *The Hustler*, it would provide a nice excuse for losing. But, in Eight Ball, you have to pick solid balls or stripes and stick with your choice. After you sink all of one or the other, you call a pocket and fire in the eight. That's usually how you win. But so many of our balls were still there on the table (all of them) that, by the time Leo got to the eight ball, he couldn't get a clear shot. When he tried to make the last shot in what should have been a decisive victory for him and his partner, he missed, he "scratched" on the eight. When a player scratches on the eight ball, he loses the game.

As soon as he missed, Leo looked real disgusted with himself and threw his cue on the table. "Well, you guys win," he grumbled.

Right away, Bryan and I started saying sympathetic stuff like, "Aw, that's a shame, Leo. That's too bad. You guys really deserved the win." But when we got back out in the main room, I remember we told several people, "We just whipped Leo Durocher and his friend in a game of pool." I don't think we mentioned the scratch.

Even though The Daisy was a private club, the membership system was very indefinite. Really, to get in, you just had to be "somebody", or know somebody who was. I mean, there would be a knock at the front door and Maurice the doorman would slide back the cover to the peephole and, if it was a regular guest or a celebrity, they would be let in. Bryan and I had never been invited to become members. We both simply happened to be good friends with the hostess.

One night, on the way to The Daisy, we found ourselves sitting at a red light at the corner of La Brea and Sunset. "Hey, isn't that Arthur?" Bryan pointed to a large black sedan across the intersection, idling at its own red light, belching what appeared to be coolant from the tailpipe. "He's in his new Bentley." But, of course, it wasn't new: it was used. A "classic". Old. Hence the smoke from the tailpipe.

"Looks like he's blown a head gasket, or something," I said. Abruptly, the smoke stopped and Arthur's light turned green. Even though the other cars around him began to move forward, his Bentley sat still. A few of the people stuck in back of Arthur started honking, then it belched again and Arthur slowly inched the giant sedan ahead. "He's still got the Porsche, right?" I wondered aloud.

LOVE in performance at Torrance High School
Los Angeles

"Oh, yeah," Bryan waved as Arthur drove past, "but he likes to take the Bentley. He's just had it a few days." Arthur, his eyes fixed on the road and his face contorted with anxiety, hadn't acknowledged Bryan's wave as he passed us. He looked ridiculous in that thing, like Jack Benny in his prized Maxwell. I guess he thought it was some kind of status symbol. The next day, rehearsal was cancelled so Arthur could take the Bentley into the shop and get the head gasket fixed. He belonged in the Porsche, anyway.

In December of 1967, we booked a concert at The Blue Law in Torrance with Canned Heat. This building was like a rec centre, located in the heart of a typical suburban Los Angeles community. The stage had no private rear entrance or dressing rooms, and the groups that were scheduled to perform simply walked through the front door, past the people that had come to see them play, and right up the stage steps.

When we arrived, about twenty minutes before Canned Heat's set was due to end, the place was jam-packed, but room capacity was only seven or eight hundred, tops. Why Arthur accepted these types of bookings was hard to figure because it seemed, throughout our career, we regularly turned down opportunities to play festivals of legendary proportions so we would be free to hang around L.A. and play gigs like The Blue Law. I think we even played a high school assembly in Hawthorne once.

We had been told by the promoter at The Blue Law that we could use the drums and amps that belonged to Canned Heat, so all we would have to do is wait for them to finish their set and then walk up on stage, plug in – I could sit right down – and start playing. Their first set was to end a few minutes before ten; ours was due to begin at ten sharp. About a quarter to ten, Arthur, Johnny, Kenny, Bryan and I walked over and stood by the refreshment bar, out of the way, to wait for them to finish.

Ten o'clock came and went and Canned Heat was still going strong with no obvious signs of wrapping up. Frankly, they had a strong following and a single on the charts ('On The Road Again') and a large segment of the audience was there to see them, not us, even though we had top billing. And they were rockin'. Canned Heat had a stage mannerism that always got the crowd going pretty good. It was the "head bob". Their bass player, The Mole, did it best. He would look down at the floor with his squinty little eyes, so you couldn't see his face at all, and bob his head real hard to the boogie beat. Bob "The Bear" Hite, Blind Owl, they all did it sometimes, but Mole did it constantly, on every song. In fact, I don't think he could not do it whenever he played. He had to do it to play right. On this night, as they neared the end of 'On The Road Again', they were all head-bobbin' and boogyin'. The crowd was going wild.

I glanced over at Arthur, standing next to me, and he was kind of smirking and glaring and shaking his head. Occasionally he checked his watch impatiently, irritated as hell to be kept waiting. Finally, around twenty after ten, Canned Heat played the last few notes of their first set and unplugged their guitars and, to enthusiastic cheers of appreciation from everyone in the audience, got the hell off the stage. We climbed the stage stairs and plugged in. I did a little rearranging of the drums. After a few minutes, we were ready to go. Arthur sort of half turned to us and barked, "John Lee Hooker!" and started counting it off.

"That's funny," I thought. "We never start with John Lee Hooker." It was our "boogie". And it was a real long song, too long for this kind of gig really. As soon as we broke into it, I had a funny feeling Arthur had something up his sleeve.

Sure enough, after only a few bars, Arthur started the "head bob". Then he looked over at Johnny and winked. Johnny started the "head bob", too – but both doing it really exaggerated: so much so, that Arthur nearly cracked his noggin on the microphone stand with every down-bob. But Arthur thought that maybe not everyone in the audience had noticed this little farce, so he grabbed his tambourine and began marching all over the stage. Stomping and marching and bobbing, driving the point home. Occasionally, he paused long enough to leer at the crowd, as if to ask, "Have you seen this bit someplace before? Doesn't it look stupid?" Then he would break into the bob again. Kept it up the whole time, too, almost.

When we finished our set, we walked off the stage to strong applause. There was enough applause for both groups. Plenty for everybody.

Chapter Seventeen

Bristol, Wolfgang and The Hells Angels

IN JANUARY and February of 1968 the group continued to work the L.A. area, in preparation for the East Coast tour that was to begin in March. We were booked into The Whisky, The Valley Music Theater, Cinnamon Cinder on Ventura, The Cheetah in Venice: local non-pressure situations where our regular fans could come see us in a relaxed atmosphere and we wouldn't have to leave home. And because it was a laid back time, spent hanging around our own area, each of us always invited a few personal friends to the gigs, and left comps for them at the ticket booth.

The dudes I always comped were four bikers named Moose and Dutch and Woody and Conrad. We met one night at The Whisky when Conrad approached me and said, "Hey, man, my name's Connie, we're neighbours. Can I stop by sometime?"

You could tell just by looking at these guys that they were real bikers, not like Peter Fonda and Dennis Hopper. Like Hell's Angels. They had the scraggly hair and the tattoos and the missing teeth, and they wore greasy Levi jackets adorned with club emblems, and rode the really loud, chain-driven Harleys, the kind of choppers that were built from scratch. You know, score a frame here, a motor and a gas tank there, spend a lot of time putting everything together just right and, after about eight months to a year, you have the finished product, each one a unique, singularly beautiful work of art. This common bond was the glue that held them together. They loved their rides. That simplicity and honesty was obvious and, in spite of their appearance, made them non-threatening and instantly likable.

So, I said, "Yeah, sure, man. You know where I live, come on over anytime." The next night, Conrad banged on my door and we sat around and listened to music and smoked some weed that he brought and he told me a little about himself. His dad was a doctor and his mom was a lawyer, and they lived back in Pennsylvania someplace with his younger brother – an upscale neighbourhood where he couldn't bear to stay, so he struck out for California. He quickly found his niche and bonded with the dudes in L.A. who rode Harleys. I soon learned that Conrad made enough money selling drugs to pay the rent and otherwise get by, so he didn't have to hold down a regular job or anything. But, mainly, Conrad was funny as hell. He would have made a great stand-up comedian, a natural. He looked a whole lot like the Zig-Zag Man. We shot the breeze for a while, then Conrad reached into his pocket and pulled out a container shaped like a machine-gun bullet. He took the cap off the shell and tapped four lines of crank onto a magazine.

"Try this shit, Michael. It's pretty good. Hey, stop by my house tomorrow. I'm only three blocks up the street. White house on the corner. You'll see my dog, Wolfgang, and my chopper parked out front. He won't bite."

Somewhere along the way, Conrad had acquired a big black stuffed wolf, which he had mounted on a platform with rollers, so that he could move it around. In the daytime, he kept it chained up to the gas meter outside his front door and at night he brought it in, just like a regular dog. He named it "Wolfgang". The taxidermist had done a real fine job on Wolfgang, right down to the expression. Arrogant, proud, ready to defend his territory, Connie's pad.

I had long ago gotten in the habit of taking my Irish Setter, Bristol, with me everywhere. Bristol loved to fight big dogs – I think he considered them a challenge to his manhood. Besides, he was a hella good fighter, so he liked to do it. I mean, he always won his fights and everybody likes to do what they do well. It's only natural. But a wolf is a pretty big challenge for any dog.

The next day, on our first visit to Connie's house, we rounded the corner and Bristol spotted Wolfgang standing out front. Right away he went into the trance he always used to psych himself up for a fight, shaking and whimpering and growling and glaring. I pulled up at the curb and turned off the engine. At the very split second I began to open my car door, Bristol forced himself between the back of the driver's seat and the door jam, squishing me against the steering wheel. He leaped through the open car door, charging full-throttle toward the immobile and defenceless Wolfgang, then slammed on the brakes mere inches short of making contact, kicking up a little dust as he slid to a stop.

"Hey, Michael, what's up?" Connie stood over the threshold of his front door, holding a can of beer. Bristol started to circle Wolfgang, growling, teeth bared, muscles taut, the red hair across his shoulders standing straight up. He was ready to go as soon as Wolfgang flinched. He would have a long wait. Wolfgang remained stoically at attention, not blinking an eye, his gaze fixed permanently on a telephone pole across the street. He didn't wanna fight.

Connie stepped out on the porch and handed me a beer. "Hey, Michael, you think Bristol and Wolfgang are gonna get it on? At least let me unchain Wolf first so he can defend himself properly, O.K.? It's only fair. Maybe I should get the water hose ready, in case we have a hard time breaking it up. Whaddaya think?"

Bristol never caught on. Every single time I took him over to Connie's house, he would go through more or less the same routine. He just couldn't figure it. Wolfgang looked so alive.

"Come on in, Michael," Connie said finally, "and bring Bristol. I don't want him to hurt Wolfgang." After we went inside and sat down on the couch, Conrad tapped out some lines of crank onto his coffee table glass, and we started watching that old black-and-white World War I war drama, *Paths of Glory*, with Kirk Douglas. There's a part in the movie where the French generals pick three scapegoats at random, to be lined up and shot as a lesson to the regiment – you know, to set an example – because everybody retreated during a battle, and the generals don't want them to do that kind of thing again anytime soon. So, the soldiers to be sacrificed are being led out to the area where they'll be executed. They're accompanied by a priest who is doing his best to comfort them and help prepare them for the next world. But one soldier is inconsolable and, being French, is full of emotion: crying, emotionally distraught, struck by the unfairness of the situation. They're walking slowly to the drumbeat of the death march. "Why, Father?" he cries, "Why me?" The priest is holding the condemned man's arm and pulling him along, offering words of support and encouragement: "Brace yourself, my son, brace yourself," he says, quietly.

Connie paused between sips of beer and snorted, "You mean I'm not even gonna get a wall?"

His favourite movie was *Electra Glide In Blue* because he just flat loved anything having to do with Harley-Davidsons, even if the central character was a cop. The part he liked the best was when Robert Blake and his partner are at the beach food stand and Robert Blake looks up at the real tall, beautiful chick next to him in line, smiles and says, "You know, Alan Ladd and me are exactly the same height, right down to the quarter-inch?" So I think he kind of identified with Alan Ladd. And Robert Blake. He liked the ending a whole lot, too, when Robert Blake gets blown off his motorcycle by a shotgun blast and dies sitting up on the highway asphalt.

One morning my phone rang. "Hey Michael, it's Connie. Can you get us in to that gig you guys have coming up in the valley, next weekend?"

"You mean The Valley Music Theater? Yeah, sure, I'll take care of it, man." So, when we hung up, I called the promoter and arranged for the tickets to be at the booth on the first night of the two-night gig. It was a theatre in the round, one of those deals where the stage goes around and around like at The Hullabaloo, but on a much smaller scale. All the paying customers have to stay seated. "Concert seating," I guess they call it. In other words: "no dancing allowed." Connie and Moose and Woody were sitting in the front row. Every time the stage rotated past them, they made faces and flipped me off and generally cut up, like bikers are prone to do. For some reason, it was the shortest gig we ever played. Just a single half-hour set. I think we were supposed to play longer, but we just didn't. At the end of the night, Arthur and I were walking out to the parking lot and Bryan, Johnny and Kenny were right behind us.

Connie was sitting next to the sidewalk on his Harley, warming things up. He waved me over. The bikes were making quite a bit of noise so, even though I was standing right in front of him, he had to yell. "Michael, you hear Woody broke up with his bitch?"

Woody shook his head and leaned back on his sissy bar, "No, man, I didn't break up with her. I just told her to get her shit out, that's all. Hey, Mike, thanks for the comp, man, but I got to know, how do you guys get away with it? You were supposed to play an hour and you didn't even play forty-five minutes. What a rip off! You're lucky you didn't have a riot. I know if I had paid to get in, I would have gone to the ticket booth and demanded my money back." Then he and Conrad laughed, but he wasn't bullshittin'. He would've.

Arthur looked aggravated, "I'll see you back at the car, Michael. Hurry up," and he started to walk away.

"Hey, nice concert, Art! You guys sounded great!" Connie yelled after him, and laughed again, loud enough to be heard over the roar of the choppers, easy. He was giving Arthur the needle because he didn't like to be "short-setted", even if he did get in for free.

The next night, when Kenny and I picked up Arthur, he asked me, "Michael, who was your biker friend?"

"That was Conrad. If you had waited around, I would have introduced you."

"Yeah, well, I don't want to be introduced, and I don't like to be called 'Art.' Tell him."

I shook my head. "I don't think he'll listen to me, Arthur. Conrad pretty much has a mind of his own. Maybe you better tell him." I'm pretty sure nobody ever told him because, every time Connie bumped into Arthur, he always called him "Art".

Later, we had a booking at the Santa Monica Civic coming up, so I gave Conrad a jingle to see if he wanted a comp. We headlined a bill with Linda Ronstadt, Strawberry Alarm Clock and a new group, Spirit. Connie had the hots for Linda Ronstadt so he said, "Yeah, sure, but ask Art if he plans to play a full set this time, O.K.? Woody and Moose are still razzin' me about that fiasco at the Valley Music Theater, and I don't want to sit by myself."

"Yeah, don't worry about it," I told him. "I have a feeling we'll be playing a full set, maybe two. Who knows?"

During the week prior to the gig, I had called Arthur several times to see if he wanted the group to get together and run over a couple of the tunes we hadn't played for a while, and he always said, "Lemme call the other guys and I'll call you right back." But he never did.

Finally, as the concert date was upon us, I realized there wasn't going to be any rehearsal and we were probably gonna skip those songs we needed to practice or just wing it and hope for the best. A few hours before we were scheduled to leave for the Santa Monica Civic, I was putting new heads on my drums, and Kenny was in the other room working on his bass, when the phone rang. It was Bryan.

"Forget the gig, tonight," he said, matter-of-factly. "I just talked to Arthur. We're not gonna do it."

"Does the promoter know?" I asked, suspecting the worst.

"Uh-uh. Nope. That's not how he's planning to handle it. We already did a last-minute cancellation with Dave Diamond a couple of months ago, remember? He might not be so understanding this time."

"Well, what's the plan then?"

"Arthur told me he wants to wait until about a half an hour before the gig is supposed to start, and then at the last minute he'll phone in a bomb threat, and then we'll be off the hook."

And that's what he did.

I forgot all about Conrad but, the day after the non-concert, he came banging on my door. He sat down on the couch with a big smile on his face and pulled a joint out and fired it up. "Oh, man, it was great, Michael!" he raved, "Linda was beautiful, she sings like an angel. I love that chick. Strawberry Alarm Clock was so-so." He took a second hit and passed me the joint. "How come you guys didn't show up? Not that anybody missed you."

"We heard there was a bomb threat."

"Oh that? They cleared everybody out for about fifteen minutes and then they brought the crowd back in, and the show went off without a hitch. Nobody blew up. Actually, I wasn't going to say anything because you always get me in free so I don't mean to be rude but it's probably better that you guys didn't play. That new band, Spirit, brought the house down. They would have blown you off the stage."

So the show had gone off without a hitch. Except for us. How embarrassing. Again. I could never understand this reluctance to play. Would it have been so difficult to get together a couple of times? I mean, that's what this was all about. The bottom line was, we were too lazy to get ready to do our job.

Conrad had a lot of nerve. He didn't care. If he was riding down Sunset and the man pulled him over for some bullshit traffic violation, he's the kind of dude that would engage the cops in a struggle to stall them long enough to give him time to swallow the dope. It happened twice that I know of. He had long ago realized that, thanks to the genes he had inherited from his folks, he was way more intelligent than just about everyone around him, so there wasn't anything he was afraid to try. He knew just how far to push it.

When Connie wasn't riding his Harley, he drove a Black '59 Corvette that had needed a paint job for a long time, but bad. One day he took it to the most expensive shop in the area and told them to paint it with their best enamel finish. When the job was complete, the night before he was scheduled to pick it up, he broke into the yard with bolt cutters, started up the Corvette with a spare set of keys, and drove it home. Stole his own car.

Next day, the shop owner called him and gave him the bad news. "Yeah, uh, Mister Sanka, sorry to have to tell you this, but last night somebody broke into our property and stole your Corvette. Only car they touched. Anyway, don't worry about it. We have insurance. Blue book on your car was seven grand, you can stop in any time tomorrow and we'll have a check for that amount ready for you."

So, Conrad got his car back with a free paint job, plus seven grand in insurance money to cover the "theft". After that, he used to drive the Corvette within a few blocks of that auto shop when he had to without a second thought. The only precaution he ever took was to keep his garage door closed when the Corvette was parked in there so nobody would see it at his house and make the connection. Or steal it.

The last time I comped Conrad and his buddies into one of our gigs was one night at The Whisky. We were already on stage, in the middle of a set, when they walked in and went upstairs to sit in the balcony where it was relatively safe to smoke weed. In those days, before the "no smoking" laws went into effect, there was so much smoke in the air, it was hard to tell who was smoking what.

Around eleven there was sort of a commotion at the front door. A guy came busting in, ran past the bouncers and the girl taking tickets and headed right for the balcony stairs followed by two uniformed cops; a second later, I lost them in the lights: they disappeared right into the area where Connie and his biker buddies had gone to sit. The crowd was momentarily distracted from our set and everybody seemed to be goose-necking in the direction of where the cops had run. Then there was another disturbance near the top of the staircase.

At the break, I grabbed a Coke and made for the stairs to see what had happened. There sat Moose and Woody and Dutch in the front row of the balcony, but no Connie. Just an empty chair. "Where's Conrad?" I asked.

"Hey, Michael," Moose shook his head, "It was really bad, man. The pigs came running up here, chasing a dude, and Connie, figuring to help him out, sort of, crossed his legs, just as the lead cop came running by. So, the cop tripped and fell, then his partner tripped and fell over him and the guy they were chasing got away. It looked like an episode of *The Keystone Kops*. So after the two cops looked around for him for a while, they came back in and grabbed Connie and dragged him outside and gave him the business and worked him over pretty good, and then they put the cuffs on him and took him away. He's been beat-up and arrested."

A couple of months later, Connie asked me to give him a lift down to the courthouse to face "Obstructing an Officer" charges. On the big day, when I pulled into his driveway, he came out looking sharp, fresh haircut, new shirt and slacks and penny loafers, all cleaned up and ready for his court appearance. He signalled me to hold up a sec, then he walked over, unchained Wolfgang from the gas meter and rolled him inside. "Let's go to court," he said, opening the passenger side door of my car and climbing in.

During the ride we smoked a joint, right down to a roach about a half an inch long, then Connie placed it in his shirt pocket. After we parked the car and got lost a couple of times, we found the right courtroom. A big cop was standing just inside the door, with his back to the aisle, at "parade rest", his helmet tucked upside down under his arm. He was engrossed in deep conversation with a female member of the court staff, smiling and nodding and occasionally reaching out and touching her arm to make a point. Not looking our way at all.

Connie nudged me and nodded towards the cop, "That's one of the pigs that busted me up in back of The Whisky. Let's go find a place to sit." We made our way past the cop, down the aisle to some seats near the front and waited for court to begin. In a couple of minutes, Connie leaned over and asked in a hushed voice, "See that desk with all the papers on it?" He gestured toward a large wooden table, located close to the judge's bench. "I have a feeling those papers are today's caseload."

The papers seemed to be laid out in some kind of order so that all the names of the defendants were visible without having to look too hard because, every once in a while, one of the prosecuting attorneys would walk over to the table and, without spending much time looking, reach down and grab a file, then walk away to confer with an associate.

"You know, I'll bet the arrest manifest is attached to each of those indictments. If mine was to get lost, I'm pretty sure they wouldn't have any record of me at all. I'll be right back," he whispered, and rose from his seat. Incredibly, as Connie pushed through the swinging wooden gate that separates the spectator section of the courtroom from the judges and attorneys, nobody even looked up. Before court is declared "in session", the scene is pretty much one of disorganized bedlam. Everybody's walking around and talking to everybody else and there's a lot of noise. Different people are going back and forth through that little wooden gate. I guess that's the reason there was no reaction at all from anyone, court officers or spectators, when Connie walked right over to the prosecutor's desk and started thumbing through the paperwork. Before long, he removed a sheet, folded it, put it in his pocket, turned and walked back through the gate. As he made his way up the aisle, I got up and followed Connie past the cop that had arrested him, and out through the courtroom door.

When we were safely outside, he removed the warrant and arrest manifest from his pocket and threw them in one of the city-owned trash barrels that line the sidewalk. Then, we headed in the direction of where the car was parked.

"Man," I said, still in awe, "I can't believe what you just did!"

"Yeah, well, it was the only way. I just wish I could be there when that cop puts his hat back on. I dropped the roach in it on the way out."

But, one day Conrad ran out of luck and met his master, one he couldn't outsmart. The phone rang and it was Conrad's good buddy, Moose. "Michael, did you hear," he asked in a sombre voice, "Connie overdosed on heroin last night. He's dead."

He didn't even get a wall.

Conrad's brother got his chopper. Moose got Wolfgang.

Chapter Eighteen

The East Coast Predicament

IN SPRING of 1968, we made final preparations to embark on the East Coast tour, set up by Elektra to promote *Forever Changes*: a trip that would last several weeks, taking us back through Detroit, Cleveland, New York and, finally, down to Miami for the Miami Pops Festival. At this point, we had never scheduled a series of performances, one after the other, for such an extended period, so this was to be a severe departure from the norm. The umbilical cord attaching us to L.A. was about to be stretched paper-thin. Our equipment guy, Neil, would travel with us only for part of the tour.

The night before we were to leave, Kenny and I spent several hours packing our clothes and equipment, double-checking all our stuff, making sure nothing was forgotten. When I was finished, I passed by Kenny's room and poked my head in. "How's it goin'?" He was sitting on his bed, with his bass partially disassembled, and holding a Phillips Head screwdriver in one hand. With the other, he was laying out twenty or so small transparent packages containing what appeared to be China White. It was no secret that Kenny had begun to use more than occasionally but, since it had never noticeably affected his performance, it was more or less a non-issue. I mean, except for acting extremely laid back from time to time, he was always the same old Kenny. No severe mood swings or anything. He always did his job.

"Michael, come on in. Check it out, man." He lifted the neck adjustment plate. "There's enough space in this compartment to hold all the smack I need to last the whole trip, easy." Then, he removed the plug-in cover from the edge of the instrument. "Look, my outfit goes right in here so, even if they search our stuff at the airport, I'm cool. They'll never find the shit in my bass." He replaced the packets and the syringe and began to reattach the cover plates. Kenny, being a coordinated, well-structured individual, had left nothing to chance, coming up with a plan that, apparently, eliminated all but the most improbable acts of fate. He was packing probably twice as much of the drug as he would need to last the whole tour. Kenny put the bass back in its case and closed the lid.

"We better get to bed," I told Kenny, "our plane leaves LAX at 9 a.m."

The next morning at six, our phone rang. "Hey, man," Arthur sounded as sleepy as I felt, "I just wanted to make sure you and Kenny were awake. Johnny needs a ride to the airport. Can you guys pick him up?"

"Yeah, man. No problem." I hung up and rolled out of bed. Then Kenny and I threw our bags together, put everything in the car and headed out the door. The drive from Laurel Canyon to Johnny's house in Beechwood was only ten or fifteen minutes, so by a few minutes past seven, we pulled into my old carport on Durand.

I opened the front door and yelled, "Hey come on, man, we're gonna miss the plane."

Johnny sprinted up the stairs, guitar case in one hand, small clothing bag in the other. "I'm ready. Let's go."

"We gotta hurry," I told him, as he closed the door. He put his stuff in the car and we drove to LAX as fast as we could through heavy traffic.

Around 8:15 a.m., we met Bryan and Arthur in the parking lot and began the long walk to the terminal. Of course, when we arrived, even though everybody had left home in plenty of time, the five of us were greeted in the American Airlines lobby by Ronnie Haran, looking distraught, practically screaming, "Where have you guys been? You have exactly three minutes to check in." So, once again, we had to literally run, like O.J. in the Hertz commercial, to get to the boarding area in time to make the plane to New York. It was our destiny. To be late, I mean.

When we landed at J.F.K., we were met in the baggage claim area by a limo driver and an Elektra rep. "Hi, guys," the rep introduced himself to each of us and we shook hands. Then, he nodded to the driver, "This is Phil. As long as you're in New York, wherever you want to go, he's the man to take you. He'll be responsible for getting you to the gigs, as well." Phil smiled and began to grab as many bags as he could carry. "The limo's right out front, fellas, the black one. Follow me." Phil bullied his way through the crowd, with us close behind, carrying what remained of the luggage.

As we piled into the limo and started to pull away from the passenger-loading zone, the Elektra rep filled us in on the immediate schedule. "We're putting you guys up in a hotel directly across the street from Central Park. There's a lot going on in that part of town, so you'll be able to enjoy some of the sights of the city. Within a several block walk or ride, you can check out some really nice restaurants, Broadway plays, great shopping... Greenwich Village is close. Coffee houses, jazz and rock clubs: there's so much to do and see. We think you'll have a good time while you're here."

The traffic was unreal, stop and go, of course, and no private cars at all, just taxi cabs and limos and delivery trucks. Message service employees on bicycles darted in and out, making much better time than any of the motor-driven vehicles. And, of course, New York is so horizontally challenged that all the buildings are constructed as high as their contemporary codes would allow. This was, after all, the place where Superman went to leap tall buildings in a single bound, right?

Soon, we were at the hotel the rep had described. One of those New York, sky-scraping brick buildings, probably constructed in the thirties, that showed absolutely no signs of neglect or deterioration, a work of art that had, in fact, over the years, retained all the elegance that had been so much a part of its original design. Extravagant architecture, giant pillars and enormous crystal chandeliers greeted the guests as they entered the lobby.

It had been decided that Kenny and I would share a room, Johnny and Bryan would room together and Arthur...? All by his lonesome.

"Well, this is where we leave you guys." The rep and Phil set our luggage on the Bell Captain's cart and we all shook hands and Phil tipped his hat. "You have a couple of days before your first booking," the rep said, "so just relax and enjoy yourselves. We'll be in touch."

By now, it had become evening, post-rush hour so, as soon as Kenny and I got up to our room, we realized we were hungry, and decided to hit the street. When we got back downstairs, and out on the sidewalk, we began to walk along in no particular direction, just looking around, taking in the amazing sight. "What do you want to do, man," Kenny asked, "try to find a restaurant or what?"

I shrugged, "I don't know, man, let's just walk and see what we run across." We kept passing those sidewalk Italian sausage-sandwich joints. They smelled good so we opted to grab a couple of sandwiches and soft drinks and go ride the subway.

The subway's a strange place because it's... what? Underground. Funny place to travel from point A to point B unless you're a mole. Day or night, it always looks the same down there. No natural-light time reference, at all. Just light bulbs. As soon as we boarded, Kenny and I went to the front car to check things out. There was a small, rectangular window located in the front centre of the lead car, next to the operator's cubicle, that looked out onto the tracks. As soon as the train reached full speed, we pressed our faces against the glass of the little window. The oncoming lights on the side of the track flew past on both sides at breakneck speed, putting on a yellow, green and red luminescent show that resembled the effect of the passage of time in space travel. So, you know, we were just tripping, the way you're supposed to do when you go to a place you've never been before, like New York City. Having fun.

In a minute, the operator opened the little door to his cubicle and asked us, "First time you guys been to New York?" He was a real friendly dude and we talked for a while. He had lived there all his life. He didn't even get on us for eating our sausage sandwiches on the subway, like he could have, because there was a big sign in every car, "No food or drinks allowed," but he was cool.

Later, we caught a cab to Greenwich Village and walked around, met some nice people and went to a coffee house and had a good time. When we got back to the hotel, around two or three in the morning, the streets were deserted, except for one cop patrolling his beat. He almost looked like he was out for a stroll; as we passed him, he nodded and smiled and twirled his nightstick, a far cry from the L.A. cops we were used to, who patrolled the streets in cars, carried guns and always seemed horny for trouble.

When we got back to the room around three a.m., Kenny went to the bass and opened the compartment which held his stash. He removed one of the small packets, unsealed it, and tapped out two lines of the powder on the coffee table. "This is some pretty clean smack, Michael, you want to try some?"

This time I wasn't afraid. In the last year, all the barriers had fallen. There was no drug I hadn't done, except heroin. It was the only one left. The last bastion.

"Yeah, sure, man. Why not?" I took a twenty from my wallet, rolled it up and, sitting on the couch next to Kenny, placed one end of the bill in my right nostril, held the left one closed, and whiffed one of the lines. Then I switched nostrils and did the other. I set the rolled-up twenty down on the coffee table, leaned back and waited. Soon, I tasted the bitter chemical as it dripped down my throat. A minute later, I felt a brief wave of nausea, then the imaginary itch. Beads of perspiration began to line my forehead. A glow of unparalleled calm descended over me.

The next day, Kenny and I did more or less the same thing, walked around and enjoyed whatever came along. That night, we returned to the Village, where we ran into a few of the same people we had gotten to know the night before. Once again, we got back to our room around two or three. As we entered, we immediately saw that the little red message light was blinking on the phone, so I picked up the receiver and pressed the button. After a few rings, Arthur picked up.

"Where have you guys been for two days, man?" He sounded irritated. "You had me worried."

"I don't know, Kenny and I were just hanging out. Did we miss something important?" I allowed a hint of sarcasm to slip through.

"We have a meeting with an Elektra rep here in my room tomorrow at ten a.m. sharp. You guys don't be late, O.K.?" Then he hung up.

We already knew that the first performance Elektra had scheduled was to take place the following night, Saturday, at a small college in the mountains outside the city, in the Catskills, I think. The college was the alma mater of one of the bigwigs at Elektra. I figured this meeting would provide further particulars. Give them a chance to pre-evaluate what was in store for the group and for the company during the tour. This first gig was a "tune-up", so to speak.

When Kenny and I arrived at Arthur's room the next morning, he and Johnny and Bryan were already in deep discussion with the Elektra rep. Not the same one that had met us at the airport. Somebody different. They paused long enough for Arthur to introduce Kenny and me, then the rep began.

"Look, fellas, the company wanted me to come here today to remind you of a few things that we feel you already know but perhaps need to be reminded of. Elektra has invested a great deal of money into the recording of *Forever Changes* – and into this promotional tour. We're familiar with the problems you've had in the past showing up on time, ready to play, and we just want you to remember this tour is extremely important to our company and to your careers." He made eye contact with each and every one of us as he spoke. "So, please, please, try real hard to avoid the pitfalls that, for some reason, seemed to have dogged the group in the past and, for God's sake, don't be rude or disrespectful to any of the promoters or fans. Let's make this a new beginning, O.K.?" The pep-talk went on for a good ten minutes or so. I think I heard the word "responsible" tossed around several times. This wasn't a meeting: it was a lecture, a warning, a not-so-subtle ultimatum. "Don't let us down or there'll be hell to pay" was the message.

I glanced over at Arthur, who sat in a chair, with his head cocked slightly to one side and his legs crossed. With furrowed brow, and feigned interest, he fixed our company rep with a glare that seemed to threaten physical violence if the little talk continued much longer. The rep finished his train of thought and paused. After a few more moments of silence, Arthur rose and said, "Yeah, well, Don, I think we understand what you're saying, man. Don't worry about it. All right? What time can we expect the limo?"

Don looked relieved that this part of the conversation had come to an end. He smiled a thin smile, "Phil, the limousine driver, has instructions to pick you guys up at six p.m. on the dot. You don't start playing until nine and the college is a little over an hour from the hotel, so that'll give you plenty of time. Your equipment will be set up for you guys before you get there."

"Let's see," I thought, "close to a two-hour time cushion? Yeah, even for us, that should be fine."

The rep continued, "Heh, heh, I mean it's not that we think you're not gonna show up for the dates or anything. Obviously you're gonna show up. We trust you guys, but this tour is really important to us both, the company and the band. So, let's get off to a good start, O.K.?"

The rep stood up and removed a Polaroid photograph from his inside coat pocket, then handed it to Kenny, "Check it out. I thought you guys might be interested to know, the *Forever Changes* album cover is on the back of every single double-decker bus in London, England." Kenny passed the Polaroid to Arthur, then around the room. Sure enough, there we were on the back of the bus.

The rep continued, "The band is getting some great publicity in Europe. There's quite a bit of fan interest in you guys. Keep the picture, O.K.? Get plenty of rest today and remember: Phil will be out front at six o'clock. You know who graduated from this school, right? 'Nuff said." Then, he shook all our hands and wished us a good tour and left.

When Don had gone, Arthur walked over to a bureau and, opening a drawer, removed a small stack of legal size 8 1/2" x 11" documents. He laid them on the coffee table. "I met with another Elektra rep earlier and he asked me if it would be all right if the company made out all the royalty checks to me, and then I can write your checks out to you guys for your one percent each. He said it would save a lot of time and make it easier to get our royalties to us sooner. Is that O.K.?"

We all nodded. "Yeah, sure, I guess," we all said.

Arthur spread the forms out on the table. "There's one here for each of you guys to sign. Thing is, there's a pretty big recording debt to be paid off first, before we start to get any royalties at all anyhow, but as soon as the debt's paid, we're cool, so be patient." Arthur handed a pen to each of us and we all signed.

"Is that why we haven't gotten any royalty checks for *Da Capo* yet," I asked. "The recording debt?"

Arthur studied the paperwork, "Huh? Oh, yeah. We still owe them money on the *Da Capo* sessions." He looked up. "Like I said, Michael, be patient."

It was still daylight when we all met up in front of the hotel. As we climbed into the limo, Phil said, good-naturedly, "Hey, it's 6 o'clock and you guys are on time. I don't know what they're talking about." Arthur shot him a dirty look. Seems our reputation had preceded us, even with the limo driver. As we headed out of the city and wound our way toward the interstate, Phil gave us an abbreviated guided tour. "There's your Empire State Building, right over there, see it? In a minute you'll be able to see the Statue of Liberty. Right at the end of this next block... There it is." He pointed out the passenger side window, to a place somewhere through the maze of skyscrapers.

Phil reminded me a lot of Huntz Hall. Same vocal mannerisms and body language. Good sense of humour. He kept up a running commentary more or less the whole time he drove. We hopped on the freeway, made some lane changes and, before long, we were headed for the Catskills. After about forty-five minutes, Phil said, "Here's our turn-off," and we made the exit from the interstate. The sun had begun to set and we were starting to lose a little light, as the limo rolled along a four lane highway, that soon became two. Trees on both sides of the road grew up and circled overhead, joining branches directly above us. We had entered the dense mountain region that had provided the magical backdrop for stories nightmares are made of. The Legends of Sleepy Hollow, Ichabod Crane and The Headless Horseman, and Rip Van Winkle were still lurking here – in spirit, anyway. Arthur removed the hash pipe from his coat pocket and packed it, then he took a hit and immediately started to fight the cough. "Here, Michael," he choked. He passed it to me as he reached over to turn up the passenger compartment stereo. "Man, I love this song." So, we rode along in the limo, in a picturesque setting, listening to music, occasionally talking, all of us together. This was what touring was supposed to be about. We should have done more of it.

Bryan extended the pipe through the little partition window to Phil, "Here you go, man. It's O.K., we won't tell, you can smoke and drive at the same time, right?"

Phil shook his head deliberately and waved his hand in a "no thanks" gesture. "No, no, no. Absolutely not, I can't. I have to keep a clear head. I can't miss my next turn-off, it's a real small road, kinda' hard to see. And I've never been out here before so..." he trailed off. "I gotta stay sharp." There was an understandable hint of concern in his voice. Time passed. Soon there was no moonlight or starlight, just headlights. Phil began to drive leaning forward, hunched over the wheel, presumably to see the road better. I checked my watch: it was already 7:45. We were supposed to start at nine. Arthur reached over and turned the music down. "Phil, we're not lost are we? If we're lost, it's all over, man."

"Hey, are you kidding? No way are we lost because, if I missed the turnoff, we'll just double back and find it. No big deal. That's why you have a professional driver. Believe me, I know what to do to get you guys there on time. Don't worry. But I think we should keep going this way a little while longer, just to make sure." So, after about another fifteen minutes, we made a U-turn and headed back from where we had come. It wasn't long before we started doing that thing that people do when they get lost in the woods. They go back and forth over the same ground, over and over; just like those folks, the more we did it, the more lost we got.

"You know," Phil said finally, "I don't think we went far enough the first time, fellas." We pulled another U-turn. Conversation faded and a feeling of apprehension swept through the limo. By now, for sure, it was out of our hands – because it was 9:30, and we were lost and a half-hour late. Visions of an auditorium full of college students staring up at an empty stage began to appear in my mind. In desperation, Phil began taking turn-offs he knew were probably wrong, just to "check it out". Finally, around eleven o'clock, at the end of a dead-end that "probably wasn't it", his persistence paid off and the limo headlights illuminated a small, hand-painted sign, nailed to a telephone pole.

"Tonight Only, 9:00 p.m., LOVE." A little further up the road, a group of buildings, a school: "College of The Catskills" or something like that. We were there! Nobody else appeared to be. The campus looked devoid of humanity. Deserted. Phil rolled the limo to a stop in front of what must have been the administration building. There was a light on upstairs, coming from a third floor window. We all just kind of sat there for a few seconds until finally Bryan said, "Well, somebody's got to go up and tell them we're here, who's gonna do it, Phil?"

"Why should anybody go up?" I interjected. "It's not gonna do any good, everybody's already gone home. You think they might let us get up on stage and play anyway, or something? Face it, man, we'll just have to go back to the city and call Elektra and tell them what happened. It wasn't our fault. How can they get mad at us?"

Phil looked down and said, "No, you guys are right. This is my fault. I should take the heat. I'll go up." He got out and closed the driver's side door behind him and disappeared into the building. We just sat in the limo and smoked, with no conversation passing between us; after a little while, Phil came trotting out to the limo with a big smile of relief on his face and climbed in. For a brief moment, I thought everything was cool.

"Don't worry about it, fellas," I thought he might say, "They're not mad. They said this kind of thing happens all the time, this place being so far out in the boonies and all. They told me to tell you the group can schedule a 'make-up' gig for whenever. Just have your manager give them a call. No big deal."

But that's not what he said. He said, "Whoa, you guys should have seen it in there!" He was breathing hard. "Soon as I started climbing the stairs to get up to that office where the light was on, a bunch of photographers came out of the woodwork and were taking my picture and yelling questions at me. I felt like a star! When I got up there, some dudes behind a desk asked me who I was. I told 'em I was your limo driver and they said you guys 'didn't even have the decency to come in and explain what happened yourselves' and that 'LOVE doesn't have any respect for its fans' and 'if this was a big school like U.C.L.A., you guys would have found a way to be here on time' – stuff like that." He put the limo into gear and we began to head back out to the main road.

"So, it sounds like it didn't go very well in there, huh, Phil?" Bryan asked.

He shook his head, "Nope, not at all."

"Did they say anything else? You were up there for a few minutes."

"Yeah, they said they were gonna sue you guys – and Elektra – first thing Monday morning."

Arthur choked on his hash, again. "But Phil, didn't you tell 'em that it wasn't our fault, that it was you that got lost and made us late?"

"Well, I started to, but they wouldn't let me get a word in edgeways. They kept yelling about how you guys have a terrible reputation for being late and not showing up, and they had made a mistake booking you in the first place, but they had been assured by Elektra that there wouldn't be any problem this time. Then they yelled at me, 'Just get out. Get out!' So I split. They're pissed off, man. Whew! I'm glad that's over."

We made it back to our hotel in about an hour and a half.

Several days later, on May eighth and ninth, the group was scheduled to play The

Generation in the city, an upscale hangout for industry professionals and recording artists. According to handbills posted near the front door, The Rascals had played there recently, as had The Blues Project, The Velvet Underground and Lovin' Spoonful. It was a concert club, sort of like The Whisky. We went by on the afternoon of opening night to get a sound check and look around, to make certain all our equipment had made it safely and to see if Neil had it properly set up.

When we arrived, another Elektra representative was on hand to meet us and to explain that the club would be filled with booking agents, promoters and executives from other New York-based record companies who had anticipated seeing us play, literally for years. The message? "Really do your best to get here, this time." The club was located just a few blocks from our hotel, so chances that we would get lost again were slim. He didn't mention the Catskills fiasco.

Arthur had written a song called 'My Flash On You' which appeared on the first album. A lot of people thought it sounded like 'Hey Joe'. I guess, to the untrained ear, it did a little, but only because the words were shouted, not sung. It was way better. More powerful, ferocious. A lyrical tirade with instrumental accompaniment.

It was a song directed at his buddies who kept offering him, encouraging him, to use heroin. At that point, he was trying his best to resist temptation. Like, "I don't want any, lemme alone about it. Thanks, but no thanks." It was a dynamic, exciting tune that, often, brought the crowd to a fever pitch. It begins with a five-chord progression, played by Bryan, which immediately grabs you by your soul and pulls you in. It was so unique, no other song we played approached its intensity, except maybe '7 and 7 Is'.

Kenny had experimented with a device called a "Fuzz Tone", occasionally used by Jeff Beck on his guitar solos. Kenny was the first guy ever to hook one up to a bass, and it did a lot more than just give the bass a fuzzy tone. It about tripled the strength and force and volume of what came out of the speakers. But Kenny would only use the "Fuzz Tone" assist one time during our set, during his bass solo on 'My Flash On You'. I think that's what made it so special, because it was such a surprise to hear it live: he didn't overuse it. As we approached Kenny's solo, Arthur would sort of half turn and shout to Kenny over his shoulder, "Lemme hear you play it one time, now!" Kenny would step on the control button for the "Fuzz Tone" and play the first few notes of the solo and... Well, a Piper Cub would be transformed into an F-16, a nuclear-driven roller coaster; the earth would shake, and the audience would grow weak in the knees. Always a powerful moment, it was an incredible solo on a hell of a great song. Made the hair on the back of your neck stand up, gave you the chills and plastered a grin on your face you couldn't shake if you wanted to. It was explosive. It was intense. It was a perfect opening tune for our New York City debut.

That night, when we were all in place, on stage, on time, and the announcer said, "Ladies and Gentlemen, LOVE!" we were met with greater than enthusiastic applause. Then, Arthur turned from the microphone and said to us, 'My Flash On You'. He didn't count it off because there is no "count off". Bryan just starts when he feels like it: five-chord progression, all alone.

Apparently, Bryan thought that, with all eyes and ears on him, this would be the perfect time for a musical practical joke. So instead of banging out the first five chords forcefully, the way he was supposed to, he kind of looked off in the distance with a straight face, and enthusiastically hit five, half-hearted, mutated versions of what was supposed to be the beginning of 'My Flash On You'. Sounded a lot like somebody dropping an electric guitar four or five times on the ground, but muffled. Then he kicked into the normal progression as if nothing out-of-the-ordinary had happened, and we joined in, trying to mend the damage.

Came the moment for Kenny's bass solo. "This'll make things all better," I thought. Only a few notes in, I realized something was dramatically wrong. "Plunk, plunk, plunk..." Still sounded like a Piper Cub, not an F-16, at all. I looked down. Kenny was plugged directly into his amp. No fuzz tone. No extra power, no jet-propelled excitement. No much-needed momentum to get the audience back on our side and carry us through the rest of the set. The song ended. The audience clapped. We played other songs from the group's first three albums, we played them well, and the crowd responded. They liked us, and everything was pretty much O.K. It wasn't a disaster or anything. It's simply that we could have grabbed 'em by the balls in a death grip. We could have ripped their throats out. The group could have made a severe impact on the New York rock scene, but we weren't struck by the importance of the moment, I guess, and so we didn't seize the opportunity. It just wasn't that important to us, so we let the chance slip through our fingers. Again.

After the set was over and we were offstage, I ambled over to Kenny, "Hey, man, where's your fuzz tone? Did Neil forget it?"

He looked kind of sheepish, "Aw, it was a pain in the ass to lug around. I told Neil not to pack it. We left it back in L.A."

Oh, O.K. I mean, the thing is a little black box, measuring, perhaps, four inches by eight, weighs maybe a pound tops. This was our New York debut. No big deal. Like they say, little things can mean a lot, particularly if they aren't there. But the *New York Times* entertainment editor gave us good reviews anyway, so I guess we didn't crash and burn totally. Still...

A few nights after we closed at The Generation, we were scheduled to play a gig at what was supposed to be a similar club on the other side of the city. We met our limo-sidekick, Phil, at the appointed hour in front of the hotel, everybody piled in and we headed off to the new club. But, right away, we noticed something was different this time. The atmosphere in the limo seemed to be a little tense. There was a stranger riding shotgun. Bryan nodded in the direction of the new guy and asked me, "Who's that?"

"Never saw him before," I shrugged.

Arthur took the hash pipe from his inside coat pocket, packed it and fired it up. After we had travelled a few blocks, Phil nervously introduced us to the new guy, "Uh, fellas, this is Sammy." Sammy turned and acknowledged us with a smile. "Fellas," Phil continued, making eye contact via the rear-view mirror, "there's been a little problem with tonight's booking. The people that own the club didn't realize that so many of your fans are under 21. You see, the club is an 'Over 21' place and they priced the tickets to accommodate a more sophisticated crowd. They wanted to keep out the hippie element. So, anyway, the bottom line is, there's a little demonstration taking place in front of the club, as we speak. Just a bunch of kids, really, walking up and down the sidewalk in front of the club, carrying signs and chanting. They're all pissed off about the 'Over 21' business and the expensive tickets. It's stupid. We don't think it's that important or anything, but Elektra and the club owners thought it might be a good idea to have Sammy ride along tonight, just to make sure you get in O.K."

Sammy was a big boy, not tall, probably only 5'6" or so, but weighing about two hundred and fifty pounds. Solid muscle, late thirties, craggy face, prison issue suit, he was, without question, a gunsel. Armed and dangerous. "The club's right around this next corner." Phil made a turn and there it was. No fewer than fifty or sixty fans walking the sidewalk in front of the club, yelling stuff like "Free Love!" over and over, and carrying handmade cardboard signs, just like Phil said. But then, Phil brought the big black limo to a stop directly in front of the club entrance, only a few feet from the picketing fans.

I thought, "What are you doing, man? Isn't there a rear entrance to this place? You're throwing us to the wolves!" But it was too late. The fans had noticed the limo. I could tell by their expression that they weren't just mad at the club owners, they were a little bit mad at us, too. They were mad at everybody.

"O.K., guys, have a good gig." There was an edge to Phil's voice, like, "Hurry up and get out, before they trash my limo."

To lighten the mood a little, and because I couldn't believe what was happening, I joked, "Hey, Phil, they're not gonna rush us when we get out, are they?"

Sammy turned in his seat and began smacking the bulb end of a blackjack into the palm of his left hand. "I guarantee you," he threatened, "they better not rush you." The smile was gone.

It was the first time I had ever seen a "blackjack" – outside cartoons, I mean. When you see one live, they don't look like much. They're really ineffective-looking little things, dark brown, maybe six inches long, floppy leather, they don't appear to have enough weight or size to really hurt someone. If I was a gunsel, I would want to carry a metal baseball bat, something you could really get some muscle into, something you could remove a couple of heads with if need be. But Sammy seemed comfortable with his "blackjack", so more power to him. Besides, I know a blackjack's advantages. They're easy to conceal or get rid of. It's hard to hide a baseball bat if the cops show up. I noticed Sammy's blackjack was wrinkled and worn, like it had some mileage on it.

Sammy got out and walked around and opened the rear door for us. "Let's go!" he growled. You could tell, he was psyching himself up for violence.

When the crowd saw we were about to get out of the limo, they picked up the volume a bit, and put the chanting into high gear. "Free Love! Free Love!" they yelled in unison. As we started to walk, Sammy began moving us in the direction of the front door of the club.

"Stay right behind me, guys. I'll lead the way." By this time he had put the blackjack back in his pocket, because he had realized he didn't really need it, after all. He was sort of like a walking blackjack, anyway: he was a good three feet wide at the shoulders. All he had to do was walk with conviction and the people fell back – were knocked back, whatever – out of the way. He quickly reached the front of the club, with us following along behind single file, like pussies. That's how we felt, anyway. I think if we had more character and a little more time to think about what was happening, we would have told Phil to take us back to the hotel. I mean, the people in the picket line had a point. They had purchased our records and supported us and here we were in the company of a professional bully who had been hired to beat 'em up, maybe.

The whole way in, we tried to make a little eye contact with the fans to give them a look, like "Hey, sorry about this, folks, it's out of our hands, though. We're still friends, right?" But most of the crowd was busy being assaulted by Sammy, so there wasn't a lot of visual communication to be had. Sammy resembled the lead engine in a slow-moving locomotive. No "Excuse us, please" or anything. Just "Get outta the way!" Brute force.

Once inside, Sammy disappeared. His job was done. An affable-looking, middle-aged dude emerged from the office, and gave each of us a big hug. "I'm really sorry about the mix up, fellas. The ownership didn't realize so many of your fans were under-21. We'll do the best we can to get through this mess. Come on over to the bar: I'll buy you a drink."

As we walked and talked, I noticed that, even though we were only a half-hour from the scheduled start time, the place was virtually empty. Maybe thirty people sitting at a few tables in the main room. "Was this another deal like Cleveland?" I wondered, where everybody had gotten arrested and taken away the night before for smoking dope?

Neil had gotten there early, as usual. He and the equipment dudes who worked for the club had all our amps and drums already set up; after we got our drinks, and the club manager had excused himself to take care of some business, we climbed up the stage steps and started checking things over. Johnny, Bryan and Kenny hooked up and did a preliminary sound check and tune up, I rearranged the drums a little, like I always had to do. Arthur tested the microphone volume. We joked around a little, trying to stay loose, but this was going to be tough. There was really nobody there, and the folks sitting at the tables wore suits and ties and evening dresses and didn't look like our crowd at all. The LOVE fans were out on the sidewalk.

About ten minutes before we were due to start our first set, I heard Bryan grumble, "This is ridiculous. I'll be back." He set his guitar down and walked out to the foyer of the club, where the bouncers and security guys were guarding the door. Keeping the fans out. They were engaged in a running argument with several of the leaders of the people demonstrating outside. Everybody was striking a hard-ass position; nobody was giving an inch.

The bouncers were patiently explaining to the fans that the club was prohibited by New York State law from admitting them and the people were saying they didn't care, they wanted to come in, anyway. It was pretty tense. So, right in the middle of this conversational melee, Bryan walked up behind the bouncer doing most of the talking and, believing he had a little leverage, us being the stars and the focus of all the attention, said, in a belligerent tone of voice, "Hey, man, why don't you just let the people in? What harm can it do, huh?"

Bryan was an accomplished talker and a manipulator. He figured, if he could get them to open the subject up to debate, maybe, somehow, we might prevail: our fans could come in and enjoy the show and we could enjoy playing. But, of course, the leaders of the group picketing outside heard this exchange between Bryan and the security guy and it gave them renewed energy and then they really started screaming and yelling. "Free LOVE! Let us in!"

The main guy, one of three trying to hold the crowd back, turned and glared at Bryan. "How would you like for me to push your teeth halfway down your throat? That's what's gonna happen if you don't shut up and get your ass back inside, where you belong." He clearly didn't really feel like putting up with any bullcrap from the peanut gallery.

Bryan, looking a little hurt and highly insulted, gave up this futile attempt to reconcile a bad situation in a way that would make us, and the fans on the sidewalk, happy. He went back into the main room and climbed up on stage, and picked up his guitar. "We may as well start playing. The motherfuckers aren't gonna let 'em in." And that night and the next and the next we played a private concert for a few Mafia members and their wives. Because this was a mob joint.

On the final day of the club gig, one of our Elektra contacts called us at the hotel and told Arthur that they had arranged for us to go ahead and cover the second Cleveland booking right away, and then fly back to New York, to fulfil our commitments there, before heading down to Miami. Otherwise we would have had a week to kill with nothing, really, to do. So, the next morning, we hopped a plane for Cleveland; after we arrived, we grabbed dinner and checked into the hotel. The gig was scheduled for two nights only.

After dinner, Arthur got everybody together in the lobby, "Hey, we don't go on for about three hours, you know? Maybe we should all go up and catch some shut-eye, so we'll be fresh. We'll meet back down in the lobby at eight. Everybody leave a wake-up call with the front desk. O.K.?"

We all went upstairs to our rooms, I don't remember who was rooming with who, but I do remember it was different than in New York. I think I roomed with Bryan. Around eight, we all met back down in the lobby and went out front, hailed a couple of cabs, and drove on over to the venue.

This wasn't the same place we had played when we were in town for the *Da Capo* tour. It wasn't a club at all. It was a large red brick auditorium: classic design, held three or four thousand people. The cabs took us around back and dropped us off near the stage entrance. The guard at the stage door recognized us and waved us over. Once inside, we were greeted by the promoter.

He put his arm around Bryan and signalled everybody to follow him down the hall. "The dressing room is down this way, guys. Tommy is waiting for you down there. He'll take care of you. Anything you want, ask Tommy. He'll go get it for you."

For the next half-hour to forty-five minutes, we sat around, ate sandwiches, drank soda, smoked cigarettes and went back and forth to the restroom and did a little individual mental preparation. Finally, a crew member stuck his head in the door, "The warm-up act is starting its last number, you guys about ready to go on?"

So, we said "Yeah, sure," and we gathered up the stuff we had to carry and headed out the door and down the hall to the backstage entrance, where we waited. When the other band was finished and had left the stage, we grabbed our stuff and plugged in and rearranged, and got all psyched up and ready to play.

Arthur peeked out through a small separation in the curtain. "Full house," he said. He walked back to his place behind the microphone and picked up his tambourine. Meanwhile, the promoter was out front doing his best to get the crowd worked up.

"Are you people ready for LOVE?"

"Yeah!" they cheered back. The stage manager looked around the edge of the curtain, "You guys all set?" We assured him we were. Arthur glanced back over his shoulder, "'7 and 7 Is'." The promoter continued to fire up the fans. "If you're ready for LOVE, then I know they're ready for you people!" More cheering. The stage manager placed his hands on the rope that would open the curtain. I looked down from the drum riser and noticed, for the first time, something didn't look right. I counted heads. "One, two, three... Lemme try that again," I thought. My heart started to race. "One, two, three..." What the hell? Somebody was missing! Who? It was Johnny.

"Ladies and gentlemen, it's the group you've all been waiting for..."

Arthur had his arm held high, ready to count off '7 and 7 Is' as soon as we were introduced to the crowd. "Hey! Arthur! Arthur!" I yelled to the back of his head, "Wait a minute! Johnny's not here." Arthur brought his arm down and looked back at the spot where Johnny normally stood.

"Shit! Hey, stage manager, hold up a sec, our guitar player's not here. We gotta find him. Kenny, you check the bathroom, Bryan, go look in the dressing room. Michael, wait here. I'm gonna go look out front!" Bryan and Kenny and Arthur set their stuff down and ran in different directions. I was left alone onstage, sitting behind the drums on the riser.

"Folks," the promoter didn't miss a beat, "I just got word we have a slight problem backstage, but LOVE will be out momentarily. I promise." He ran around the edge of the curtain, arms outstretched, palms up. Imploring. "What happened? Where is everybody? They told me you were all ready! What are you doing to me?!"

"Well," I explained calmly, "we don't know where our lead guitar player is at the moment, but we're looking. He's around someplace. Don't worry, we'll find him in a minute."

He looked exasperated, "I can't wait. I've got to put another group on." He waved to the stage manager, "Get this equipment off to stage left, and see if the other guys are ready."

Arthur trotted back in, "I can't find him. Only thing I can figure is that he's back at the hotel for some reason. I'm gonna grab a cab and check it out." And he was gone.

When Kenny and Bryan came back from their search, I told them what had happened. They just nodded. We went back to the dressing room to drink sodas and smoke and wait.

About a half-hour later, Arthur and Johnny came charging in, all shook up but ready to go – when the other guys finished, of course. Arthur jerked his thumb in the direction of Johnny, who was hurriedly removing his guitar from its case. "Motherfucker was at the hotel, asleep! I'll be right back. I'm gonna go tell the dude that we're all here, finally." He shot Johnny a glare and walked out the dressing room door, shaking his head.

"What happened, man?" we all asked Johnny when Arthur was gone.

"I don't know. Sleep deprivation, I guess. Whatever, I was really tired, and I forgot to leave that wake-up call request with the front desk, like Arthur told us to do, so... I overslept. But talk about a bum trip, to wake up to that big gorilla standing over my bed screaming at me, like that? I thought I was having a nightmare."

We finally got to play our set. From that point on for the rest of the night, everything went off without a hitch. But you may wonder how the group could possibly have met down in the lobby of the hotel, climbed into a couple of cabs and ridden to the venue, sat around the dressing room for over a half an hour and walked out on stage and not, until the last possible moment, realized that Johnny wasn't with us. The answer is, I don't know. Except that he was always off somewhere buying a pack of Kools or in the bathroom or making a call or something. Usually nearby and ready to play, but out of sight. Not this time, though. He was out of sight and not ready to play.

It wasn't just Johnny. More and more, we were each all off in our own little world, not really caring what the other guy was doing. I always felt sorry for the promoters in these situations. They would go way out on a limb, put their asses on the line and book us, in spite of the bad reputation for dependability and everything, and then we would go right ahead and mess up and fulfil their worst nightmare. These people had to end up over in a corner, kicking themselves and saying to nobody in particular, over and over, "I knew it! I knew it! I knew I shouldn't have booked 'em."

After the Cleveland date, we flew back to New York to play our remaining gigs there, before heading down to Miami to do the Pops Festival. When Kenny and I got up to our room, at the hotel, he immediately laid his bass on the bed, took out the Phillips Head screwdriver and removed the neckplate. "Gotta check my resources, here, Michael." He pulled out the remaining packets and counted them. His face dropped. He was visibly stunned. I think he had been pulling them out of the hiding place one by one, never taking inventory to see how many were left. Now only three remained.

He sat on the bed next to his bass, speechless for a moment, then placed all the packets in the top dresser drawer, next to his works. "Oh, man. I knew I was getting low but.... Hmm, not looking good, and we won't be back in L. A. for another couple of weeks. No way is this gonna last until we get home."

"Why don't you check with Johnny?" I offered. "Maybe he'll front us some, 'til we score."

"Uh-uh. Johnny's almost out, too. I already asked him. We're gonna have to score some shit here, before we leave New York."

This wasn't exactly a bolt from the blue. In the three-week period since we first hit town, the tour had lost its original upbeat atmosphere. It was all business, now. Just hang around the hotel rooms, do the smack and watch TV. By this time I had gotten used to the warm, relaxed glow and the surge of power that comes from doing the world's most dangerous drug. Now, it was a habit with me, too. I had told myself that if I stayed away from the needle, then I couldn't really get hooked. But I was wrong. Every night I looked forward, more and more, to the lines of smack Kenny laid out for me from the seemingly limitless supply he had brought from L.A.

Kenny and I no longer strolled through the theatre and club district or rode the subway in the middle of the night or grabbed fast food from the sidewalk sandwich shops. Now the group was in a survival mode. We had been gone from L.A. for weeks and we were all a little homesick. Then, as drug supplies got low, a mood of concern descended on us. Again and again, potential connections fell through. I mean, you can't exactly put an ad in the classified section of the newspaper for that kind of thing. Fact was, we were due to leave for Miami in a couple of days and we were almost out of dope.

Several nights later, Kenny placed the final remaining packet back in the bass and looked up. "Well, Michael. This is the last of it, man. This is all there is. Not even a whole dose. The stage manager over at the Generation, that guy Eric, said he would bring over a taste in a while. He's almost all out, too. I told him if he would set us up with his man, you and I would buy his third of a quarter. O.K? His connection's got our phone number. He told Eric he would call here when he scored."

So, Kenny and I turned on the hotel TV and just kicked back and waited for Eric. In a little while, there was a knock.

Kenny opened the door and in walked a big dude with long greasy hair, wearing dirty Levi's, T-shirt and moccasins. Eric found himself a place on the couch and sat down.

"What's happenin'?" he asked, without a whole lot of enthusiasm. Then, without waiting for an answer, he took a paper container from his sock and, laying it on the coffee table, began to unfold it. "This is all I have left." He dumped the contents on the coffee table, then taking a playing card, he divided the powder into three equal piles. I rolled up a twenty and horned mine, then Kenny took his pile and made preparations.

"Hey, Eric, thanks for sharing what you had left with us, man. We appreciate it, really," Kenny said.

Eric laughed, "Yeah, I know you appreciate it. That's why you guys are buying my part of the quarter that's coming in later. It's only around ten right now and this new stuff won't be here 'til after midnight, so after I geez my third of what I brought over, I'm just gonna hang out here and wait for the new shipment."

Kenny and I took a couple of popsicles out of the hotel room fridge and sat down to enjoy the high and watch TV and wait.

Eric stood up and removed a black leather pouch from his coat pocket, and unzipped it and laid it face up on the bed. Then he went in the bathroom and got a glass of water and set it on the coffee table and started to set all the crap you need to shoot up next to the glass. He took his works out of the pouch and held them up. They were those, "do it yourself" kind, a baby pacifier attached with string and rubber bands to the shaft of an eyedropper and then to the needle. He dumped his portion of the powder into the spoon and squirted some water from the outfit into the contents and stirred it up good. Then he tied himself off with his belt. After he cooked the stuff up, he drew it back up into the works, then cinching the belt tight and holding it secure with his teeth, he laid his arm across his knee and placed the tip of the needle against the vein on the inside of his elbow, where tracks and scar tissue, the results of years of untreated abscesses, dotted the injection site. Eric tapped the pacifier once and the needle moved inward. But there was no cloud of blood to signal him it was time. "Fuck, man, this thing's collapsed." He removed the needle and reinserted in a different spot further down. "All right, baby," he smiled. Then he squeezed. Then he squeezed harder. But the harder he squeezed, the more nothing happened, until, in a lightening-fast sequence, the rubber band holding the spike to the dropper, broke or came off, or something, and everything went "kablooey!" all over the place. Eric grabbed and fumbled frantically at the falling mess but no amount of effort could prevent the last of the precious fluid from hitting the floor and, almost immediately, soaking into the hotel carpet. I guess the point of the spike was plugged.

For a second, everyone sat stunned, as Eric appeared to be trying to formulate a plan for extracting the heroin from the floor; then, realizing the futility of the situation, we said stuff like, "Oh, man, Eric, what are you gonna do? That was your last one, right?" You know, we all felt sorry for him, especially because he had shared the last of what he had with us. Now, it was all gone.

Staring down at the brownish stain on the carpet, Eric's eyes grew big. Suddenly, he turned and flung what remained of his outfit at the wall. Then he commenced waving his arms and stomping around in circles, yelling, "Fucking shit god damn!" at the top of his lungs. In a downtown New York hotel room. In a little while, there was a knock at the door, "Hotel security! Everything all right in there?"

"Yeah, yeah, everything's O.K., we just had a little accident, that's all," Kenny answered. Then turning to Eric, "You tryin' to get us busted? Keep your voice down."

Eric sat down heavily on the couch and buried his face in his hands. He understood, completely, the gravity of the situation. Out of dope and the new shipment wasn't due for another three hours, if at all. Even if it came in right on time, when you need a fix, three hours can be a lifetime spent in hell. Giving up a bird in the hand can be a big mistake in the drug world, where nothing is sure. Things looked bad.

Things looked bad for another five or ten minutes, at least, until the morbid atmosphere was punctuated by the ringing of the telephone.

Kenny picked it up. "Yeah? That's cool. Come on over. We're in room 305." He placed the receiver back on the cradle and smiled. "That was your man, Eric. He scored early. He's on his way over with the goods."

Chapter Nineteen

LOVE (minus Arthur) Meets The Military

THE TIME CAME when our scheduled commitments in New York were complete and we checked out of our hotel, and into the limo, to catch a flight for Miami.

"Hey, listen man," Arthur said, on the way to the airport. "I've got some business to take care of back in L.A. We're about to have three days to kill, after the group gets to Miami, before we play on the eighteenth. So, I booked a flight for myself to head back home for a couple of days, then I've arranged passage to get me back to Miami on the morning of the 18th, in plenty of time for the gig that night. But you guys'll be going straight to Miami. O.K.? You don't mind, right?"

We all said, "Yeah, sure, whatever, that's cool, see you in Miami." So, when we got to La Guardia, Arthur headed for one terminal, and we went to another, and Johnny, Kenny, Bryan and I boarded the plane for Miami.

Elektra had arranged for us to stay with a company A&R man, and his family, in a home located on one of the canals. Before Arthur said goodbye, he told us the guy owned a boat. He had more or less mapped out an itinerary of things for us to do during the three day wait: fishing, water-skiing, visits to some of the local clubs. Sounded like fun. A working vacation.

As soon as we arrived at the Miami airport and went to the luggage pick-up area, we saw a limo driver holding a sign that read, "LOVE". We made eye contact. He recognized us and walked over. "Hi, fellas. Welcome to Miami. I'll be your driver while you're in town. Follow me, I've got the limo right outside. I'll take you over to where you'll be staying. It's not far, maybe fifteen minutes."

As we pulled out onto the Florida interstate, the driver told us the A&R man was named Jake, and he was a big LOVE fan. We shot the breeze with him for a while on the way over, and asked him how he liked living in Miami, and stuff like that. You know, making polite conversation. When we got to Jake's pad, he came out and opened the limo door and gave us a warm welcome, and, after introducing himself, he said, "Come on inside, quick guys. It's about to start raining, again. We don't want your guitar cases to get wet." Because it rains quite a bit in Florida, I guess.

So, without further ado, he and the limo driver grabbed our luggage for us and took it in the house. All the way in he was telling us how great it was that we could stay with him and how much he liked our music. Jake was a real nice guy. I guess he made pretty good money doing A&R work because his house was right on the water and his boat was docked maybe ten feet beyond the rear limit of his property, and he had a pool in his back yard.

"Come right this way, fellas. I have a couple of bedrooms set aside for you." He led us down a hall and put our bags down next to the laundry room. "We're all really looking forward to seeing you play. I understand Arthur's scheduled to fly in near the end of the week. I can't wait to meet him. Come on back into the dining room. We can fix something to eat. I'm hungry. You guys hungry?" He was laid back and relaxed.

On the way back down the hall, we passed some framed pictures of Jake taken when he was a few years younger, posing with a group he had recorded with back in the early sixties. He was holding a guitar and everybody had razor cuts. They looked like a surf group: each guy was wearing a shortsleeve shirt with stripes, like the Beach Boys wore on their album shots. Jake made us sandwiches and we sat around the dining room table and talked for a while, then he rose from his chair and went to the sliding glass door and opened it, and yelled for his wife and kids to come inside. "I'll introduce you guys to some of your biggest fans," he said.

Two little girls, seven or eight years old, came running into the house from the pool area and stood self-consciously in the kitchen, hugging themselves to keep warm, bathing suits dripping small puddles of water on the tile floor. His wife followed closely behind, carrying a half-full pitcher of lemonade. The two kids politely told us they were happy to meet us and looked forward to having us stay there for as long as we wanted. Then they told us they had tickets to the Pops Festival and that we were their favourite group, except for The Beatles. "All right," Jake's wife finally said, "now you two go back outside so I can mop the floor." So, the two little girls, squealing and laughing, ran back outside to play in the pool, and Jake's wife started drying the floor and clearing off the dining room table.

Jake motioned for us to follow him into the den. "I think there's a good baseball game on. The Giants and the Dodgers. Let's check it out. These guys hate each other." After we sat down on the couch, he reached over to turn on the TV, then he started switching channels with the remote until he found the game. "You guys like to fish?" he asked us, not taking his eyes from the action, "Heck, man, tomorrow morning we'll take the boat out and do some heavy-duty fishing, and maybe some water-skiing, too." He looked at Johnny and Bryan, seated to his left, then at Kenny and me. "You guys are gonna have a good time while you're here, I promise. Wait and see."

The next morning, we got up early, because that's when you usually have good luck fishing, and we all went out with Jake on the boat and putted around for a couple of hours. We didn't catch anything except a sunburn but, while we were out, he talked about his years recording and what had led him to decide to give it up in favour of a "behind the scenes, regular job" type gig with the company.

"You know, it's funny. People look at you up on stage and think you have it made, that a musician can do whatever he wants to do: 'Artistic freedom, freedom of expression' and all that. I don't know about you guys but, when I was a musician, I never had so many bosses. Managers, booking agents, concert promoters, record producers... There's too many fingers in the pie, and when you come right down to it, they're all your 'boss'. I mean, they're constantly telling you what to do, or what you should do and how and when you should do it. Isn't that what a boss does? It just got old, having so many people clamouring for a piece of the action and making sure you earn it for them.

"To me, the touring was so damned hectic and boring, and uncomfortable, but you have to travel and play to sell the records. A musician really isn't in charge of his own destiny at all. So after a couple of years, I just got to the point where I wanted out. It never really was that much fun, anyway. I mean, some people are cut out for it and some aren't. You guys like it, though, right?"

Jake appeared to have made the right decision for himself. He had a nice home and a beautiful wife and two well-behaved kids. He seemed to be absolutely happy, and in control of his life.

As we drifted along the calm surface of the bay, he played with the boat's gearshift lever and studied the horizon, "Of course, sometimes I look at groups like yours and I'm envious. You guys get up on stage and make music and it's a thrill to do that. Believe me, I remember. Or, sometimes if I'm driving and listening to the radio and a song comes on I really dig, the switch is tripped, then I get that old feeling and, for a little while, I almost wish I hadn't given it up. I spent all those years learning to play the guitar well enough to be a professional recording artist, and then, just to walk away from it like that? Well, it felt really strange. Still does, sometimes. I wasn't a hundred percent certain I was making the right decision. I just went with my instinct.

"You guys know, it becomes a part of your being, the most important segment of your identity. After I stopped playing, it took me a while to get on my feet, emotionally, and find my new self. It was hard to make the adjustment to the real world. A few of the guys in my old rock group are studio musicians now. I know I could do that, if I wanted to, but why should I? For the thrill of playing? My theory is, the thrill goes away after a while, anyway. So, the only way to come out a winner is to get the jump on the situation and leave it before it leaves you. Find something else you like almost as much. Then study it and learn to do the new thing well enough that other people will pay you to do it for them, like you did music. It's cool. It works. At least it did for me."

Jake started the motor and eased the boat into a trolling gear. "A big, beautiful world exists out there. I found out long ago you can't do everything in this life, so there comes a time when you have to choose one thing over another. Hopefully, the thing you choose is in your own best interest. Something rewarding, that will help you enjoy the future." He smiled, "Anyway, I think older dudes look funny trying to play rock'n'roll. It's a young man's game." Then he glanced briefly up at the sun, now almost directly overhead, "You know, I don't think we're gonna catch a thing, it's too late in the day. You guys want to try some water-skiing?"

So, we did that for a while, then, after another hour, we headed back to shore. Bryan was the best skier. What I mean is, Bryan could water-ski. It's hard to get up on those things, and stay up. It's like: "Here, have a face full of water while I drag you through the ocean at the end of a long rope." It's like being keelhauled, actually. Kenny and Johnny and I took turns looking like we belonged in a clip from "The Three Stooges Go Water Skiing". We didn't have the knack, so to speak. There was a lot of falling down and getting wet.

When we got back to the house, Jake barbecued lobsters out by the pool, and we laid around until eight or nine o'clock that evening, then he came into the bedroom where Kenny and I were watching TV. "Michael, my wife and I are going out. After the baby-sitter gets here to watch the kids, you guys are welcome to take our other car, and just go hang out in town or do whatever. There's some great clubs down near the beach. The Pops Festival starts in a few days, so you'll probably run into some of the other groups while you're out. Anyway, have fun, go enjoy yourselves. The keys are hanging by the garage door."

Kenny and I asked Bryan and Johnny if they wanted to go, but Bryan said his sunburn hurt too bad and Johnny was into laying around and watching TV, so Kenny and I went alone. He drove. When we were in the car and headed to the strip, I smiled and looked over at Kenny, "How about that Jake, huh? He's a hell of a nice guy. Nicey-nice." Kenny shook his head, "I can't believe his attitude, man. He's so cool and relaxed; his wife, too. I mean, to bring strangers into your home like that, and treat 'em practically like old friends – or family, even? Too much."

We hit a couple of clubs and ran into some of the guys in The Mothers. They were kind of rough-looking dudes, a lot like my biker friends, Conrad and Moose and Woody. Frank wasn't there. I motioned for them to come on over and Kenny and I bought them a drink, even though they were already real drunk, and we talked for a while. And in a minute, I leaned across the table, so I could be heard, "Hey, you guys are playing Friday, right?"

The Mothers guy nodded and yelled back, "Yeah, so are you, I saw the schedule. I think you go on right after us." We talked a while longer and then they went over to the edge of the stage to harass the band, so I said to Kenny, "Come on, man, if we're supposed to play Friday, we better get back to the house. Arthur might try to call tonight." We went back to Jake's and watched TV for a while and fell asleep around 2 a.m. No call from Arthur.

The next day, Jake took us out on the boat, again, but we just rode around and checked out the sights from the water. No fishing or water-skiing or anything. Just a tour. He let each of us drive the boat for a while. After a few hours, we went back to his house again and laid out by the pool. At noon, Jake got up and stretched, "Well, Arthur's plane is due in at one. I'm gonna go ahead and leave for the airport right now, so I'll be there in plenty of time." He threw on some blue jeans and a T-shirt right over his wet bathing trunks and grabbed the car keys. In a minute, we saw him pull out of the driveway and head off down the street.

After only about five minutes, we heard the phone ring. Jake's wife opened the sliding glass door and leaned out, "Michael, Arthur's on the phone, he wants to talk to you." When I got inside, she pointed to the master bedroom, "You can take it in there if you want." So I did.

"Hey, Michael, what's happening?"

"Hey, Arthur, Jake just left to go pick you up. Are you at the airport, already?"

"No, man, I'm still in L.A."

"Whaddayamean?" I was starting to get a little nervous. "Why are you still in L.A.? We play tonight, don't we?"

"Listen, there's been a problem and a change of plans and, since I'm here and you're there, you're gonna have to take care of it, O.K.? The promoters promised us top billing on our night, but I just saw a handbill and we're like second, not first. The Mothers have top billing, so we're not gonna play. Hey, I been thinking it over, this Miami Pops Festival is a bullshit gig, anyway. It wasn't gonna do us any good. So, just tell that dude Jake what's going on and you guys catch the next plane back home, O.K.?"

"Yeah, I guess," I mumbled, and we hung up. Of course, the posters were all printed up and distributed all over Miami and they had "From L.A., LOVE!" prominently displayed in large letters right up near the top. I mean it looked like top billing to me. Close enough. And they had been playing segments of our songs on the radio, night and day, in ads for the Festival, but never mind all that. We were outta there.

"WHAT THE HELL IS THIS?" I wondered. "Even if we didn't get top billing, so what? Playing music is fun! Let's go play anyway!" But it was too late. Arthur couldn't hop a plane and get to Miami in time for our set now even if he had wanted to. Which he didn't.

So, I guess I'm supposed to say, "Hey, Jake, thanks a lot for the free room-and-board, and the use of your boat and your pool and your car and the hospitality, but we've decided not to play the Pops Festival, after all, because we didn't get top billing." I mean, it had gotten to the point where nothing really surprised me any more, but this was a little much.

So, I called Johnny and Bryan and Kenny inside and gave them the strange news. They thought I was joking at first. When Jake got back home from his futile trip to the airport, I gave him a watered-down version of the rude crap that Arthur had told me to tell him, along with a genuine apology on behalf of the group. And he was cool, naturally. He was too polite to say so but, because of our reputation, he probably knew from the get-go almost anything could happen, until we actually got up on stage and started playing. And even then... Sure was embarrassing, though. Again.

Ronnie Haran was still doing some booking and management work for the group and she had flown in special, that morning, just to catch our set. Before we left Jake's, she called and told us she had heard the news and already booked us a flight later that afternoon: she would be making the flight home with us. We packed our bags and called a cab. When we left, Jake shook each of our hands and told us he was happy to have met us and that maybe someday he would see us play. Then we left.

During the cab ride, Johnny and Kenny and Bryan and I didn't talk a whole lot. We were pretty worn out from the tour and now simply looking forward to getting back home. In a while, we met Ronnie at the Miami airport and she was upbeat and understanding about having wasted the airfare and the time to come all the way across country to see us not play. She was a good sport, too. I guess you had to be a good sport if you had a business association with our group and expected to keep your sanity. It was a prerequisite.

When we arrived at the terminal, we joined up with Ronnie in the restaurant. "Yeah," she said, "as soon as I stepped off the plane, and I didn't see Arthur, I got worried, so I called his house back in L.A. and he gave me the word that you guys weren't gonna play, after all. That's when I called Jake's house, and here we are. You guys hungry? I'm buying." She wasn't upset, at all. She seemed downright chipper, in fact.

Looking at Ronnie across the table made me wonder how jet lag works. I mean, if you make the long trip, cross country, and you arrive with jet lag but then turn right around and go back, before your body has a chance to start to suffer from the new time frame, do you get rid of the jet lag you were about to accumulate before you get it, or do you arrive back home with "double jet lag"? I think it must be the former, because Ronnie didn't look tired at all. She nipped that jet lag in the bud.

Around seven o'clock, we boarded the plane for the all-night trip back to L.A., the trip that marked the end of our East Coast tour.

An hour or so after we departed Miami, the 727 landed in Georgia and everybody got off the plane except us. Then, after a few minutes we took off again. The captain came on the intercom and joked around, a little, about how we had the whole aircraft to ourselves for the trip back to L.A. and they ought to have charged us more for our tickets, and we should be careful, if we had to get up to go to the bathroom, not to throw the plane out of balance. Stuff like that. But the flight was nice and peaceful. Kind of like it was our own private jet.

We put the armrests up and sat in several seats each, stretching out crossways with our feet dangling in the aisle, eating snacks and drinking Cokes, and listening to music on the earphones. From time to time, we looked out the windows at the blackness and at the moon and the stars and, occasionally, down at the lights below and just enjoyed the solitude. And in a little while, we all fell asleep. We were finally going home.

"Can I have your attention, folks?" The captain's voice cracked over the intercom, disrupting our tranquillity. "We've been requested to make an unscheduled stop in Denton, Texas, to pick up a regiment of Army personnel. They had a problem with their flight, so we're going to give them a lift on out to L.A." The Captain's tone of voice wasn't friendly anymore. Now, it was all business.

"They'll be taking another plane directly from LAX to Viet Nam. These people are going to war so they'll be dressed in full battle gear and carrying rifles and equipment backpacks. Unless you want to lose something important, like a knee or an elbow, please keep all arms and legs out of the aisle while they're boarding."

"Well, excuse us," I thought. I mean, what happened to Captain Happy? Just a few minutes ago, this guy was our newest best friend and now he sounds like he's about to hand us all parachutes and kick our asses out the cargo door.

This was, of course, a period of great discontent in our country's history. Our nation was virtually split down the middle, trying to decide what, if any, purpose would be served by continued intervention in, what many perceived to be, an internal conflict in a strange land, half a world away. There were really hard feelings between the members of the two major philosophical camps: one believing this was a noble endeavour and a worthwhile investment of American lives and resources, the other believing it was a suicidal waste of time and energy. People felt strongly, both ways. Television news reports of demonstrations by throngs of anti-war protesters had made one thing obvious to the people who supported our country's participation in this military exercise in Southeast Asia: individuals with long hair and unusual clothes appeared to be irresponsible drug-crazed hippie draft-dodgers, who were willing to let other people's sons go fight and die in support of our government's policies while they stayed home where it was safe. So, now, in Denton, Texas, it appeared these two diametrically opposed worlds of opinion were gearing up to collide in the cabin of a 727 passenger airplane – with us inside.

After we landed and taxied to a stop, Kenny and Johnny and I found seats together and Bryan and Ronnie sat with each other, across the aisle and in back of us. We looked out the window to the tarmac, where the soldiers stood in a kind of "boarding line". A regiment, a battalion, whatever: a long olive-drab cable of humanity stretching almost as far as the eye could see. The cabin door was opened and they started to file on. It was just like the captain had said it would be, a marching melee. Guns and combat boots and helmets and packs filled with fighting gear. Everybody was pushing and grunting and clanking and laughing as they boarded, secure and jovial in their relatively newfound common-interest brother-and-sisterhood bond of making war on the southeast Asians. Some located seats near the door where they entered but most had to walk past where we sat on their way to the rear of the plane. As they did, they noticed us, tie-died, buckskinned and bleary-eyed. They poked each other and laughed even harder than before, and some made cracks only the others could hear. Most of them simply looked at us and shook their heads in wonderment.

It was an uncomfortable situation for the group, to say the least. After what seemed an eternity, they were all seated, the pilot fired up the engines again and we took off. I soon realized the soldiers had no intent to cause us a long-term problem or anything. They simply had made a few comments to one another about the way we looked, then went about the business of getting seated and flying to L.A., reading magazines, drinking soda, each guy listening to music or talking. Once in the air, Johnny, Kenny and I hunkered back down in our seats and put the earphones on. It looked like, despite our philosophical differences, they were gonna live and let live. All was peaceful once more.

After a while, I leaned forward and twisted in my seat to release the tangled earphone cord from its spring-loaded mechanism. In doing so, I was able to steal a peek in the direction where I knew Bryan and Ronnie were sitting together. I couldn't believe my eyes. "You gotta be kidding!" I thought. They were locked in a very physical lovers' embrace, hugging, passionately kissing, groping, fondling: "making out" in front of the soldiers. Making a spectacle of themselves. As long as I had known them, they had been like siblings, never lovers at all. This was, quite obviously, a show.

"What is he doing?" I whispered to Kenny.

Kenny shook his head, "I don't know, man. Trying to make trouble, again, I guess."

Was it that Bryan simply couldn't pass up any opportunity to cause a little commotion, maybe stir things up some? Provide entertainment for everybody? A fistfight at twenty-thousand feet would be nice. Anything to break up the monotony. So, he was heavy-duty acting and Ronnie, ever the good sport, was going along with the gag. They kept it up for a while longer, and then Bryan removed his arm from around Ronnie's shoulder and picked up a magazine and started to read.

Nobody responded one way or the other. Nobody laughed, nobody got mad. Maybe a little silent disgust drifted through the cabin, because what Bryan had seemingly done – at least temporarily – was validate the low opinion most members of straight society had of musicians and hippies. At least, that's the way it appeared. But that wasn't it, at all. Bryan simply had a distaste for the separation that results when one group, holding one set of values, isolates itself from the others. He felt compelled to bring opposing groups that had no apparent common interest whatever together, whether they liked it or not, just to see what would happen. And he found that the most interesting method of accomplishing this goal was to interject himself, uninvited, into private social situations. He often accepted the role of "sacrificial catalyst", readily giving himself up in order to help initiate this kind of social metabolism. He liked to bring people together.

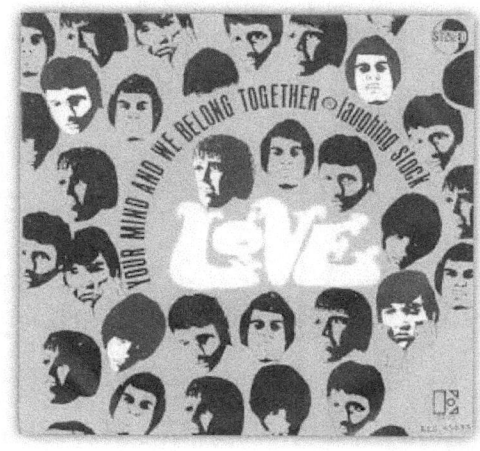

He would jump at the chance to throw a wrench in the works of the status quo without hesitating. He was always perfectly willing to relinquish his own dignity – anytime, anyplace – just to observe the reaction of regular folks to his outrageous behaviour; with a little luck, maybe even fix things some. He hated structure. He was addicted to shaking things up. I guess you could say he was as much an experimental social scientist as he was an artist.

Bryan was a gifted writer who was endowed with extraordinary vision, and his compositions captured the emotions and the imagination of most who ever heard them. But he was also two opposing forces trapped in one body: the ridiculous clown and the serious artist. It's just that, I guess, his was an extreme case.

His philosophy worked, too, even on that plane ride from Denton, Texas to Los Angeles, California. Because, before long, their curiosity piqued, the soldiers came one-by-one and sat down with Bryan and Ronnie and the rest of us, and we all began to talk: they told us about themselves, their lives and families. Most of them were familiar with LOVE, and some of them were fans.

By the time we landed in L.A., we got to be pretty good friends with a few of those soldiers. Bryan did it.

Chapter Twenty

"Arthur *IS* LOVE!"

THE MORNING after we arrived back in L.A., Arthur called me. "Hey, Michael, while you guys were in Miami, I was contacted by the U.C.L.A. film department. They want to do a documentary on the group. The dude I talked to said, to compensate us for our cooperation, we would have access to any part of the completed project to use for promotion, or whatever, as long as we give the film school credit for the production. Anyhow, they want to get started right away, so let's meet here at my house at noon tomorrow. Tell Kenny, O.K.? I'll call Bryan and Johnny." We hung up.

Sounded like a pretty good deal, and it was coming at a good time. Before we had left L.A. to do the East Coast tour, around late January or early February of 1968, we had recorded two songs, 'Laughing Stock' and 'Your Mind And We Belong Together'. Elektra had planned to release them as a single and I figured the group might be able to use the film to promote the new record. TV spots or something. The film school had learned that Arthur's pad had been the location for the Fonda-Hopper flick, *The Trip*, and they told Arthur it was their plan to use it as a setting for some of this film, as well.

Fact was, it was a cinemagraphically convenient place to shoot because there were no other houses within eyesight or earshot.

Promptly at 11:55 a.m. the next day, Kenny and I left our house and made the short drive up Kirkwood, along the single-lane, blind-curve dirt road that dead-ended into Arthur's driveway. The last hundred yards or so, Bryan and Johnny were right behind us, both cars arriving at Arthur's house precisely at noon. A large station wagon was parked in front. As our cars came to a stop in the driveway, the two occupants got out and approached us. They had long hair and wore blue jeans and plaid flannel shirts and tennis shoes. They looked a lot like college students, actually. The dude leading the way extended his hand to introduce himself.

"Hi, guys! I'm Tim and this is David," he added, jerking his thumb in the direction of his trailing partner. "We'll be filming the first segment of the project today, then some other crew members'll finish up, hopefully before Friday. We have light reflectors and stands to set up but, otherwise, we're all ready to go. Our cameras are in the car and loaded. By the way, we knocked on the door when we got here, maybe around a quarter to twelve. Arthur's not home yet, I guess, huh?"

I checked the carport. Sure enough, no Porsche. So, Bryan and Johnny and Kenny and I, and the two film crew guys, stood around out front while they gave us a rundown on what they felt would be a good basic format for the project, camera angles, stuff like that. As we talked, I couldn't help but think, "This is probably a complete waste of time. Whatever we decide, Arthur's just gonna veto it when he gets here and make them do it the way he wants it done." But I suppose it was a good way to get to know the film crew guys, and it helped to pass the time while we waited.

After a few minutes, we all wandered over to the area near Arthur's front door, where it was cool and shady, then, during a lull in the conversation, I noticed Bryan kind of staring into a crevice between the porch and the house. "Hey, look at the spider," he said. "Is that a Black Widow?" He pointed down and we all gathered in for a closer inspection because it's not often you see one. It was real shiny and black, with a small red hourglass tattooed on its back. Total body diameter, including the legs, was about the size of a nickel – pretty big for a Black Widow. It was completely motionless. That's how spiders are, they don't move around very much. Mostly, they stay put and wait for food to come to them. One day, of course, spiders die, and they don't move at all after that. They find a good place to be, and their biological clock expires, and then they just sit there. That's the way this one looked: dead.

Tim picked up a large rock and dropped it near the Widow, then he did it a second time. We all watched closely for movement. There was none. "Yeah, he's dead," Tim volunteered, "or he would have jumped, or something."

"You got that right," we all chimed in. "Yeah, he's deader than a doornail." Bryan, his courage bolstered, slowly leaned forward and cautiously nudged the Black Widow with his foot. Suddenly, the spider wheeled around and grabbed onto Bryan's sandal and began to crawl over the top strap. At first, frozen in terror, Bryan did nothing, apparently hoping the spider would crawl off his foot without prompting. But then his eyes began to widen as it crawled, not off, but further up, nearer the ankle. The next 30 seconds probably made Tim and David wish they hadn't left their cameras in the car.

"Aauugaragh!" Bryan screamed. "Get him off me!" Then he was off to the races, violently shaking his foot and hopping and running in circles. I mean, everybody felt bad, because we had all assured each other that the Black Widow was absolutely and positively dead, but, even if we had been able to catch up with Bryan, there wouldn't have been a whole lot we could do. I mean, when you have a Black Widow on your foot, you're pretty much on your own. So, everybody just stood back and waited for the scene to play itself out, while he ran around lickety-split, kicking up a cloud of dust in the process.

Eventually, he stopped, shook the Black Widow off his sandal and stomped several times, rendering the spider harmless. Dead for real, this time. Then, he slowly returned to the group, all out of breath and distraught.

"Sorry, man," I offered. "You O.K.?"

He shot us a vicious stare, then sat down heavily on the front porch to catch his breath, resting his elbows on his knees and rubbing his closed eyes with the palms of his hands. "Dead, huh?" he puffed.

In a few minutes, Arthur's Porsche came around the corner and pulled into the carport. "What's happenin'?" he asked through the driver's side window. Then he shut off the engine, got out and walked over to where we were standing.

"Hey, man, I'm Arthur." He shook hands with the film guys, and then everybody hung around outside for a few minutes, while Tim and Dave discussed the stuff they had in mind for that day's shooting. Finally, Arthur turned and began to mount the porch steps, signalling us to follow. "Let's go inside and talk where we can sit down." He placed his hand on the doorknob, looked down, paused and withdrew it. Then, glancing briefly back at us, he pressed his fingertips against the door and pushed. It swung open. As we all stood on the porch, his brow furrowed: "Did one of you motherfuckers go into my house while I was gone?"

Tim hesitantly raised his index finger, "Actually, when David and I first got here we knocked on the door and it wasn't closed all the way, so it opened when I knocked, and we came on in and, sort of, called for you. But when we realized you weren't home, we went on back outside and waited in the car. I hope we didn't do anything wrong, Arthur."

Arthur walked in, looking around, suspiciously, "Well, I'll tell you, man, the word 'wrong' really doesn't cover it. 'Dangerous' is a little more like it because, if I had been here and I heard somebody come into my pad, uninvited, I would have gone for my gun. You think it's all right to just go walking into a man's house, like that? Are you guys fuckin' crazy? You're lucky to still be alive! You know that?"

He was yelling now. Tim and David glanced nervously at one another, probably wondering how far and how long this might go. Was he about to wind it up? Or was he just getting started?

"I'll tell you something else. I'm gonna stop right now, before we go any further, and check things out. Just to make sure nothing's missing, you know what I mean? You guys go ahead and sit down. I'll be right with you." Arthur began to wander through the room, lifting things, opening drawers and examining the contents to see if anything was missing or broken or vandalized. An uncomfortable few minutes for everybody, to say the least.

Suddenly he discovered what he was looking for. "Now, you see?" He pointed at the kitchen counter. "That's exactly what I'm talking about. I definitely left a twenty-dollar bill sitting right there, and now it's gone. Did one of you guys take it?" He wiggled his finger at Tim and David. They shook their heads innocently. Arthur continued, "I don't know. Maybe you did, maybe you didn't. I'm not accusing you or anything, all I know is, the twenty was here and you two were in my house and nobody else was here, and now it's gone." He was starting to run down, a little. "Well, I guess it's too late to worry about it anymore today so," he threw up his hands and took a deep breath, "let's get started on this film thing, O.K.?"

Oh, O.K. After leading these two respectable and well-educated dudes through a fifteen-minute labyrinth of humiliation, designed to cut them down to size, Arthur figured his point had been made and it was time to move on. Not that easy, though. Now, there was this enormous wall between us. They appeared shaken and a little scared. Tim and David had arrived expecting to complete the first day of filming on a project which was to be a well-coordinated, imaginative, joint creation between the U.C.L.A. film school and LOVE. Something enjoyable. Now, they were just looking to survive.

"Well, Arthur," Tim began, bravely, "David and I thought we might start with some outside stuff. The light's pretty good right now." But he was hesitant. Now you could hear, by the tone of voice, that his priority was not to successfully create something special, but to not get hollered at, again. To avoid any further conflict, at all cost, was his new goal.

"Of course, it doesn't really matter where we start, you know? The film'll be edited later, so scenes can be rearranged into whatever you think the proper order should be. So, if you had rather we started with some interviews in here, we can do that."

This was bad. The mood had already shifted from "Let's work hard and have fun and create something special together that'll blow the audience's minds" to "Tell us what you want us to do, Arthur, just don't get mad and yell at us anymore, O.K.?"

"No, that's cool," Arthur politely acquiesced, "we can start outside, if you guys want to."

David and Tim picked up their cameras and we all headed back out front to patch up the heavy atmosphere as best we could and get on with the job of making the film. I can't remember very much about the content or the direction of what we tried to accomplish that day, except there was some running around and hiding behind rocks and other inappropriate stuff that didn't fit the character of the relationship we had with one another, at all. Actually, I think Tim and David had seen a few too many episodes of *The Monkees* because they tried to implement that feel onto this first segment. You know, "Gosh, we're having fun. This band thing is a blast!" I don't think it came across though.

I'm pretty sure nobody in the room had believed that "missing twenty-dollar bill" story Arthur made up, either. It was as if, in the middle of getting all excited about Tim and David coming in his house, Arthur realized, "Hey, I can really make these dudes understand how pissed off I have a right to be if I pretend something is missing. Then, they'll realize what a big mistake they made, barging in here, like that." So, he devised that crock of shit about the twenty. It was his version of an object lesson. So obvious.

After a few hours, David said, "Well, hey, guys, that's a pretty good start. I know we got some great footage." He and Tim began packing up their equipment and loading it into the station wagon. "We're gonna take this back to the lab and develop it, go over what we have, then we'll get back to you and set up a time and date to do the remaining segments, O.K.? We feel it's gonna be a tremendous film. It was nice working with you guys today." Then, they left. They never called back, of course.

A few weeks later, a funny thing happened. Arthur, always reluctant to accept bookings, anyway, suddenly started turning down offers altogether. In desperation, booking agents in L.A. and San Francisco began calling Kenny and me to complain that the group was committing "professional suicide" by continually rejecting opportunities to work and promote our recordings. They weren't telling us anything we didn't already know. What could we do? Accept the bookings and show up without Arthur? We sure felt like it sometimes.

The money started to run low and, not surprisingly, Kenny started to fall behind in his payments on his Jaguar. He came home one day and told me he had made arrangements to move out of our house and into a less expensive pad up the street on a tiny, almost completely hidden cul-de-sac. I helped him pack his stuff and we loaded it into both cars and I went up to the new pad to check it out. He slowed the Jag to a stop and signalled me to park in the driveway. Then, he got out, opened the garage door, and waved me in. The garage held a few bedroom-type items: bed, end table, portable fridge, stuff like that. He climbed back in the Jag and pulled it in next to the bed. "What do you think, Michael? What a score, huh?"

"Whaddaya mean?"

"Well, the finance company sent me notice they plan to repossess my car, so I thought I better move, to make it harder to find me, you know? Then, I discovered this garage that these people were willing to rent me for fifty bucks a month, so I figured, 'Hell, I'll just park my Jag in it, and I'll live in it, too,' so that's what I'll be doing. I get to sleep right next to my car every night."

So, I told him, yeah, he was real lucky to have found the new place – and take care of himself and I would see him later – and I left. But I didn't exactly know when I would see him later because, without really talking about it among ourselves, it was more or less understood that the group was breaking up. Bryan was putting together a solo project, I had begun considering recording offers from Atlantic Records to play with other groups I had met in L.A. and Seattle, and I hadn't even seen Johnny or Arthur in about a month.

In fact, the next time I spoke with Arthur, he stopped by my house, one day, to have a good laugh over Kenny's new living situation. "Can you believe the motherfucker's living in a garage? Haw, haw! Hey, Michael, dig it. Yesterday, me and Echols went over to Kenny's pad and, when we were getting ready to leave, I said, 'Forssi, I need to borrow your car, O.K? I'll bring it back in about an hour.' So, Johnny and I took it over to the West Side and drove it around and went to see a flick and I got my hair done, but, like eight hours later, when we finally brought it back to his garage-home, Kenny's out front, sitting on the curb, looking all scared like he was about to cry.

"So, Kenny walks up the car and says, 'Where have you guys been?'" Arthur mocked, in a high-pitched, wimpy voice. "Hey, man, I just got out and threw the keys to him and I said, 'What are you so fuckin' worried about, man? Didn't you think I'd bring it back in one piece?' And he says, 'I'm sorry, Arthur, but now my car is all I've got left.' Haw, haw, haw! Can you believe that? How pitiful. Kenny's really hit the skids. What a fuckin' loser!"

There was nothing wrong with Kenny that a regular performance schedule wouldn't have cured. He was talented, imaginative and his creativity was boundless, but Arthur had eroded his confidence with relentless criticism and ridicule, and had effectively cut his legs out from under him, and now he didn't have respect for him anymore because he didn't have any legs.

Why didn't Kenny make a few contacts and record with other people, like I had started doing? I don't know. Maybe he thought eventually the group would start accepting bookings again and then everything would be all right. Or maybe he realized that scouting around for a new gig would require him to take his prized XKE out in public, where he was sure to be spotted by the repo men. And then what? He might be chased down and humiliated, like William Holden in *Sunset Boulevard*. I guess he figured it was better to simply hunker down and wait it out and hope for the best.

And, then, one day, my phone rang: it was Bryan. "Michael, did you hear the news? Arthur put a new group together to record the last album we owe Elektra. It's just gonna be him and a bunch of new guys, but he's still calling the band 'LOVE'." Bryan told me about a party he had been to. Jimi Hendrix was there and he mentioned to Hendrix that he thought it was a rip-off for Arthur to call the new group, "LOVE".

"Arthur is 'LOVE'!" Jimi had yelled. "He can do what ever he wants!"

"Yeah," Bryan laughed and shook his head, "You should have seen him. Several of his people had to hold him back or he would have jumped me. He was all excited. You know what? I don't even care, but if Arthur thinks he can fool the public, he's mistaken. That would be like Mick Jagger trying to pass himself off as 'The Rolling Stones': he may be the main guy, but he's not the only guy. Mick's not The Rolling Stones. He's just Mick Jagger... of The Rolling Stones."

We talked for a little while longer and, when we hung up, I remember I felt free. Three years can seem like a very long time if you're not having fun, and I wasn't. At least, not for the last year. I picked up the phone and notified my contacts at Atlantic that I wouldn't have to schedule our recording and club dates around any proposed LOVE gigs, anymore. They were relieved, and so was I. Now I could move on.

Several months later, I saw an ad in *Billboard* announcing the new "LOVE" album, *Four Sail*, the group's last on Elektra, with a picture of Arthur and the three new guys. Once, when I bumped into Arthur at a restaurant on Sunset, I asked him, "Hey, what's with the Four Sail?"

He told me, "Well, it was gonna be the last album on Elektra, and we were looking for a new label, so the group was 'For Sale', or 'Four Sail' because there was four of us."

"And as soon as you found that new label, you guys would be 'Sail'-ing off, right?" I asked.

"Yeah."

"That's pretty good," I told him.

During the next five or six months, I continued to work with new people and started to enjoy playing music again. From time to time, I saw ads or handbills for Arthur's new group and the places they were scheduled to perform. I even went to see them play once at a gig they did at The Shrine. Arthur sang 'Signed, D.C.' a la José Feliciano. I guess it was supposed to be "a joke". Luke Warm was in the audience that night.

His final album for Elektra was in the stores and seemed to be doing all right, but I don't think it was ever on the charts or anything, and the FM stations never played any of the cuts on the air that I know of. So, you might say, it wasn't the success he had hoped it would be.

Then, one day, a few months after the release of *Four Sail*, my phone rang, and it was Arthur. "Michael, I have something I want to talk to you about. Where can we meet? It's important."

"What's up?" I asked.

"Well, you know I just landed a new contract for the group with Blue Thumb Records, but they don't like this new sound I got on *Four Sail*. In fact, they've more or less told me to do everything possible to try and get the original members back together. That's the LOVE they want. They don't think the new guys are marketable. Anyway, you're the first dude I called, because I know you have other things going and I wasn't positive you'd be available. Soon as we hang up, I'll call Bryan, then I'll try to locate Kenny and Johnny. You think you might be interested?"

"I don't know, man," I told him. "I'm on a retainer with Stigwood- Fitzpatrick and Atlantic, so my first commitment is to them, but I'll ask and see if something can be worked out that won't conflict, O.K?"

Arthur said that was cool and he would give me a call back after he talked to Kenny and Johnny and Bryan to set up a time and place to meet with the Blue Thumb representative. When I spoke with my contacts at Atlantic and Stigwood-Fitzpatrick, they agreed to grant me whatever flexibility necessary to continue my ties to the old group for as long as I thought it was worthwhile. They figured whatever continued success I had with LOVE could only help the record sales of any new group I recorded with.

When Arthur called back, he told me he had found Kenny and Johnny, and they were all for a reunion, but he didn't think Bryan had sounded up for it. "But, Michael, whatever happens with Bryan," Arthur told me, "Blue Thumb is still enthusiastic about reforming as many members of the original 'LOVE' as possible, so it's not critical if we have Bryan or not. Anyway, eight o'clock tomorrow night, at that little Italian joint below the Canyon Country Store, the Blue Thumb guy wants to meet with us. Can you make it?"

The next night at eight o'clock, Arthur and Johnny and Kenny and I all met with the Blue Thumb rep at the Italian restaurant to talk over the plans for the new-old group. Bryan didn't show. The company rep was a cool guy: you could tell he was happy to have us join back up for the next album. We worked out a tentative rehearsal schedule and I found out Johnny and Kenny didn't have instruments anymore, so Arthur said he would rent a guitar and bass from Studio Instrument Rentals. Kenny and Johnny could buy their own equipment after we played a few gigs. "No guitar or bass?" I wondered. "That's crazy. How do they survive? How do they pay the bills and buy food?"

The next day around noon, we got together at Arthur's new house, up in the hills above Sherman Oaks, I think. It was a large ranch house-type place, but real fancy and kind of L.A. faux western-opulent, not at all like his other house. Bigger pool, too. Gone were the pigeons. Now, he owned peacocks, which were allowed to roam the property at will. Arthur's Black Lab, Self, had run away from home, so he bought matching Russian Wolfhounds to fill the dog-man void.

After we set up, the group began to run over some of the old songs from the first three albums. We actually sounded pretty tight, considering we hadn't played with each other for a while, and that Johnny and Kenny were using instruments they'd never seen before. Johnny was even able to do double-duty, filling in most of Bryan's licks when he had to, so the sound was pretty much complete – even without Bryan. He was always super-talented. He could do it all.

When we had played a few songs, we took a smoke break. "Hey, guess what," Arthur smiled. "Our first gig is this weekend, and we have two more lined up the weekend after that, and the week after that. Whaddaya think? Can you guys handle it?"

We all laughed and slapped each other five. It was an upbeat rehearsal. I think we were all starting to believe, "Well, this isn't so bad. Maybe we can make this thing work, after all. Hell, maybe it'll be almost as good as before, who knows?"

After rehearsal was finished, while Kenny and Johnny were packing away their equipment, Arthur and I went out on the patio. He picked a basketball up off the seat of a lawnchair and tossed it to me. "Let's play some one-on-one, Michael, O.K.?" He grinned and positioned himself between me and the basket.

"Look out, man, coming through," I warned. Pushing off hard with my left arm, I dribbled past him and took it straight to the hole. He laughed and stumbled backward a couple of steps. No ref around, so no harm, no foul. As Arthur lined up a shot from the perimeter, I seized the opportunity. I had been patient.

"Tell me, man. What the hell ever happened to our royalty checks we were supposed to get from *Da Capo* and *Forever Changes*? Don't tell me that stupid recording debt still hasn't been paid off."

"Bronggg!" Arthur's shot bounced off the rim. "Oh, yeah. I know, Michael, it sounds ridiculous but believe it or not, we still owe Elektra money on those two albums. They really haven't sold that well, and the recording debt on *Forever Changes* alone was over twenty thousand."

I fired up a shot, "When the debt's paid off?"

Arthur grabbed the rebound, "You'll get your royalties, man, I promise. No bullshit."

When the night of the following weekend's performance came, Arthur asked if I could give Kenny a lift because he didn't have the Jag anymore; he picked up Johnny up. I don't even remember where the gig was, except somewhere in the L.A. area. But I do remember, we played well and the audience liked us, and we left the stage feeling like this, in some ways, might be the beginning of an even better LOVE than the one we had before. I mean, we were tight. No mistakes. On every song, Kenny was all over the fretboard, once again the master of the sophisticated bass runs that had always defined his playing style, punctuating my bass drum licks with his own seamless phrasing. Working the foundation. Laying it down.

Johnny's technique was as flawless as ever. He was blowing the audience away on every tune. Occasionally, he made eye-contact with me and smiled that Johnny-smile. He was totally in control. The guitar master. That had never gone away.

And another thing: Arthur seemed to be a little more relaxed without Bryan around. A little less on edge. Not as threatened. The atmosphere was calmer now.

We were in a groove.

After we were through playing, one fan came up and asked, "Where's Bryan?" but that's all. Just one. Then, Kenny and I went to get something to eat and we talked for a while. Later, I dropped him off, back at his garage-home. "I'll see you next week," I told him. Arthur had lined up a bunch of gigs for the new-old LOVE.

"Yeah, Michael, next week." He removed the rental bass from the back seat of my car and went inside and closed the garage door.

The next Thursday, my phone rang, "Michael, it's Arthur. Bad news, man. We're in a little trouble for this Saturday's gig."

"How come?" I asked.

"Johnny and Kenny were supposed to return their guitars to the rental shop during the week and pick 'em up again for the weekend gigs, just until they got back on their feet, you know? A couple of hours ago, Studio Instrument Rentals called and told me they never brought 'em in on Monday, like they were supposed to. So I drove over to the pad where Johnny's been staying, and the people he's been living with told me he had moved out on Tuesday. So, I jumped back in my short and went to Kenny's garage-pad and he was gone too, man! And check it out: I went down to Western Pawnbrokers – you know, Echols' favourite pawn shop – and the bass and guitar I rented them are sitting in the front window. You know what? The motherfuckers pawned 'em the day after our very first gig, man!"

"Wait a minute," I thought. "Something's fishy, here. That story sounds made-up. What really happened?" I wondered. We had been too good for Kenny and Johnny to up and disappear for no reason. It didn't make any sense. Something else was going on. Another of Arthur's "hidden agendas" maybe? A blow-up over the money? Probably.

"But Michael," he continued, "as far as this weekend is concerned, a couple of the dudes I used on the *Four Sail* album can step right in. They know all the songs as well as Johnny and Kenny. So, let's meet up here tomorrow to run over a few of the tunes. I'll introduce you guys. You can sort of get acquainted. We'll just do the gigs we have booked with them on bass and guitar."

I said, "Yeah, sure, man," and we hung up, but the wheels were turning. I mean, no Bryan was one thing but no Kenny or Johnny? What would be the point? Sounded like hanging onto the ledge by your fingertips to me. Let's call it a day, you know?

But I went ahead and rehearsed with Arthur and the two strangers from the "New LOVE", to see what would happen. They were hella fine musicians, no doubt about it. And no doubt about one other thing. You could have wound 'em up and they would have played every single song exactly the same every time. Note-for-note. Because that's what they did. That weekend and the following one, the fifty-fifty split of the old and new LOVE flew up the coast to somewhere in central California and played good music. We got along well, too. But, after the second week, I called Arthur and told him that I had scheduling conflicts with some recording dates I had been committed to with another group for some time, and he would have to find somebody else to play drums. "It might be better if you found someone who could devote full time to the group," I said. So, that was that. The end.

Because me and Arthur and the two new guys? That was no fun. It was an exercise in futility at best...a mythical journey with no predetermined destination. The truth was, everybody knew LOVE's epitaph had already been inscribed on vinyl in the fall of 1967.

The people at Blue Thumb, as determined as they had been to put the old LOVE back together, were philosophical – it was worth a shot, right? Honouring their contract with Arthur and allowing him to record with whoever he wanted so long as he called them "LOVE". That was the deal, I think.

Occasionally, I saw even newer, more updated "LOVE groups" on the store shelves; and, after a while, I began to realize that it wouldn't be long before Johnny and Kenny and Bryan and I were lost in the shuffle. Before long, the fans would only think of one guy as "LOVE": Arthur Lee. Bryan's songs would quickly be forgotten, they were so few in number. Sweep 'em under the carpet, quick. Get enough new faces and names on the liner notes and who knows? Jimi Hendrix was a prophet, wasn't he? "Arthur is LOVE, man!" That's what he said. That's the way it would be, after all.

From that time on, as long as I remained in music, I had plenty of opportunity come my way for session and performance work with groups from southern California to Seattle, and it was steady. One day, when I was in L.A., I ran into Kenny at a restaurant at the bottom of the hill near my new house in the hills above Old Cahuenga on the Valley side. "Hey, man, what's goin' on?" I asked him. We gave each other a big hug. He looked to be in good shape and healthy. "I'm clean, now," he said proudly. He told me he had a brand new job at Hanna-Barbera Studios. "Remember?" his voice brimmed with enthusiasm, "I was in art school when I joined up with Arthur so this is perfect. I'm just picking up where I left off. See? I'm a professional artist, finally."

Suddenly he laughed and shook his head. "Hey, man, did you hear that ridiculous story circulating a while back about me and Echols going around holding up Winchell's Donut shops with a toy gun?"

I nodded, "Yeah, I did. That's what Arthur told me."

Kenny looked concerned, "I hope you didn't believe any of that crap. I mean, if I ever decide to hold up a donut shop, I'll be sure and do it with a real gun, you know?"

"No, man. I didn't believe the stories. I stopped believing what Arthur says a long time ago. To him, 'the truth' is something you make up as you go along, to suit your needs."

We sat at the table and talked for a while then he said, "Michael, I'm glad I bumped into you, man, because I need a big favour. I've been staying in an apartment on the other side of Hollywood and it's gonna be real hard to get to my new job from there because I don't have a car anymore. I have to take the bus. Would you mind if I stayed with you for a few weeks until I get my first paycheck? Then I can find a place of my own, closer to work."

I punched him on the shoulder, "Yeah, sure man. Remember? You let me move in with you once upon a time. I have a spare bedroom, so no problem. I'll help you move in tonight if you want." Later, I drove him over to get his things and then back to my place, where we set him up in his new digs.

On the first night in my pad, we were sitting and smoking weed, like in the old days, listening to Miles.

"Hey, Michael, you know what's perfect about this?" he said, " Hanna-Barbera is right down the hill, so I can walk to work everyday 'til I get a car. I don't even have to take the bus." But I told him it was easy for me to give him a lift to work in the mornings, no big deal. And he was appreciative, and said he would make it up to me, somehow, some way.

Around nine that night, I told him, "Kenny, let's go get dinner down at Tiny Naylor's, we'll celebrate your new job. My treat, O.K?" So, we drove down the hill to the corner of Laurel Canyon and Ventura Boulevard, and we parked around back of the coffee shop, in the lot, and went inside.

After we ordered, Kenny said, "I gotta go to the shitter, man. I'll be right back." He scooted out of the booth and walked away in the direction of the head, and I began to think about the recent turn of events in our lives.

This was exactly what Kenny had needed. If he was good enough to land a job drawing for Hanna-Barbera, then he must have been a damn fine artist. I mean, he was a great musician too, but music and drugs share too great a proximity. If you're predisposed to use drugs to excess, then the further away from the music business you can take yourself, the better. In music, drugs are everywhere. Self-discipline does you no good, whatsoever. If you are a mainstream musician in Hollywood, the chances that you will someday have a drug problem stop just short of inevitable.

Five minutes had passed since Kenny had gone to the restroom. Then ten minutes. Our food came and I started to eat. Kenny's Steak-kebab sat on the table in front of his empty side of the booth getting cold. Soon, I started to wonder when he was coming back.

"Hey, Michael. Sorry I took so long, man. Is that my food already?" Kenny slid back into his seat and began pulling his kebab things off the skewer. As soon as I looked across the table, I could see the reason for the delay. "Sorry. I got hung up in there. Time flies, when you're having fun, you know," he forced a shallow laugh. His eyes were glazed and his voice had that husky glow.

I was incredulous. "What did you do, man? Shoot up in the restroom? I thought you weren't geezing any more."

He slowly cut a small bite of his steak and grinned. "Yeah."

"Are you outta your mind? Why didn't you do that before we left the house? Or wait 'til we get home? Why here?"

He looked up, "I don't know. I guess I just like the public restroom thing. It's fun. I like the oscillating hum the fan makes, when you're on the shitter and you start to come on. It goes, 'Woh, woh, woh, woh...' Sounds unusual." He laughed again, "Don't worry, man. I'm not doing any serious geezin', just chippin' a little. I've got it under control."

"Oh, well," I thought. High as a kite or straight arrow, Kenny was my buddy and a fun dude to be around. I certainly wasn't about to pass judgment. I was just glad to be helping him get back on track.

About that time, a small group of people entered through the back door from the parking lot. You could tell right away they were pretty drunk because their voices were loud and they were all falling over each other on their way in. A little out of control. Then I realized one guy seemed to be quite a bit drunker than the rest of his friends. Someone on either side held him by his arms and manoeuvred him in between the tables to a seat at a table near the kitchen door. He looked strangely familiar.

"Kenny, turn around and check out the dude they're helping in. Who is he?" I knew he was an actor in films but I couldn't think of his name. Kenny's face lit right up. "Oh, man, that's Dana Andrews: you remember, *The Best Years of Our Lives*?" So, Kenny and I began watching the action. There was something odd going on but what? They all ordered the same thing, spaghetti and salad. I began to see that the others weren't nearly as drunk as Dana was. I mean, he was way over the edge, practically unconscious. And everybody at his table was slapping him on the back and pretending to be as drunk as he was, but it was an act. They weren't. Dana's friends were doing practically all the talking, too. He wasn't saying much of anything, just nodding occasionally and smiling non-stop. And eating.

About the time they finished their salad and started on the spaghetti, Dana was having a hell of a time keeping his head up. He was sort of bobbing and weaving and smiling but not contributing anything at all anymore to the conversation. And, then... "clank", before anybody could grab him, he went face down in the spaghetti. And it was a real mess. He splashed it all over himself. But the coffee shop manager saw what was happening and quickly sent the waiter over with the check to clean up the table and get Dana and his friends out of there.

After the waiter laid the check down, everybody started saying stuff like, "Ha, ha, come on, Dana, stop clowning around." They pulled him up out of his plate, and took their napkins and wiped his face off. Then, one of his friends reached into Dana's inside coat pocket, took some money out of his wallet and paid the bill. "It's time to go home, buddy, let's go." I looked at Kenny and shook my head, "That's cold-blooded, man."

Dana's friends helped him to his feet and dragged him back out the rear exit to the parking lot, the whole time talking to him like he was still conscious, slapping him on the back, laughing. The most amazing part of this whole scene was this: if these people were going to take advantage of a big movie star like Dana Andrews, why didn't they cart him over to The Brown Derby or some other class restaurant, where they all could dine in splendour? Why Tiny Naylor's? Unless maybe they figured if they took him somewhere reputable, the restaurant manager might see what was going on and call the cops, and maybe they'd all get arrested for "drunk and disorderly" or "aggravated rolling of a drunk". Tiny's was a little safer, in that respect.

The next morning, I gave Kenny a ride to his first day at the new job. When we pulled up out front, he pointed to a guy getting out of a BMW, "That's my supervisor, Gary. He's a real nice dude. Hey, thanks for the lift, man." Kenny got out of the car and went inside to draw pictures. For the next couple of weeks, it went on like that just about every day. After I dropped Kenny off at his job, I would meet one of my new bandmates for breakfast, then drive on over to the rehearsal hall to go over a few songs, or to the studio. From time to time, Kenny would come home from work, go into the bathroom and stay for a while. When he came out his eyes had the familiar glaze and his voice was husky, so he continued to "chippy".

My new group had booked a two-nighter someplace in Arizona to fine-tune the material and help get it ready for the studio. We arrived back in L.A. several days later. As I unlocked my front door, I could hear the phone ringing and ringing, which I thought was strange: Kenny should have been home. It was early Monday morning, way too early for him to have left for work. After I finally got the door opened, I got to the phone as quick as I could. I hate phones. You're the slave, they're the master. They ring, you gotta jump up. You can't ignore the stupid things, and it's nearly always bad news or a wrong number or somebody selling something. I don't like the recording machine or voicemail either, because then the bad news is just waiting for you.

"Yeah, hello!"

"Michael, my name is Gary. You don't know me but I work with Kenny at Hanna-Barbera and, to be blunt, we're a little worried about him. He took a draw on his first paycheck last Friday afternoon and he was supposed to work on Saturday but he didn't show up. Is he there, by any chance?"

I didn't have to look.

"No, Gary, he's not here but, when I see him, I'll have him give you a jingle, O.K?" We hung up, then I walked back to his bedroom. He was gone. I looked around and all his stuff was gone. I went to his closet and opened the door. All his clothes were cleaned out. Then, on a hunch, I went to my closet in my own bedroom and opened the door. All my stuff was gone, too. The nice things, anyway. The leather coats and articles with resale value of any kind. Gone. I just stood there.

I felt like Dana Andrews must have felt when he woke up with a headache and an empty wallet the morning after his friends picked his pocket for a free spaghetti dinner at Tiny Naylor's. I have to admit, I was completely fooled. I mean, Kenny had been given still another precious opportunity to start fresh – as an artist this time and without the hindrance of being dragged down by somebody else who was too damned lazy to work. I thought, "No way is he gonna do anything stupid." Incredibly, he had blown it. I mean, life usually gives you a few chances to save yourself from certain disaster and then, after a while, you jump on the downhill slide and ride the thing all the way to the bottom. Kenny was on it and picking up speed. Not surprisingly, I never heard from him again.

Chapter Twenty One

Endgames

IT WAS mid-morning, around December of '69, when there came a knock at my door, and it was Jefferson, the lead guitar player in the C.K. Strong group, a band I was playing with at the time. I invited him in and we sat down and, after we fired up a joint, he began to relate to me the following story...

A couple of large, intimidating-type dudes had come to his house and asked if I lived there, and Jefferson noticed, as they stood in the doorway talking, the visitors seemed to be sort of trying to look around him, you know... as though they were trying to spot some evidence of my having been there, perhaps, like maybe my silver Ludwigs, or whatever. They claimed to be friends with Arthur, and when they learned I wasn't there, they went away.

After Jefferson left, I gave Arthur a jingle to see what was going on, and he says, "Yeah, Michael man, somebody broke into my house a couple of days ago and took some money and my stereo and a few other things, so you know...." As he trailed off, his voice had an indefinable edge to it.

"And, what... you think I did it?" I asked. "How about I come over to your place and we'll talk about it, OK?"

"Uh...OK.," he responded, with a note of apprehension. "Alright man, see you in fifteen," I said, and hung up.

So, in less than fifteen, actually, I swung my Porsche through the wide-open security gate of Arthur's house on Avenida Del Sol; and being careful to avoid flattening one of the many peacocks and Afghan hounds running hither and yon, I maneuvered my car to a spot close to the front door.

Right away Arthur came out to meet me, and then, walking ahead of me back into the house and into the living room, he offered, "Have a seat on the couch, man." So I did. But even before I had fully completed the sitting-down process, he began his explanation. "See man, my new bass player Frank actually brought your name up when we were trying to think who could have pulled this off or who had reason to do it. Frank said it might be you because of the royalties thing."

"Really?" I replied. "What did you say was taken?" Arthur wandered off around the corner and into the kitchen, but he raised his voice level a bit, so we could continue to communicate, only not face-to-face.

"Some hash, a few hundred dollars and my stereo," he said. I heard a few pots and pans clanging, so I figured maybe he was starting his dinner.

"You mean the stereo that hasn't worked for a long time... that stereo?" I asked, because it hadn't. Then I added, in a voice loud enough for him to hear around the corner in the other room, "But I have lots of money and hash of my own and a really nice stereo that works great, so what would I want with your stuff?" Arthur stood for a moment in the kitchen doorway, thoughtfully wiping a pan with a dishtowel.

"Yeah, OK Michael, I guess you got a point. But look here, man, just so you'll know, there's something else that made me think it was you. Whoever ripped me off, took my assault rifle out from under my bed and put it in the middle of the hall, pointing toward the front door. They even chambered a round, you know... like a challenge."

"And that seemed like something I would do?" I pressed on.

"I don't know," he responded quietly, a vestige of suspicion still lingering in his voice.

I was suddenly feeling kind of pumped-up. Somehow Arthur had arrived at an oddly misconceived image of me as some kind of dangerous and crazy lunatic who would burgle his house to get my royalties. I was a little shocked actually, but of course flattered and somewhat proud that he would view me as such an extreme example of a "take charge" kind of guy. How could he be so far off? I wanted to savour the moment as long as possible, but sadly it was time to wrap things up. "So, now that you know that it wasn't me after all, I guess you owe me an apology, right?" Because he did, after all, and he knew it, but nevertheless he began to pace defiantly back and forth across the living room floor; and then shaking his head in the negative, he says, "No man, I don't owe you any apology! I had every right... you know... you kept hassling me about your royalties...!" On and on he went.

About that time I sort of stopped listening, because I could tell where the rant was headed anyway, and also, you see, what I haven't mentioned yet, is that Arthur and I weren't the only ones there in his living room at the house on Avenida Del Sol that day. Because all this time, sitting quietly on the other side of the L-shaped black leather couch, only several feet away, expressionless and silent, and not moving a muscle, was... I don't know... I guessed maybe one of Arthur's friends from the old neighbourhood, or maybe one of the guys that came looking for me over at Jefferson's house. It could have been either or neither, because, you know... Arthur didn't introduce us or anything. Very rude. Was this guy Arthur's "back-up"?... like, I was on my way over for a potential confrontation, and if by chance I had been the one, then the confrontation might conceivably turn violent or something, because I was, after all, unpredictable to say the least. Better call what's his name, to, you know... be there, just in case there's trouble.

Shaking his head, Arthur strode deliberately back out of the living room, off into the kitchen and out of sight again, ... and suddenly I had a thought. Making brief eye-contact with Arthur's friend from the old neighbourhood, and purposefully putting my index finger to my lips, I reached toward the wooden dope box that always sat on the coffee table, I opened the lid, and removed the chunk of hash I knew would be there. Then I picked up his glass pipe and loaded it, placed the remaining chunk in my coat pocket, and closed the box lid, just as Arthur re-entered the room.

"Hey, uh, Michael," he began, "I've been thinking... and you know, you're right man, I do owe you an apology, but I'm just trying to think who the motherfucker is who could have done it, you know? But I am sorry. I know it wasn't you." He reached out and we shook hands.

Over already? Too bad. I felt a slight letdown.

"No problem," I obliged, "Hey, check it out..." I handed him his pipe and lighter, "I brought over some nice Turkish. Go ahead." He fired it up and took a long pull, then, letting it out slowly, commenced with the inevitable coughing spasm.

"Hey, look," I said, standing up, "I gotta get going. Here... keep this." I took the hash chunk from my pocket and set it on top of the box. I glanced briefly over at the friend from the old neighbourhood. No expression, punctuated by a blank stare.

"Cool, man," Arthur said, smiling and shaking my hand again. "Take it easy, Michael." Then I walked outside, got in my Porsche, and left.

What was really cool, of course, was what I didn't get to see... the look on Arthur's face when the friend from the old neighbourhood told him I had just turned him on to his own hash.

The next day, I got a call from Craig Tarwater, the dude who replaced Randy as lead guitarist in The Sons of Adam, after Randy quit.

"Hey, Michael, I know a guy in Seattle who's looking to form a group to record an album. You want a gig?" I knew Craig was a hell of a fine guitar player and I had respect for his opinion, so we headed north to be part of a group headed up by Danny O'Keefe.

You know that song that Dandy Don Meredith used to sing at the end of every Monday night football game, when the outcome was no longer in doubt? Sort of a country and western ditty. "Some gotta weeein... some gotta lose. Goodtime Charlie's got the blues." Danny O'Keefe wrote and recorded it.

Danny was funny. He had a super-resonant normal conversational voice, like Kenny's old actor-neighbour in Laurel Canyon, the one with the German shepherd. He always talked like he thought somebody might sneak up and try to record him on the spur of the moment. So he wanted to be ready and "in vocal-character".

Danny was a meditator, a fact I had a hard time remembering. Sometimes, I would walk into the living room and see him out of the corner of my eye, sitting on the couch, and would say, "Hey, Danny, what's happenin'?" to be polite, but I wouldn't get a response. Then, I would look at him a little more directly and he would be... wearing his rainbow skull cap, legs crossed yoga-style, head tilted back, eyes closed, thumb and forefingers of each hand forming circles atop his knees. Then, I would remember... Oh, yeah. Meditation time. "Whoops, sorry," I would say, tip-toeing out of the room. Don't want to break the trance.

The sax player in the group was Billy MacPherson. He was the best I ever heard. A genius. Real skinny dude, because all he ever ate was a bowl of white rice once or twice a day, great big afro that he only washed once the whole time I knew him: he was gifted. We used to climb into my Porsche every night, around eleven, and go looking for a club we hadn't been to yet, so he could sit in with the house band and blow everybody's mind. I mean, I would sit in too, but when Billy was onstage nobody else got any attention. Like, Billy would start to play and everybody else would just kind of disappear. Anybody that hadn't heard him play yet would simply stare in awe. Especially the other musicians. As soon as he started to take a solo, the house band would look at him and smile and shake their heads in wonderment. He was that great. On the way out of the club, I always had the feeling people were watching us leave and thinking, "Shit, that drummer's lucky. He gets to hang out with one of the best sax players in the world." I always felt the house band wanted to leave with us, too.

How is it Billy and I were able to go club-hopping every night? All part of Danny's master plan. Everybody in the group lived in one house, so we qualified for food stamps and financial aid as long as we didn't work. Danny thought we should just use our time to practice the material for the upcoming album and not waste our energy working a club gig four or five hours a night.

Anyway, I finally went to Danny and said, "Look, man, why don't we forget the food stamps and find ourselves a little club to play in at night and fine-tune the album in front of a live audience?"

But nevertheless, we soon thereafter landed a club gig over on the wrong side of the tracks in a beat little dive where the crowd was pumped and there were fistfights at the door every night. A joint called The El Roach Club. What I remember most about The El Roach Club was a hand-written sign over the urinal in the men's room that said: "You are the person your mother warned you about." My mom liked that one.

Danny saved a guy there one night. What happened was, the door man/bouncer was a tough dude who was fond of showing off his belt buckle, which had been sharpened to a razor edge, so he could take it off and use it as a weapon on somebody who wouldn't cooperate, if need be. "I could cut somebody up pretty good in a fight," he would say. Then, he would take the belt off and swing it around and around over his head menacingly. So, one night a guy went outside for a smoke and when he tried to come back in the bouncer says, "Sorry buddy, policy says you can't come back in, even if you have a stamp." But, the patron wasn't going for it, and they started to have words and before you know it they were in a fight for real. And the patron, who was much larger than the bouncer, was immediately getting the better end of the deal because the bouncer didn't have time to get his belt out. So, without a moment's hesitation, Danny runs over and gets right in between them and he settled things down. After that, the bouncer was walking around for the rest of the night, saying, "Did you see that? The only guy that came in to help me was the singer in the band," because everybody else just stood there and watched what was happening. I kept thinking the bouncer was going to somehow get his belt out and even things up a bit, but no could do. He was too busy being overwhelmed. Anyway, Danny was the hero that night. No doubt about it. He was.

Danny was an excellent singer-songwriter and had a contract in place with Atlantic but I bailed out about a month before we were to start recording the album and headed back to L.A. Over the course of the next couple of years I worked with some extremely talented people and participated in a lot of worthwhile projects, but two irrefutable realities had become evident. In the first place, the magic was gone. The music business was just that, another business. Maybe a little more cut-throat and unregulated, perhaps more dangerous to be a part of, but still just a business. In 1965, when I decided that professional music was where my heart was, this wasn't what I had in mind – or heart. What changed, reality or my perspective? Probably both, but so what? It didn't matter, because it just wasn't fun and exciting any more. Secondly, drugs proliferated. They were everywhere. They were a major component of every social and professional contact. "Hi, glad to meet you. Here, check it out, man. I got some bad coke, smack, crank, whatever. Have some." And they would line it up.

The worst part was that, after a long, long time of being the squarest dude in the group, of resisting drugs, of not even really being that interested, I had begun to buy into the drug mentality. Smack, coke, reds, crank... The list went on and on. Now, being under the influence of anything was a lot better than being on the natch, which had begun to feel scary. And getting high was so time-consuming. A different drug for each situation. The approach-avoidance. The guilt. You know it's not good so, when supplies start to run low, you ask yourself, "Do I want to score any more of this shit? If so, how much? Maybe I should make the call now. Maybe I should wait so the dude'll run out and I can't get any more and I'll be forced to stop getting high. I can stop. I'm strong enough if I have a little push." If you're not at peace with doing drugs, there's a lot of decision-making type thinking that goes into it. Anguish.

It's summer. No rehearsals scheduled today. And it's hot, well over a hundred. Hot as it gets in L.A. Why does it get hotter in the flats of Hollywood than it does in the hills? My air conditioner is on the fritz, too. It works, then it doesn't work. I'm just gonna lay here in my pad and eat a popsicle and wait for my connection to call. He's harder than hell to get hold of. When you need the drugs you have to call his answering service and leave a message for "Louise Hettig". That's what he calls himself, to throw the cops off. Then he calls you back when he's good and ready. I made the call over two hours ago, so... Guess I may as well turn on the TV and channel surf for a while to pass the time, because he'll be calling any minute. Any second, actually, so I better not go out or I'll miss the call.

Hmm. What do we have here? KCOP, Channel 13, this looks interesting. Good old black and white movie. Check the newspaper TV guide... Let's see... "Stars Cameron Mitchell. Story of a man who comes home from the war with an addiction to morphine. Title... *Monkey On My Back*."

Next day, go to the studio, sniff a line of coke, smoke a little weed, lay down a track.

Smoke a little more weed to get really hungry, then go eat lunch, snort another line, go back to the studio to work.

That's the problem with drugs: you start by being afraid of them all. Then, little by little, you lose the fear and your conscience and you begin to use each one to "enhance" life's experience or to counteract the other. Before long, you start to believe that you can't really have a good time or do your best effort or relax without drugs. And that's when they kick all the other little birdies out of the nest. Then, it's just the drugs. That's what remains. There is no "real world". There's just the phoney one that you and the drugs have created. So I began to rethink my direction. I mean, when I was drawn into music, I entered it with no preconceived timetable. I just knew I wanted to be a professional musician, that's all. For how long? I didn't think in those terms. I suppose if somebody had asked be in the beginning how long I planned on staying in the music business – forever? For the rest of your life? – I would have responded, "Well, no, not forever, I guess. I don't know."

Sometimes you don't become aware of the end until it comes. You don't recognize it because you never saw it before. But I began to think maybe this was it. This growing ambivalence I was feeling in the pit of my gut to the "business" side of music had started to result in a funny kind of self-destructive career mannerism. Something that I know must have made me appear irrational to other people in the industry.

Just when a group I had been working with was about to sign contracts and enter the most lucrative and rewarding part of their schedule, the structured touring and recording, I would save up the last three or four thousand dollars of the retainer checks I had been receiving, walk into the corporate office of the management group and lay the checks on the desk and I would quit. It happened more times than I like to recall.

I remember my conscious reasoning at the time exactly. I would think, "What am I doing? I don't want to play with these guys exclusively, and I certainly don't want to get locked into any kind of a contractual obligation. I don't even like their music." But, looking back, I realize that was my way of easing myself out of the business. When I decided to get into professional music, I never thought, "I'll do it for five years." It was more open-ended. I could feel myself reaching the end of the line. I just didn't want to be there any more. It was suddenly becoming stale. Cue: 'The Party's Over'.

One day, before I had come to a hard-and-fast decision, a friend who was the equipment manager for Neil Diamond called me. "Hey, Michael, Neil's looking for a drummer. I told him I knew you. He's interested in talking to you about a permanent gig. He has a European tour coming up next month and he wants to replace the guy he's got now before the tour starts. It could be a lot of money for a long time to come. Neil's closing tonight at The Troubadour. If you think you might want to do it, he asked me to bring you down to check out his act, you know, his stage presentation, and all. Our names will be left at the door. I'll meet you in the bar at ten, O.K?"

So, around ten o'clock that night, I pulled up to the curb in front of the club and, after turning my car over to the valet, I went in and had a couple of drinks with Neil Diamond's roadie at the bar. Then we went inside. Neil was onstage in the middle of a set. He was singing 'Cherry, Cherry' and all the ladies were grinning big, watching his every move and clapping along with the beat and mouthing the lyrics. They were stoked. Neil was wearing his signature black sequined shirt and his guitar was way out of tune (which, as I learned later, was the way he played all the time). "Close enough for rock'n'roll," Bryan used to say, when he was tired of tuning up.

In a minute, Neil finished up 'Cherry, Cherry' and went into a between-songs, informal-style-rap with the audience. He swung his guitar around his back and, stepping closer to the microphone stand and caressing it with both hands, he began: "You know, sometimes people ask me how I felt, the first time I ever heard myself on the radio. Well, all my life I had dreamed about hearing myself on the radio and, when it finally happened, I was walking out of a record store." Neil was smiling a wicked smile. "They had one of those sidewalk speakers set up, see? My song came on and I looked down and this dog was urinating on a fire hydrant." Much hilarious laughter. "So that's what I always think of when I remember myself on the radio for the first time. I think of that dog urinating on a fire hydrant next to the speaker." More laughter.

Then, he broke into 'Holly Holy' and all the ladies went bonkers, whereupon Neil, after removing the microphone from its anchor at the top of the mic stand, executed a deep bow from the waist and kept singing. Then, after 'Holly Holy', he started reeling off his hits, one by one: 'Sweet Caroline', 'Brother Love's Travelling Salvation Show' and so on. I remembered that I had never liked one song Neil Diamond had ever recorded, not even a bit. Songs for girls is what they were.

As the waves of tittering began to subside, his road manager leaned over, "According to the guys in the group, that story about the dog urinating is true. He told it to an audience a few years back and it got a big laugh so he's been using it ever since. He calls it 'his' joke."

"Really?" I asked. "How many jokes does he have?"

"Just the one," he nodded earnestly.

Neil had a girl playing guitar in his backup group. Between songs, he put his arm around her waist and pulled her to him and looked out into the crowd and, as he brought his lips seductively close to the microphone, Neil asked, "How many singers can make love to their guitar players, huh?" And she giggled real loud. More laughter from the ladies in the audience.

"Now, folks," Neil said, while making a game but unsuccessful stab at tuning his E-string, "we're gonna play a song for you that's very close to my heart. I call it 'Gorilla, Be A Woman Soon'," he laughed. "One, two, three, four!" The band broke into the intro to 'Girl, You'll Be A Woman Soon'.

After what seemed an eternity, Neil's set was finished. He came over to where we were seated and introduced himself and he told me a little about the upcoming performance schedule. "Yeah, Michael, we'll be leaving for Europe next month, so go ahead and arrange for your passport application right away."

I told him I would, but I was thinking, "I don't know, man. We'll see. If what I witnessed tonight is any indication of things to come, I may have to try and get out of this somehow."

That part about it being a long-term gig was already beginning to bother me a little, too. Even if I accepted his offer, I didn't think I could play this material for more than a couple of weeks, but I agreed to meet with everybody the next day at a rehearsal hall on Cherokee.

When Neil left our table to rejoin the group onstage, my buddy and I got up and left. "Neil told me he likes your drumming a lot, man," he said on the way out the door. "He's heard your records and he's really looking forward to having you in the band." I was tempted to level with him on the spot and tell him that I really wasn't interested, but I was already committed to the next day's rehearsal, so I made up my mind to go anyway and give it a try.

"Who knows?" I thought, "I might find something to like about this group, after all. I'll give it a shot. What can I lose?" I was trying not to be prematurely judgmental. I was trying to be fair, you know? Maybe I was just starting to get hard up.

The next afternoon around three, we met at the VA Hall in Hollywood. Before the rehearsal started, everybody introduced themselves and we sort of got to know each other a little. Neil wasn't expected for another hour or so because he was hung up in a meeting, so the group used the time to run over a few of the tunes they thought he would ask us to play. After a while, the bass player suggested we take a break and, as I got up from my drums, he silently waved me over to a corner of the backstage area and pulled a leather pouch from his coat pocket. "Want a quick snort of some good coke, Michael?" I could tell, it was sort of like the new office employee being invited to have an after work drink with one of the office old-timers. It was a sociable gesture.

"Yeah, sure, I guess," I responded automatically. He filled a silver nose spoon with the white powder, held it up to me and I whiffed it. Then, the other side. The now all-too-familiar scent of hospital-grade disinfectant rose up through my nostrils. Almost immediately, I started feeling nauseated. This drug thing was really getting old. It was always the same. I didn't realize it for years but the truth is, drugs don't help you have a good time at all; in fact, they get in the way of a good time. Everything is more fun without the drugs. Believe it.

If you're a musician, they don't help you perform your best. They keep you from performing your best. Big time. There's no such thing as a "performance-enhancing drug". That's an oxymoron.

After everybody in Neil's backup band had partaken of the coke, someone from the office came down and told the bass player that Neil's personal manager was on the phone and wanted to speak to him. So, he left and came back a couple of minutes later looking worried. "Hey, everybody, Jack wanted to warn me that Neil's on his way over to the hall. They had a disagreement of some kind and Neil's all pissed off, so he advises us to be low-key and don't say or do anything to get him more pissed off 'til he cools down a little. He'll be O.K. in a little while."

The girl guitar player, who had been keeping an eye out the front door, suddenly turned around, "Neil's here!" She scrambled back to the stage and picked up her guitar. "C'mon, we better be going over a song when he comes in." They grabbed their instruments and I sat back down at the drums and we began to play one of his ugly-ass hits. When he walked in, I checked his expression and, sure enough, he looked all mad.

Approaching the edge of the stage, he waved his arms to stop us, "All right, all right. Never mind that," he scowled, "I've got something else I want to show you people. This is something I wrote just last night. It has a heavy African influence. I call it 'Soolaimon'."

Then he picked up his always-out-of-tune black acoustic and began the caterwauling. After he finished pouting his way through it a couple of times, Neil took off his guitar and leaned it against the drum riser. "Think you people can learn that tonight?" The next morning, I called the bass player up and told him to tell Neil "thanks but no thanks."

I used to look at the nameless, faceless, drummers in bands backing up the big-name singles and vocal group acts and think, "Well, it's not a bad gig, but personally I wouldn't care to do it." The bottom line is: I had been having a pretty good time at U.C.L.A. I never would have quit school to go on the road as a professional drummer in a back-up band for anybody but I had begun to realize, the longer I stayed in the music business, the greater the probability that the day might come when I couldn't turn down a job opportunity like the one Neil Diamond had just offered me. In fact, I might one day be sitting by the phone, praying for an offer like this. It might be my dream gig. I mean, this situation was my own doing. I had turned down so many respectable opportunities, I had lost count. I had thrown away so many chances to record with groups with promising futures and recording contracts and tours in place until, right here and now, at least for the moment, this is what I was left with: a long-term gig with Neil Diamond.

I remembered the circumstances that led me to think of professional music as something I wanted to be a part of. The special feeling I got when I listened to music I liked, the surge of adrenaline I got when I played. The admiration and encouragement of my fellow students in high school and college when they saw me drum, the jazz and rock groups that had recruited me and inspired me to drop school and try to jump on the wave of the British invasion; the personalities, the names and faces of the members of groups that were, essentially, my musical role models, the great early rock heroes, like James Brown and Little Richard and The Everly Brothers and then the more contemporary recording artists like The Beatles and The Rolling Stones.

But the magic that surrounded these groups had long since vanished. Now, it was just a business like any other. In the end, professional music turned out to be a lot like Disneyland, a great place to visit but you wouldn't want to live there. Or work there, for that matter.

I thought of the A&R man, Jake, in Miami and the pictures he had on the wall. Not because he wanted to keep playing, but because it was nothing more or less than a fond memory. Jake had a handle on it. He began to see participation in professional music as a limitation to his future, not an enhancement. It came time for him to move on, and he did. "Besides, I think old guys look funny trying to play rock'n'roll": that's what he had said. Still, he had lamented the time and effort he had put into learning the guitar and the strange feeling of having to walk away from the thrill of making music. I mean, there are no easy answers.

It's like the NFL football players who get too old or get hurt or who have to stop playing for whatever reason. No more running a kick-off back for a touchdown in front of seventy-five thousand screaming fans. One day it just comes to a sudden halt. Then what? Become a coach? That's not exciting. Buy a franchise? Nope. There is no natural progression to something else because there's nothing like playing. It's the same with music. If you decide you don't want to play anymore, that it's not in your best interest, what can you move on to? A&R? Production or engineering? Promotion? Run your own label? No thrill in any of those things. Those are just jobs, and not one of those jobs is remotely similar to playing music in front of an audience. Being a professional musician is a walk of the plank. When you stop playing, it's like hitting the ice-cold surface of the water after you take that last step.

You're flying down a one-way street at a hundred miles an hour and suddenly you see a bunch of garbage cans and a brick wall up ahead. And, on that wall, there's a sign. "Dead End", it says. Nowhere to go, and no room to turn around or time to slow down, much less roll to a controlled stop. Boom! You just hit it, full speed.

But I was simply at a crossroads. I knew I either had to come to terms with being a back-up musician for the rest of my musical life or learn to do something else.

"Hey, all is not lost," I thought. "You're only in your twenties, fool. It's just time for a change, man, that's all."

Like Jake said, "It's a big world."

"You're not shackled to this gig," I told myself. I knew it would be impossible not to miss playing music, but that's tough. Life is tough. I mean, there's something to be said for hanging in there forever, no matter what. Ask Mick Jagger. But did I really want to grow up to be a drummer in a senior citizen band? I guess I always knew sooner or later I would have to change direction. "Better sooner than later," I decided, "While I still have a little flexibility."

I called Ronnie and told her of my plans and she mentioned there might be an assistant engineer position opening up with a studio owned by a friend of hers. "After you get your feet wet as an engineer, you can work your way into production." Sounded promising, but I gave it a try and realized it wasn't for me. It felt too strange being on the other side of the control booth window.

And I knew in my heart I had to get further away from the drugs. They were everywhere in Hollywood. I had to find something to do that would take me completely away from the business altogether, away from constant temptation. Because, truth be told, by the time I left music, I was moderately addicted to several different drugs, and severely addicted to the "getting high" solution. Doing drugs is a lot like being a member of the Mafia. It's a lot easier to join up than it is to quit. Besides, I was truly, in my heart, fed up with the music business. To me, it was just time to move on.

After a few months, when I felt I was sufficiently clean, I took the entrance exams for law school and was admitted. I did well, but dropped out after only a couple of semesters. I couldn't concentrate. Physically I was clean, but psychologically I was still addicted. Truth be told, it took me years to completely divest myself of all my drug habits. It can't be done quick. Ever try to pull a tick out of a dog's hide? If you don't take your time and do it carefully, the head breaks off under the skin and it grows a new body. Same thing.

So I found regular work, you know, standard jobs, and I liked them all, really. In fact, I can honestly say I never had a job I didn't like. I just enjoy working. A wise man once said, "Work is play you get paid for." I subscribe to that concept.

I ran an offset print machine in downtown L.A., a job I landed while in law school. I worked as a product inspector on a shipping and receiving dock, and I climbed poles and pulled cable for the phone company for a few years. Great jobs, all; working with down-to-earth, cool people. No pretence. No arrogance. Just normal, relaxed, well-adjusted human beings. I like normal. It's a normal world. I crammed enough of the other into the six-year period between 1965 and 1971 to last me the rest of my life. A little abnormal goes a long way.

I realize you can't just walk away. Not completely. An undeniable part of my self-identity will always be "a musician", and a dissonant confluence of assorted patterns of notes and rhythms will always regularly greet me like old friends when I wake up in the middle of the night, then, after a while, if I'm lucky, serenade me back to sleep. "Normal", in its pure form, doesn't exist, anyhow. Nobody's totally normal. Some are just closer than others, that's all. It's a conceptual goal. Something to shoot for. The way I figure it is, as long as I'm having a good time whacking away at it, what difference does it make? I'm abnormal but happy. I loved the music. I hated the drugs and the business. I had to go.

Arthur, Bryan, Johnny, Kenny and I had all lost touch with one another by 1970. I knew that Bryan had dedicated himself to the solo project he had always dreamed of, Johnny and Kenny dropped out of sight and Arthur continued to record and tour with different groups he always called LOVE.

One Saturday morning in the late eighties, a friend who knew of my past called me. "Mike," he said excitedly, "your old band buddy, Snoopy, is being interviewed on the radio right now. Turn it on, man!" He told me the station numbers. When I tuned in, Snoop was starting to hype a percussion seminar that he and some other guys were going to host the next day at a local parks and recreation centre.

"I know you'll have a great turnout, tomorrow," the D.J. was saying, "but tell us, Snoopy, what an honour it must have been for Hal David and Burt Bacharach to have written a song, 'My Little Red Book', just for your group. That's amazing!"

Snoop laughed, "They didn't write it for us, man. They wrote it and we took it."

Undaunted, the disc jockey pressed on. "Well then, it must have felt good to be such a big part of the hippie era, helping to represent peace and love and all. My aunt told me all about it. She was one of your biggest fans. She had most of your albums."

Snoop laughed again. "I'm sorry, man, your aunt had it all wrong. There wasn't any love in that group. It had nothing whatsoever to do with love. It was all about hate. That should have been the name of the band."

"Oh," the D.J. said.

After the interview was over, I called the station, and the station manager put me in touch with Snoop. We met the next day and talked and smoked some weed and drove around. He told me he lived near Spokane, Washington, and he was happy. That was the last time I saw him.

I recently learned, over the internet, that Kenny died in December of '97, in Florida, of a brain tumour.

Thanks to the efforts of the writer, Kevin Delaney, I met with Bryan in August of '98, after not having spoken with him for thirty years. We spent an afternoon together. The following Christmas Day, Bryan was having lunch with Kevin in a small restaurant across the street from Canter's, when he suddenly rose from his seat, excused himself from the table and went into the bathroom, where he collapsed and died of a heart attack.

When people as talented as Arthur and Kenny and Bryan die so young, you find yourself wondering what would have happened if they had been allowed to live longer and happier lives, free from chemical encumbrances, and free to instead focus on creative productivity with a clear mind. But then, maybe that part of their beings, the emotional frailty and the subsequent tendency to fall back on crutches like drugs and alcohol to dull the pain and soothe the senses, were a necessary component of what made them what they were, and there was simply no escaping what lay ahead. It was kismet. The inescapable conclusion.

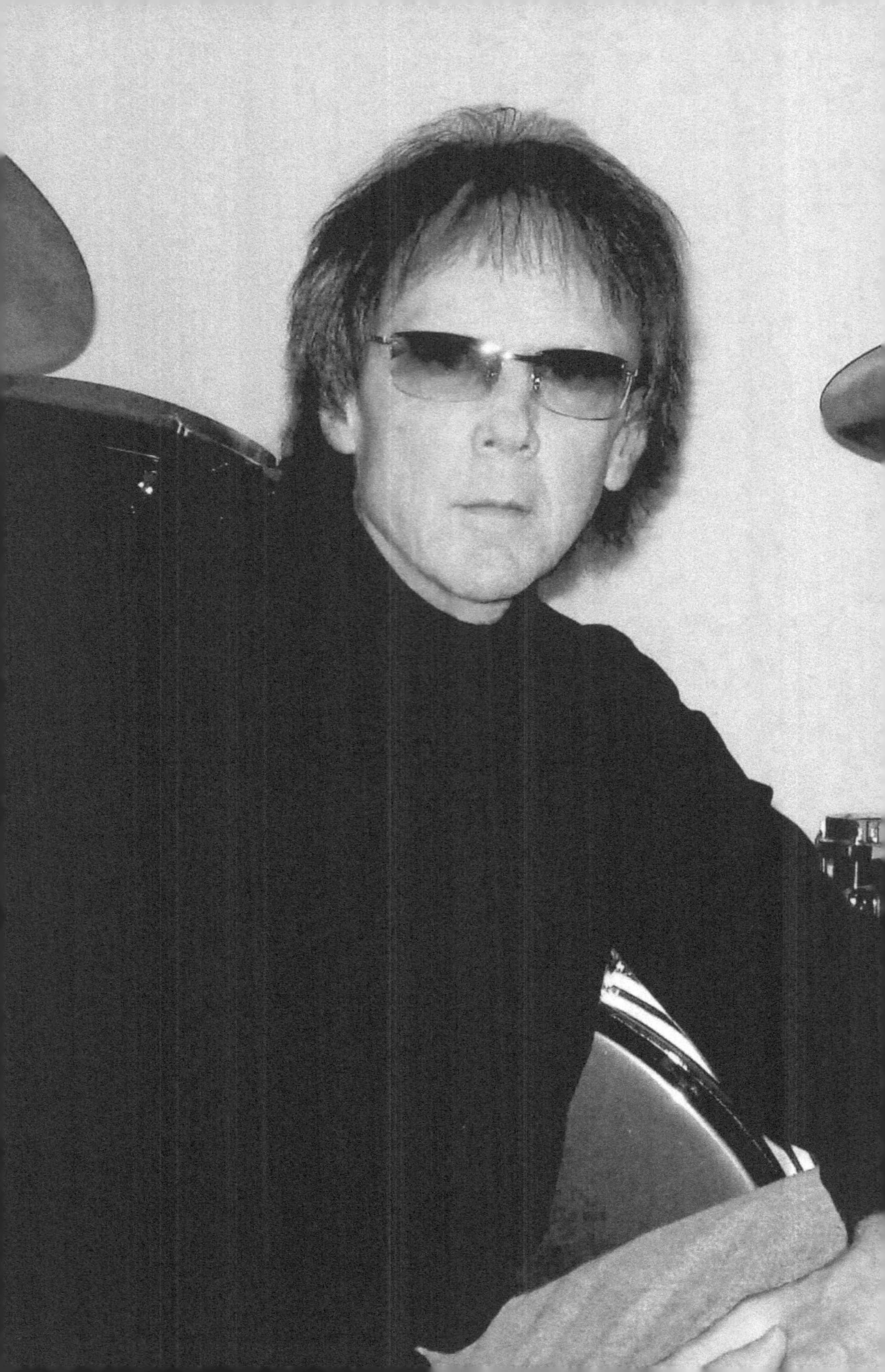

Epilogue

TO FULLY UNDERSTAND what happened to Arthur, I guess you have to stop and remember that we live in a society set up to answer the needs of the majority, and that members of the nonconformist-minority, therefore and unfortunately, live their lives at somewhat of a disadvantage.

Because how in the world are the majority-regulars going to avoid being inconvenienced by the minority non-regulars? Like, what's their leverage? Laws are their leverage, actually... and the law doesn't really care about any mitigating factors, like if you're a creative contributor to the happiness and well being of the people of the world, or if you merely used poor judgment once or twice and you didn't really hurt anybody. The law just cares that a citizen broke the law. That's all. Very straightforward, it is.

Because, late one night in the mid-nineties, while relaxing at home with a guest, Arthur got to playing his stereo a little bit too loud, and in doing so, aggravated one of his neighbours in the apartment building where he lived. So, the neighbour complained to somebody, then Arthur got aggravated and did the only reasonable thing he could think of at the time... he grabbed his gun, walked out on the balcony and fired off a couple of rounds... you know, to let the neighbour know what "loud" really was... to create some perspective, as it were. Then, of course, the neighbour called the cops and everything went downhill from there. I mean, Arthur's guest that night kindly tried to take the fall by claiming that the gun they found was actually his, not Arthur's, and that he, in fact, was the one that had fired off the rounds, but the cops weren't buying it.

Then things went further downhill, because Arthur, being a convicted felon, wasn't supposed to even own a handgun. So, when the cops came in, they naturally went right to the closet, found the gun, put the cuffs on Arthur, and that was pretty much that. I think he got convicted of being a felon in possession of a firearm and discharging a firearm within the city limits, while intimidating a taxpayer, or whatever.

Therefore, although Arthur didn't hurt anybody, or anything, he nevertheless got sent up, and, being a three-strikes felon, he served five and a half years of a twelve-year sentence at Pleasant Valley Correctional Facility, just north of L.A., right across Interstate 5 from that foul-smelling, disgusting, insult to beef eaters the world over. "Harris Ranch," the place is called...where, on any given day, around 30,000 head of cattle lay and stand, knee-deep in faeces and urine-soaked mud, waiting to be slaughtered. It stinks bad for miles around.

But like the song says... Arthur served his time...served it well... and in early 2002, he came out with a vengeance, right-away hooking up with his old manger, Gene Kraut, and the musicians who had been his touring group before he got incarcerated... a group known as Baby Lemonade... for, "The *Forever Changes* Tour."

It went on like that for three or so years, the new LOVE/Baby Lemonade touring all over Europe and the United States, finally, and once and for all, giving fans of the group what they had longed for since 1967... a full dose of the music Bryan and Arthur had written all those many years ago.

But in late 2005, Arthur took sick, and in January of 2006, he was diagnosed with acute lymphoblastic leukemia, which the dictionary defines as, "one of a group of cancers of the blood that results in an uncontrolled proliferation of white blood cells, usually resulting in death." In other words, it was bad.

By this time, Arthur and his "*Forever Changes* Tour" group had experienced some disagreements and he was living all the way back in his original home of Tennessee, working with still another group he was calling LOVE. So, Arthur went into the hospital for treatment there... not in L.A., where he had lived most of his life.

Two benefit concerts were soon organized to help Arthur with his hospital bills, one in New York, and one in June of '06 at the Whisky on Sunset in Hollywood. At a rehearsal for the West Coast benefit, a few days before the event, I met up with Johnny, for the first time in thirty-eight years, at a warehouse in downtown L.A. called, The Brewery, and it was so good to see the dude. He looked fantastic, and he played? – well he played with the ferocity of a rampaging lion. As soon as we kicked off the first tune I could tell Johnny hadn't lost a thing. Still the psycho-blues jazz master extraordinaire, he still had the gift... the power to send chills down your spine... thunder and lightening in a bottle... and simply one of the greatest to ever pick up a guitar. There was nothing he couldn't do. Just like always.

So, on the night of the sixth, Johnny and I played some LOVE tunes for a set, with Arthur's tour group, Baby Lemonade, and sometime during the night, Johnny went to the microphone and announced that he had spoken with Arthur that very day and he was feeling much better and things were looking up and the crowd gave a big hooting cheer.

Then, only a couple of months later... on August third, 2006, Arthur up and died.

They flew his body back to Los Angeles, and the funeral was set up at Forest Lawn Cemetery. I took Bryan's mom Elizabeth... picked her up in my dad's Toyota Rav 4 from over at her place in Los Feliz. Being August in L.A., it was sweltering hot, and when we got to Forest Lawn, we parked and walked over and found a cool place to sit on a little bench in the shade of a tree outside the chapel where the memorial service was to take place, and we sat and waited while a previous group finished up the service for their loved one, and then waited a little longer while the workers there got set up for Arthur.

As Elizabeth and I waited, I looked around. Some of the people were arriving in long black limousines... a few old fans of the group, dressed in tie-died clothes of the sixties, they were... and people who looked to be Arthur's family and friends from his childhood. Everybody was kind of commingling with each other, laughing and telling stories. It wasn't a sad time, by any means. Arthur would have liked it.

Then finally, a man in a suit came out of the chapel and announced it was time for Arthur's service to start and everybody began to file slowly in and find seats. Elizabeth and I sat a few rows from the front and on the aisle, which is always good, you know... so you don't feel pinned-in.

There was a stage, and on the stage sat a closed black coffin with two hats resting atop the lid. They were the two hats Arthur wore during his last years... a cowboy hat with a scarf where the headband should be, and the black top hat he wore for the animated caricature on the cover of the "*Forever Changes* Tour" album.

There was an electric piano and a guitar sitting in front of a couple of chairs on the stage, and before long a young lady came out and performed one of Arthur's compositions on keyboard, and then somebody else sang and played the guitar. Pretty soon, Arthur's good friend and personal manager, Mark Linn, came from behind the curtain and stepped to a microphone and invited anybody who wanted to share their experiences with Arthur to do that, so sure enough, a few people rose from their seats and began to form a little line down on the floor, stage right.

First up was a lady who said she went to school with Arthur, and she told a story about how when she first met Arthur his name was Arthur Taylor, and they met during a game of dodgeball when they were kids. "I remember he threw the ball so hard at me, it knocked me down and then he laughed," she said. "...and if you had a problem with Arthur during classes, he would be waiting for you after school... because Arthur was the school bully." Everybody kind of smiled and nodded.

Then, another childhood friend told about how one time he was being harassed by another kid at school, and Arthur told him, "Man, if you don't take care of it, that dude will be on your ass every day." So, Arthur taught him a couple of fighting techniques. "Arthur taught me the value of a left-hook," he said proudly. Bottom line, the next day at school, he kicked the guy's ass and they went on to become best friends after that.

Arthur's buddy kind of choked-up near the end of the story, and when he sat back down in his pew-seat, directly in front of Elizabeth, she leaned forward and patted him on the shoulder. When he turned around and smiled at her, I noticed he had tears in his eyes. It was good he ended the story when he did because he was right on the verge of you know... losing it, big time.

After the service ended, everybody filed past Arthur's casket and most touched it and said a short goodbye, and then we met out back of the chapel and paid our respects and gave our condolences to Arthur's widow, Diane.

Then Elizabeth and I left in my dad's Toyota Rav 4 and I took her back home to her pad in Los Feliz, and that was pretty much that. We didn't stick around for the actual interment. Dang, it was hot!

And now here it was, three years later... August again, and as Dennis and I sat next to Arthur on the green green grass of his home overlooking the little valley, our one-sided conversation had finally begun to wind down.

Pretty soon I said, "Well, we better get going," so we stood up and started to leave. Then I turned back and said, "See you later, man," and Dennis said, "Yeah Arthur, see you later," and we left.

Later that evening, around ten o'clock, I met up with Johnny and sat in with him and his backup group, Baby Lemonade, at The Bootleg Theater in Echo Park. Then a few nights later, I played on a few tunes at Alex's Club in Long Beach.

Maybe only a third of the people in the clubs were experienced LOVE fans. The rest were younger club regulars who had probably only heard of LOVE but had never before actually heard any LOVE music. And while we were playing, I looked out at the faces of the people moving to the music and enjoying Arthur's compositions, some for the very first time, and I remember thinking, "Well, I guess that's about as close to achieving immortality as a human can get. You know... because even though the artist dies, the product of his being lives on virtually forever."

So it does, changes notwithstanding, and that's about all you can ask.

That night, back at my dad's house, I had my favourite recurring dream. In that dream I'm walking alongside the little stream that runs gently down below the Bronson Caves, in the hills above Hollywood, when suddenly I catch a glimpse of something rusty-red, coming from off in the distance, fast toward me. Then, just as suddenly, I realize it's my dog, Bristol. And as he gets nearer, I see his tongue hanging out and off to one side, like it always did when he ran, and he's running full blast like the wind; and as he reaches me and skids to a stop, I kneel down and throw my arms around his neck and give him a big long hug. "Bristol, I dreamed you were dead," I always say; and I kiss his soft furry ears and he smells so sweet. Then I stand up and say, "Well, come on, let's go, man."

Then, he and I turn and continue walking happily together along the path next to the little stream that runs gently below the Bronson Caves.

IN LOVING MEMORY

Claude Thomas Ware
"Claudio de Pablo"

1919-2009

"I shall be telling this with a sigh
Somewhere ages and ages hence:
Two roads diverged in a wood, and I –
I took the one less traveled by,
And that has made all the difference."

Robert Frost, "The Road Not Taken"